国际中小学数学能力
检测试题解答

（初中组）

朱华伟 孙文先 付云皓 编译

科学出版社
北京

内 容 简 介

本书收录了第1届(2011~2012年)至第6届(2016~2017年)国际中小学数学能力检测(初中组)的全部试题,对每一道试题均给出详解,有的给出了多种解法,目的是使读者开阔眼界,加深对问题的理解,培养举一反三的能力.

本书可供初中数学资优生、准备初中升高中数学考试的考生、准备参加各类初中数学竞赛的选手、初中数学教师、高等师范院校数学教育专业大学生、数学爱好者及数学研究工作者参考.

图书在版编目(CIP)数据

国际中小学生数学能力检测试题解答. 初中组/朱华伟, 孙文先, 付云皓编译. —北京: 科学出版社, 2018.1

(奥数题库精选)

ISBN 978-7-03-056253-1

Ⅰ. ①国⋯ Ⅱ. ①朱⋯②孙⋯③付⋯ Ⅲ. ①中学数学课–初中–题解 Ⅳ. ①G634.605

中国版本图书馆 CIP 数据核字 (2018) 第 005481 号

责任编辑:李 敏／责任校对:彭 涛
责任印制:肖 兴／整体设计:黄华斌

科学出版社 出版
北京东黄城根北街16号
邮政编码:100717
http://www.sciencep.com

天津文林印务有限公司 印刷
科学出版社发行 各地新华书店经销

*

2018年1月第 一 版 开本:720×1000 1/16
2021年5月第四次印刷 印张:11
字数:220 000

定价:56.00元
(如有印装质量问题,我社负责调换)

主要作者简介

朱华伟,二级教授,特级教师,博士生导师

美国加利福尼亚州立大学洛杉矶分校高级访问学者.湖北省十大杰出青年.享受国务院政府特殊津贴专家.

兼任国际教育数学协会常务副理事长,国际数学竞赛学术委员会副主席,国际中小学生数学能力检测学术委员会副主席,中国教育数学学会常务副理事长兼秘书长,全国华罗庚金杯赛主试委员.多次参与中国数学奥林匹克、全国高中数学联赛、女子数学奥林匹克、西部数学奥林匹克及青少年数学国际城市邀请赛的命题工作.曾任国际数学奥林匹克中国队领队、主教练,率中国队获团体冠军.

在国内外学术期刊上发表论文100余篇,出版著作100余部.

张景中谈奥数

华伟教授认为，竞赛数学是教育数学的一部分．这个看法是言之成理的．数学要解题，要发现问题、创造方法．年复一年进行的数学竞赛活动，不断地为数学问题的宝库注入新鲜血液，常常把学术形态的数学成果转化为可能用于教学的形态．早期的国际数学奥林匹克试题，有不少进入了数学教材，成为例题和习题．竞赛数学与教育数学的关系，于此可见一斑．

写到这里，忍不住要为数学竞赛说几句话．有一阵子，媒体上面出现不少讨伐数学竞赛的声音，有的教育专家甚至认为数学竞赛之害甚于黄、赌、毒．我看了有关报道后第一个想法是，中国现在值得反对的事情不少，论轻重缓急还远远轮不到反对数学竞赛吧．再仔细读这些反对数学竞赛的意见，可以看出来，他们反对的实际上是某些为牟利而又误人子弟的数学竞赛培训．就数学竞赛本身而言，是面向青少年中很小一部分数学爱好者而组织的活动．这些热心参与数学竞赛的数学爱好者（还有不少数学爱好者参与其他活动，例如青少年创新发明活动、数学建模活动、近年来设立的丘成桐中学数学奖），估计不超过约两亿中小学生的百分之五．从一方面讲，数学竞赛培训活动过热产生的消极影响，和升学考试体制以及教育资源分配过分集中等多种因素有关，这笔账不能算在数学竞赛头上；从另一方面看，大学招生和数学竞赛挂钩，也正说明了数学竞赛活动的成功因而得到认可．对于青少年的课外兴趣活动,积极的对策不应当是限制堵塞,而是开源分流.发展多种课外活动,让更多的青少年各得其所,把各种活动都办得像数学竞赛这样成功并且被认可,数学竞赛培训活动过热的问题自然就化解或缓解了.

摘自《走进教育数学》丛书总序

前　　言

国际中小学数学能力检测（International Mathematics Assessments for Schools, IMAS）是一项为小学中年级、小学高年级与初中学生所举办的世界级数学检测，旨在以国际宏观的尺度衡量学生在三项认知层面——知识、应用与推理上的表现，为参加者提供在不同领域、不同难度、每年一次的公开数学检测，测试学生的数学能力，挑战学生开阔数学视野的能力，评估学校、国家与地区之间的数学水平，给予聪颖与能力强的学生能透过大众认可的检测评价他们在数学上的能力，支持资优教育的发展.

IMAS 针对小学中年级（即三、四年级）、高年级（即五、六年级）与初中（即七、八年级）程度的学生分别命题进行检测，参加者可以根据自己的能力，自行选择检测项目的内容与难度，即学生可以跳级或降级参加检测，即小学三年级学生可以参加小学高年级组检测，九年级学生可以参加初中组检测.

IMAS 分第一轮检测和第二轮检测.

IMAS 第一轮检测：包括 25 道题，答题时间为 75 分钟. 前 20 题为选择题，最后 5 题答案为 000 至 999 整数的填空题. 题目的难度等级分布情况为：第 1～10 题为容易题，每题 3 分；第 11～20 题为适中题，每题 4 分；第 21～25 题为难题，每题 6 分. 总分为 100 分. 考试时间 75 分钟. 学生将根据其所在考区同年级学生 IMAS 第一轮检测的成绩给予以下奖项：一等奖——成绩在前 10% 者；二等奖——成绩在前 11% ~ 前 25% 之间者;三等奖——成绩在前 26% ~ 前 50% 之间者.每位学生都可得到一张个人的详细成绩报告,报告列出整体平均标准及个人成绩的百分等级,提供学生在不同层次技能的表现,检测所显示出的强项与弱点可督促学生的学习.这些珍贵的讯息将对各地区的数学教育研究有很大的帮助.

IMAS 第二轮检测:邀请各考区参加 IMAS 第一轮检测成绩在前 10% 的学生参加.试题共有 15 题,其中第 1 ~ 5 题为选择题,每题 4 分;第 6 ~ 13 题为填空题,每题 5 分;第 14 ~ 15 题为详答题(必须写出详细演算过程),每题 20 分,部分答对给予部分分数.总分为 100 分. IMAS 第二轮检测成绩达各考区前 5% 者颁发金牌,成绩达前 6% ~ 15% 者颁发银牌,成绩达前 16% ~ 30% 者颁发铜牌,以及相应的证书.

根据各考区 IMAS 组织工作、参加检测人数及第二轮检测成绩综合评估居前的考区获邀派队参加 IMC(International Mathematics Competition, IMC),中国可以派中学、小学各四个队参赛,每个队由四名学生、两名教师组成,IMC 组委会免费提供受邀学生、教师在比赛国家期间的所有食宿,自行负担出国的往返交通费用.

本书收录了第 1 届(2011 ~ 2012 年)至第 6 届(2016 ~ 2017 年)国际中小学数学能力检测(初中组)的全部试题,对每一道试题均给出详解,有的给出了多种解法,目的是使读者开阔眼界,加深对问题的理解,可以从中得到有益的启发,培养举一反三的能力.

本书可供初中数学资优生,准备初中升高中数学考试的考生,准备参加各类初中数学竞赛的选手,初中数学教师,高等师范院校数学教育专业大学生,数学爱好者及数学研究工作者参考.

参加 IMAS 命题工作的有:Andy Liu(加拿大亚伯达大学)、朱

前　言

华伟、孙文先(中国台湾)、郑焕、付云皓、邹宇、张传军、张红兵、陈泽桐、杨姗、周弋林、李苹芳、刘阳、刘凤鸣、罗芳等.

在本书的编校过程中,广州市教育研究院郑焕博士提供了很大的帮助,在此向他表示真诚的感谢.对于本书存在的问题,热忱希望读者不吝赐教.

朱华伟
2018 年 1 月

目 录

张景中谈奥数

前言

第1章 第1届国际中小学生数学能力检测(IMAS)试题(初中组) 1
    1.1 第一轮英文试题 1
    1.2 第一轮中文试题 7
    1.3 第一轮试题解答与点评 13
    1.4 第二轮英文试题 18
    1.5 第二轮中文试题 21
    1.6 第二轮试题解答与评注 25
    1.7 第1届国际中小学生数学能力检测样题 31
    1.8 第1届国际中小学生数学能力检测样题 33

第2章 第2届国际中小学生数学能力检测(IMAS)(初中组) 38
    2.1 第一轮英文试题 38
    2.2 第一轮中文试题 43
    2.3 第一轮试题解答与评注 47
    2.4 第二轮英文试题 51
    2.5 第二轮中文试题 54
    2.6 第二轮试题解答与评注 56

第3章 第3届国际中小学生数学能力检测(IMAS)(初中组) 63
    3.1 第一轮英文试题 63
    3.2 第一轮中文试题 68
    3.3 第一轮试题解答与评注 72

3.4	第二轮英文试题	78
3.5	第二轮中文试题	80
3.6	第二轮试题解答与评注	82

第4章 第4届国际中小学生数学能力检测(IMAS)(初中组) — 88

4.1	第一轮英文试题	88
4.2	第一轮中文试题	92
4.3	第一轮试题解答与评注	96
4.4	第二轮英文试题	101
4.5	第二轮中文试题	105
4.6	第二轮试题解答与评注	108

第5章 第5届国际中小学生数学能力检测(IMAS)(初中组) — 115

5.1	第一轮英文试题	115
5.2	第一轮中文试题	119
5.3	第一轮试题解答与评注	122
5.4	第二轮英文试题	126
5.5	第二轮中文试题	129
5.6	第二轮试题解答与评注	132

第6章 第6届国际中小学生数学能力检测(IMAS)(初中组) — 140

6.1	第一轮英文试题	140
6.2	第一轮中文试题	143
6.3	第一轮试题解答与评注	147
6.4	第二轮英文试题	153
6.5	第二轮中文试题	156
6.6	第二轮试题解答与评注	159

第1章 第1届国际中小学生数学能力检测(IMAS)试题(初中组)

1.1 第一轮英文试题

考试时间:75分钟

Questions 1–10, 3 marks each

1. What is $2011+1102\times(1-3)$?

   (A) 193   (B) 4215   (C) 6226   (D) –193   (E) –6226

2. Which number is the largest?

   (A) 3.14   (B) π (C) $\dfrac{22}{7}$ (D) 3.135   (E) 304%

3. The temperature on the shady side of a certain planet is $-253\,°\!C$. The temperature on its sunny side is only $-223\,°\!C$. Which of the following statement is an accurate description of the relation between the temperatures on the shady side and on the sunny side?

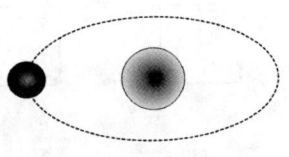

(A) The temperature of its sunny side is 30 °C higher than its shady side;
(B) The temperature of its sunny side is 30 °C lower than its shady side;
(C) The temperature of its sunny side is 476 °C higher than its shady side;
(D) The temperature of its sunny side is 476 °C lower than its shady side;
(E) The temperature of its sunny side is the same as its shady side.

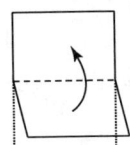 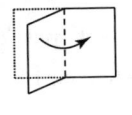 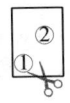

4. The given diagram shows a rectangular piece of paper folded in quarters along two perpendicular folds. If a cut is made around the corner marked 1, which of the following **cannot** possibly be the shape of the resulting hole in the piece of paper?

(A) Octagon　　　　　(B) Quadrilateral
(C) Hexagon　　　　　(D) Triangle　　　　　(E) Circle

5. Around 550 BC, the Greek mathematician Pythagoras discovered and proved a theorem which now bears his name. To celebrate this achievement, he had 100 cows killed for a feast. Thus the result is also known as the One Hundred Cows Theorem. What is the anniversary of this result in 2011? (There is no Year 0.)

(A) 2562　　(B) 2560　　(C) 2561　　(D) 1460　　(E) 1461

6. A rectangle is 6 cm by 8 cm. It is revolved about an axis on the rectangle itself. What is the number of different cylinders that may be obtained in this way?

(A) 2　　(B) 4　　(C) 6　　(D) 8　　(E) Infinity

7. There is a pattern to the given sequence of figures:

(1)　(2)　(3)　(4)　(5)　(6)　(7)

Which of the following will be the 2011-th figure of the sequence?

(A)　(B)　(C)　(D)　(E)

8. The given diagram shows two overlapping right triangles having a common vertex O. If $\angle AOD = 123°$, what is the measure, in degrees, of $\angle BOC$?

(A) 33　　(B) 53　　(C) 57
(D) 60　　(E) 66

9. A greengrocer is having an apple sale. The price is \$6 per kilogram. If the total purchase exceeds 3 kilograms, a 20% discount is applied to the portion over 3 kilograms. There is no discount if the total purchase does not exceed 3 kilograms. If Leith buys 8 kilograms of apples from this greengrocer, how much does he pay?

(A) \$32　　(B) \$36　　(C) \$42　　(D) \$44　　(E) \$21

10. The given diagram shows a pocket knife. The shaded part is a rectangle with

a small semicircular indentation. The two edges of the blade are parallel, forming angles 1 and 2 with the shaft as shown. What is the measure, in degrees, of ∠1+∠2?

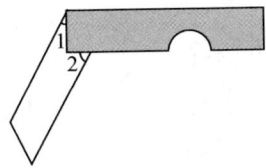

(A) 30 (B) 45 (C) 60
(D) 90 (E) could not be determined

Questions 11–20, 4 marks each

11. The given diagram shows the projected sale and actual sale of a certain toy company for the fourth quarter of the year. The achievement percentage is equal to $\dfrac{\text{actual sale}}{\text{projected sale}} \times 100\%$. What is this achievement percentage?

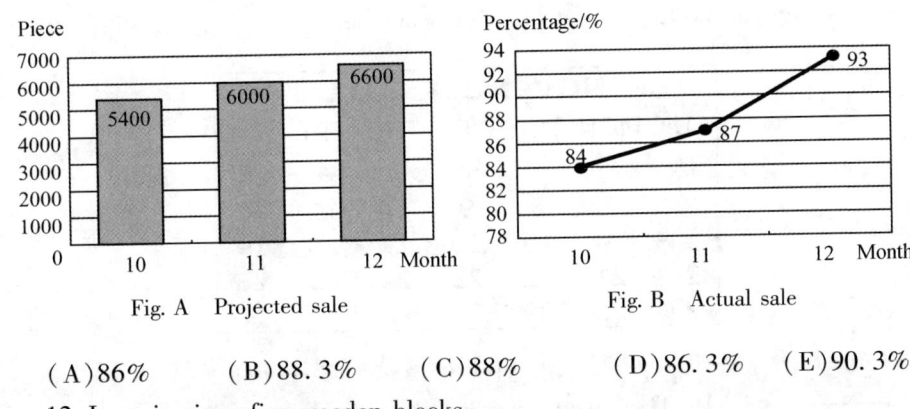

Fig. A Projected sale   Fig. B Actual sale

(A) 86%   (B) 88.3%   (C) 88%   (D) 86.3%   (E) 90.3%

12. Leon is given five wooden blocks:

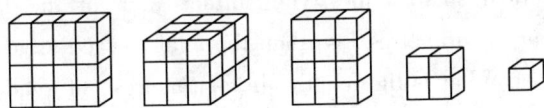

Which of the following blocks should be added so that he can make a 4×4×4 cube? (None of the blocks can be dissected)

(A)   (B) (C)   (D) (E)

                    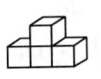

13. The given diagram shows how a square ABCD may be dissected into six pieces by three straight cuts AC, BD and EF, where E and F are the respective midpoints of AB and BC. The pieces are then rearranged to form the given

shape. What is the total area, in square centimetres, of the shaded part of the given shape?

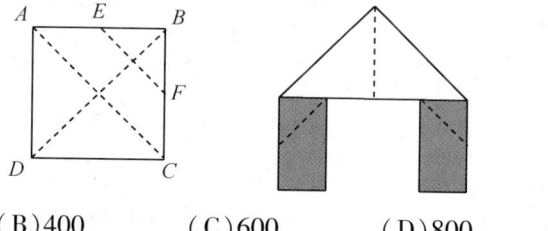

(A) 200   (B) 400   (C) 600   (D) 800   (E) 1000

14. The given diagram shows the calendar for the month of November, 2011. Three consecutive numbers from the same column are chosen. Of the following number, which can be the sum of three such numbers?

(A) 21   (B) 37   (C) 38   (D) 40   (E) 54

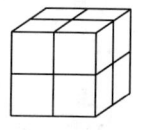

15. The given diagram shows a large cube formed of eight identical small cubes. The surface area of the large cube is 216 square centimetres less than the total surface areas of the eight small cubes. What is the length, in centimetres, of a side of a small cube?

(A) 2   (B) 3   (C) 4   (D) 5   (E) 6

16. In an NBA basketball game, a player scores 44 points, 5 of which come from 5 foul shots (each shot scores 1 point). He makes more 2-point shots than 3-point shots. Of the following number, which **cannot** possibly be the total number of 2-point and 3-point shots made by this player?

(A) 15   (B) 16   (C) 17   (D) 18   (E) 19

17. The given diagram shows a rectangle $ABCD$ being folded along a straight segment AE with E on CD, so that the new position of D is on AB. Triangle ADE is then folded along DE so that the new position of A is on the extension of DB. The new

position of *AE* intersects *BC* at *F*. If *AB* = 10 centimetres and *AD* = 6 centimetres, what is the area, in square centimetres, of triangle *ABF*?

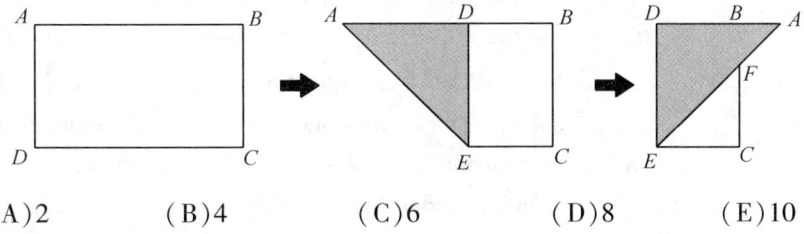

(A)2　　　(B)4　　　(C)6　　　(D)8　　　(E)10

18. A child is operating a remote-controlled car on a flat surface. Starting from the child's feet, the car moves forward 1 metre, makes a 30° turn counterclockwise, moves forward 1 metre, makes a 30° turn counterclockwise, and so on. When the car first time returns to its starting point for the first time, what is the total distance, in metres, that it has covered?

(A)4　　　(B)8　　　(C)12　　　(D)16　　　(E)24

19. Each interior angle of a regular convex polygon is greater than 100° and less than 140°. Of the following numbers, which **cannot** possibly be the number of sides of this polygon?

(A)5　　　(B)6　　　(C)7　　　(D)8　　　(E)9

20. In the given diagram, each vertex of the hexagon *PQRSTU* is labeled with 0 or 1. Starting counterclockwise from a vertex, he multiplies the labels by 3, 7, 15, 31, 63 and 127 respectively and add the six products. If the starting point is *P*, the final sum is 1×3+1×7+0×15+1×31+0×63+1×127 =168. What is the starting point if the final sum is 180?

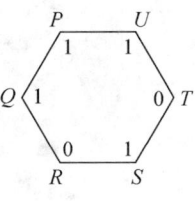

(A)*Q*　　　(B)*R*　　　(C)*S*　　　(D)*T*　　　(E)*U*

21. A drunk walks 1 metre east. Then he stops, makes a 90° turn clockwise or counterclockwise and walks 2 metres. Then he stops, makes a 90° turn clockwise or counterclockwise and walks 3 metres. He continues in this pattern, stopping, making 90° turn clockwise or counterclockwise and walks 1 metre more than the preceding segment. What would be the longest distance, in metres, between his initial position and his position when he makes his seventh stop?

22. In the given diagram, *ABCD* is a rectangle with $AB = 25$ cm and $BC = 20$ cm. *F* is a point on *CD* and *G* is a point on the extension of *AB* such that *FG* passes through the midpoint *E* of *BC*. If $\angle AFE = \angle CFE$, what is the length, in cm, of *CF*?

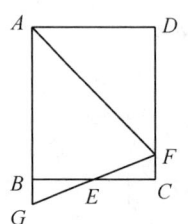

23. Consider all five-digit numbers using each of the digits 1, 2, 3, 4 and 5 exactly once, possibly with a decimal point somewhere. Starting with the smallest such number, namely, 1.2345, they are listed in ascending order. What is 1000 times the difference of the 150th and the 145th numbers?

24. On a straight line are 6 counters, each either black or white. We operate the row of counters as follow: for two consecutive counters with the same colour, a white counter is placed between them, for two consecutive counters with different colour, a black counter is placed between them. And then the original counters are removed. This is one operation. After a total of three operations we are left with three white counters. What is the number of possible colour patterns of the six counters initially?

An example is attached.

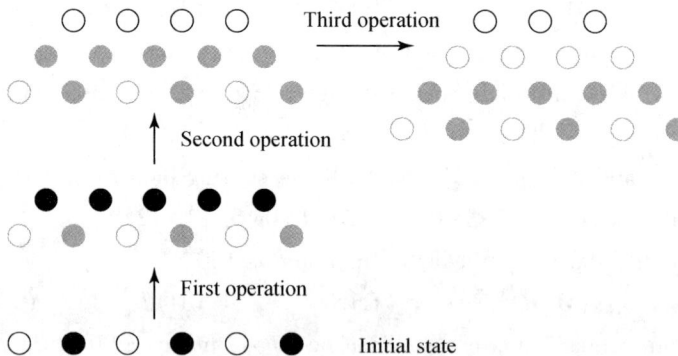

25. Mickey lives in a city with six subway lines. Every two lines have exactly one common stop for changing lines, and no three lines meet at a common stop. His home is not at one of the common stops. One day, Mickey suddenly decides to leave home and travel on the subway, changing trains at least once at each stop before returning home. What is the minimum number of changes he has to make to accomplish this task?

1.2 第一轮中文试题

注意事项

一般规定

1. 进入试场后,未获监考老师许可之前不可翻开此测验题本.

2. 不可以使用计算器、对数表、数学图表、手机与任何电子计算器具. 作答时可使用直尺与圆规,以及两面全空白的草稿纸.

3. 题目所提供之图形只是示意图,不一定精准.

4. 最前20题为选择题,每题有五个选项. 最后5题要求填入的答案为000至999的正整数. 题目一般而言是依照越来越难的顺序安排,对于错误的答案不会倒扣分数.

5. 本活动是数学能力检测而不同于学校测验,别期望每道题目都会做.

6. 请依照监考老师指示,谨慎地在答案卡上填写您的基本数据. 若因填写错误或不详所造成之后果由学生自行负责.

7. 须等待监考老师宣布开始作答后,才可以打开题本进行答题.

作答须知

1. 限用B或2B铅笔填写答案.

2. 请用B或2B铅笔在答案卡上将您认为正确选项的圆圈涂满(不是在题本上).

3. 您的答案卡将由计算机阅卷,为避免计算机误判,请不要在答案卡上其他任何地方涂划任何记号. 填写答案卡时,若需要修改,可使用软性橡皮小心擦拭,并确定答案卡上无残留痕迹.

特别约定

为确保竞赛之公平性及认证成绩优异学生,IMAS主办单位保留要求考生重测之权利.

1–10题,每题3分

1. 算式 $2011+1102\times(1-3)$ 的值等于

(A) 193　　(B) 4215　　(C) 6226　　(D) −193　　(E) −6226

2. 请问下列哪个数的值最大？

（A）3.14　　　（B）π　　　（C）$\frac{22}{7}$　　　（D）3.135　　　（E）304%

3. 某个星球的背阳面温度低至-253℃,向阳面也只有-223℃. 关于向阳面与背阳面的温度的叙述,请问下列哪一项正确(图1-1)？

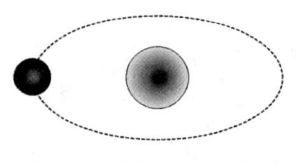

（A）向阳面的温度比背阳面的温度高30℃；
（B）向阳面的温度比背阳面的温度低30℃；
（C）向阳面的温度比背阳面的温度高476℃；
（D）向阳面的温度比背阳面的温度低476℃；
（E）向阳面的温度与背阳面的温度相同.

图1-1

4. 将一张矩形的纸对折再对折,如图1-2所示. 然后用剪刀将折后的纸的左下角（标记①的区域）剪下,请问将剪下的部分展开后所得到的平面图形不可能是下列哪一项？

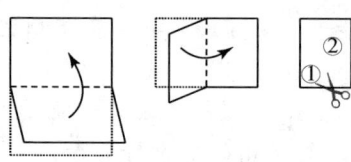

图1-2

（A）八边形　　（B）四边形　　（C）六边形　　（D）三角形　　（E）圆

5. 勾股定理(Pythagoras Theorem)传说是由古希腊的毕达哥拉斯于公元前550年首先发现并证明,当毕达哥拉斯证明了这个定理后,即杀了一百头牛作庆祝,故此定理又称为"百牛定理". 请问2011年是毕达哥拉斯发现并证明勾股定理的多少周年？（注：不存在公元0年）

（A）2562　　（B）2560　　（C）2561　　（D）1460　　（E）1461

6. 给定一个长和宽分别为6 cm和8 cm的长方形,以它上面的某一条线段为轴进行旋转,请问能够得到多少个不同的圆柱体？

（A）2　　　（B）4　　　（C）6　　　（D）8　　　（E）无限多

7. 下列图形的排列有一定的规律：

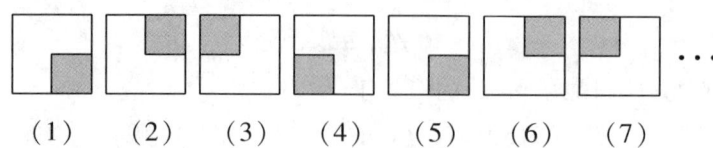

　　（1）　　（2）　　（3）　　（4）　　（5）　　（6）　　（7）

按照这个规律,请问第 2011 个图形是下列哪一个图形?

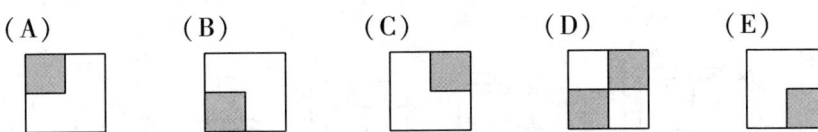

8. 将两块直角三角板的直角顶点 O 重合,已知 $\angle AOD = 123°$,请问 $\angle BOC$ 为多少度(图 1-3)?

(A)33   (B)53   (C)57   (D)60   (E)66

9. 某家水果店举行苹果特卖活动,如果购买的苹果不超过 3 kg,则每 kg 按原价 \$ 6 出售;如果购买的苹果超过 3 kg,则超过 3 kg 的部分之售价按原价减 20% 优惠. 小李购买了 8 kg 苹果,请问他应付多少钱?

(A) \$ 32   (B) \$ 36   (C) \$ 42   (D) \$ 44   (E) \$ 21

10. 图 1-4 是我们常用的折叠式小刀,刀柄外形是一个矩形挖去一个小半圆(阴影部分),刀片的上缘和下缘是两条平行的线段,转动刀片时会形成如图 1-4 所示的 $\angle 1$ 与 $\angle 2$,请问 $\angle 1 + \angle 2$ 等于多少度?

(A)30   (B)45   (C)60   (D)90   (E)不能确定

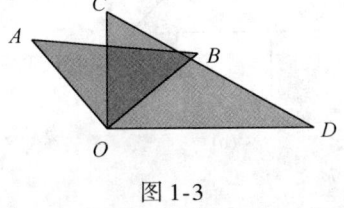

图 1-3

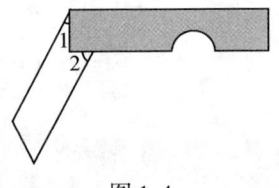

图 1-4

11—20 题,每题 4 分

11. 某儿童玩具公司去年第四季度计划的销量见图 1-5,而实际完成率见图 1-6,已知完成率 = $\dfrac{\text{实际销量}}{\text{计划销量}} \times 100\%$,请问该公司第四季度的总完成率是多少?

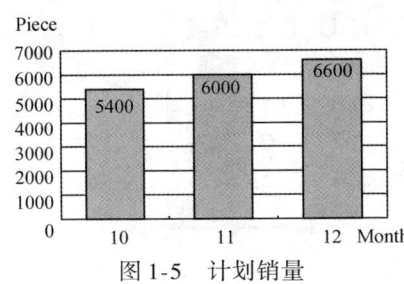

图 1-5 计划销量

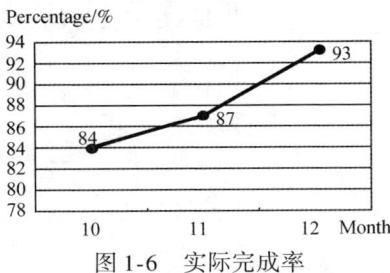

图 1-6 实际完成率

(A)86%   (B)88.3%   (C)88%   (D)86.3%   (E)90.3%

12. 小亮有以下五块积木：

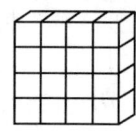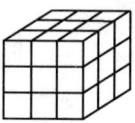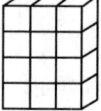

请问他再添加下列哪一块积木就能拼成一个 4×4×4 的正方体？（注：这些木块不能再分拆）

(A)　　　　(B)　　　　(C)　　　　(D)　　　　(E)

13. 如图 1-7(a) 所示，边长为 40 cm 的正方形木片 ABCD，其中点 E、F 分别是 AB、BC 的中点，若沿图中的虚线全部切开，拼成图 1-7(b) 的形状，请问图中阴影部分的面积是多少 cm²？

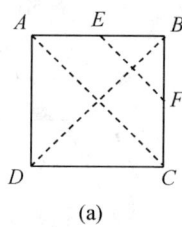 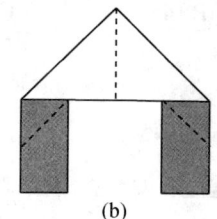
　　(a)　　　　　　　　(b)

图 1-7

(A)200   (B)400   (C)600   (D)800   (E)1000

14. 图 1-8 是 2011 年 11 月的月历，任意圈出一竖列上相邻的三个数，请问这三个数的和可能是下列哪一项？

NOVEMBER 2011						
SUN	MON	TUE	WED	THU	FRI	SAT
		1	2	3	4	5
6	7	8	9	10	11	12
13	14	15	16	17	18	19
20	21	22	23	24	25	26
27	28	29	30			

图 1-8

(A)21　　(B)37　　(C)38　　(D)40　　(E)54

15. 如图 1-9 所示,若将 8 个相同的小正方体拼成一个大正方体,则大正方体的表面积比原来的 8 个小正方体表面积的总和少 216 cm²,请问小正方体的棱长是多少 cm?

(A)2　　(B)3　　(C)4

(D)5　　(E)6

图 1-9

16. 在 NBA 某场篮球比赛中,某位球员共获得 44 分,其中他由罚球得到 5 分(每罚中一球只能得 1 分),他命中 2 分球的次数比命中 3 分球的次数多,请问他命中 2 分球与命中 3 分球的总次数不可能是下列哪一项?

(A)15 次　(B)16 次　(C)17 次　(D)18 次　(E)19 次

17. 有一矩形纸片 ABCD,AB = 10 cm,AD = 6 cm,将纸片折叠,使 AD 边落在 AB 边上,折痕为 AE. 再将 △AED 以 DE 为折痕向右折叠,AE 与 BC 交于点 F,请问 △ABF 的面积为多少 cm²(图 1-10)?

图 1-10

(A)2　　(B)4　　(C)6　　(D)8　　(E)10

18. 一位小朋友在平地上玩遥控车,遥控车从他脚下某点向前走 1 m,逆时针转 30°再向前走 1 m,再逆时针转 30°再向前走 1 m,如此下去,直至第一次回到原出发点为止,请问该遥控车共走了多少 m?

(A)4　　(B)8　　(C)12　　(D)16　　(E)24

19. 一个凸多边形的每个内角都大于 100° 小于 140°,请问这个多边形的边数不可能是下列哪一项?

(A)5　　(B)6　　(C)7　　(D)8　　(E)9

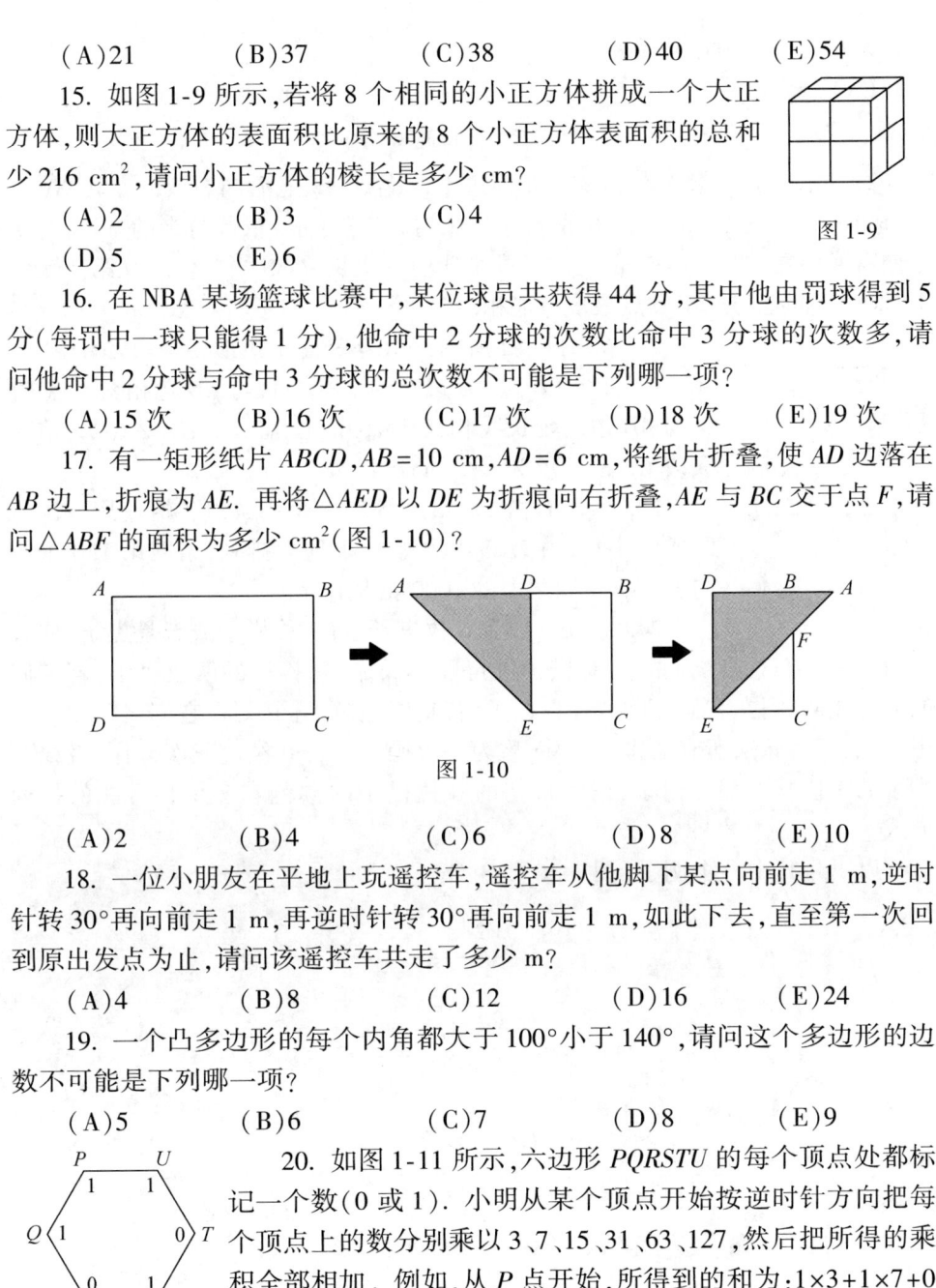

图 1-11

20. 如图 1-11 所示,六边形 PQRSTU 的每个顶点处都标记一个数(0 或 1). 小明从某个顶点开始按逆时针方向把每个顶点上的数分别乘以 3、7、15、31、63、127,然后把所得的乘积全部相加. 例如,从 P 点开始,所得到的和为:1×3+1×7+0×15+1×31+0×63+1×127 = 168. 如果小明得到的和为 180,请问他是从哪一个顶点开始的？
(A) Q (B) R (C) S (D) T (E) U

21–25题，每题6分

21. 街上有一名醉汉，他先向东前进 1 m，停下来，然后向右或向左转 90°再前进 2 m，停下来，然后又向右或向左转 90°再前进 3 m. 依此行走的方式，每次都向右或向左转 90°，每次前进的长度都比前一次长 1 m. 当这位醉汉第 7 次停下来时，请问他与原出发点最多可能相距多少 m？

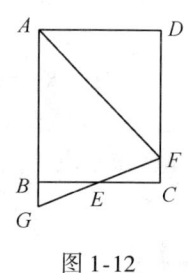

图 1-12

22. 如图 1-12 所示，$ABCD$ 是一个矩形，$AB = 25$ cm、$BC = 20$ cm. 直线 FG 过 BC 边上的中点 E 且与 CD 边相交于点 F，又与 AB 边的延长线相交于点 G. 已知 $\angle AFE = \angle CFE$，请问线段 CF 的长度为多少 cm？

23. 将所有由 1、2、3、4、5 与一个小数点各恰使用一次所组成的小数，由 1.2345 开始从小到大排列，请问第 150 个数与第 145 个数之差的 1000 倍是什么？

24. 直线上放有 6 枚棋子，每一枚棋子或者是黑子，或者是白子．我们对直线上的所有棋子进行以下操作：每相邻的两枚棋子，若它们的颜色相同，则在它们之间放一枚白子，若它们颜色不同，则在它们之间放一枚黑子，然后将原来所有的棋子移除，称为一次操作．若共经过三次操作，直线上剩余的 3 枚棋子都是白子，请问最初的 6 枚棋子的颜色有多少种可能的排列方式？

以下是其中一个例子（图 1-13）．

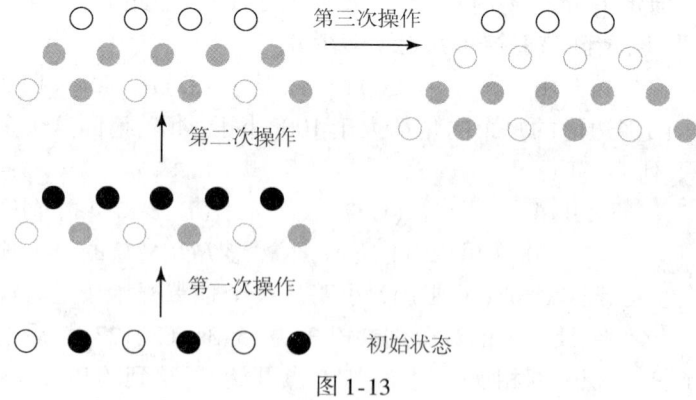

图 1-13

25. 小明所在的城市有 6 条地铁线路,每两条线路恰相交于一个换乘车站,每个换乘车站都恰只有两条线路经过. 某一天,小明突发奇想,他想从家出发,在每个换乘车站都至少进行一次换乘,最后再回到他家. 小明家的地铁站不是一个换乘车站,那么他要想达到目的,至少要换乘多少次?

1.3 第一轮试题解答与点评

1. 答案:(D).

解 $2011+1102\times(1-3) = 2011+1102\times(-2) = 2011-2204 = -193$ 或者 $2011+1102\times(1-3) = 2011+1102-1102\times 3 = 3113-3306 = -193$.

2. 答案:(C).

解 因为 $\pi = 3.14159\cdots$、$\frac{22}{7} = 3.14285\cdots$、$304\% = 3.04$,所以这五个数的大小关系为: $\frac{22}{7} > \pi > 3.14 > 3.135 > 304\%$,显然 $\frac{22}{7}$ 最大.

3. 答案:(A).

解 由 $-223-(-253) = -223+253 = 30$ 知向阳面的温度比背阴面的温度高 $30\,°C$.

4. 答案:(D).

解 展开①部分后会有两条互相垂直的折痕,显然这两条折痕都是①部分的对称轴,因此①部分具有中心对称性(图 1-14).

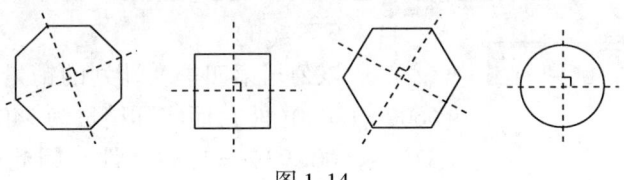

图 1-14

八边形、四边形、六边形和圆都有可能是中心对称图形,而三角形不可能是中心对称图形.

5. 答案:(B).

解 若公元前用负数表示,则有 $2011-(-550) = 2561$,因为不存在公元 0 年,故有 $2561-1 = 2560$(周年).

6. 答案:(E).

解 只要分别以平行于长方形的四条边的线段为轴进行旋转就可以得到

不同的圆柱体,因为长方形上与其四条边平行的线段有无限多条,所以能够得到无限多个不同的圆柱体.

7. 答案:(A).

解 观察这些图形的排列,我们发现有下列规律:大正方形内的小正方形从第一个图形开始,按逆时针顺序依次出现在大正方形的四个角落上. 它们以4为周期出现,由 $2011 = 4 \times 502 + 3$ 知,第2011个图形与第三个图形一样.

8. 答案:(C).

解 $\angle AOC = \angle AOD - \angle DOC = 123° - 90° = 33°$,则 $\angle BOC = \angle AOB - \angle AOC$,即 $\angle BOC = 90° - 33° = 57°$.

评注 另一种解法,$\angle BOD = \angle AOD - \angle AOB = 123° - 90° = 33°$,则 $\angle BOC = \angle DOC - \angle BOD$,即 $\angle BOC = 90° - 33° = 57°$.

9. 答案:(C).

解 小李购买的苹果超过了3 kg,则他购买的前3 kg每kg的售价为 \$ 6,超过3 kg的部分售价为 $6 \times (1-20\%)$,即每kg的售价为 \$ 4.8.

所以小李应付的钱为 $3 \times 6 + (8-3) \times 6 \times (1-20\%) = 18 + 5 \times 6 \times 0.8 = \$ 42$.

评注 小李购买的苹果超过了3 kg,超过部分减价20%优惠,因此他超出的5kg实际应付的钱等于 $(8-3) \times (1-20\%) = 4$ kg 苹果的价钱,故应当付 $3+4 = 7$ kg 苹果的原价,即 $6 \times 7 = \$ 42$.

10. 答案:(D).

解 如图1-15所示,经过点E作 $MN//AB$,那么 $\angle 1 = \angle 3$ 且 $AB//CD$,所以 $MN//CD$,得到 $\angle 2 = \angle 4$;因此 $\angle 1 + \angle 2 = \angle 3 + \angle 4 = \angle AED = 90°$.

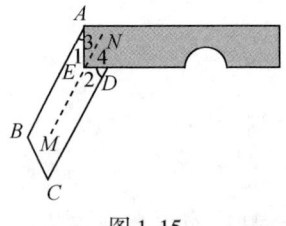

图 1-15

11. 答案:(B).

解 该公司第四季度计划的销量为 $5400 + 6000 + 6600 = 18000$(件),而实际销量为 $5400 \times 84\% + 6000 \times 87\% + 6600 \times 93\% = 15894$(件),因此可知第四季度完成率为 $\dfrac{15894}{18000} \times 100\% = 88.3\%$.

12. 答案:(C).

解 从反方向来考虑问题,要从 $4 \times 4 \times 4$ 的正方体积木中切下小亮拥有的五块积木,还会剩下什么样的一个形状. 先切下第二块积木,剩下一个由三个 $1 \times 4 \times 4$ 的面拼成的积木(但有部分重叠,如图(1)),再切去第一块积木,这时剩下由两个 $1 \times 3 \times 4$ 的面拼成的积木(有一个重叠的 $1 \times 1 \times 3$ 部分,如图(2)). 下面再切去第三块积木,剩下的只能是一个 $1 \times 3 \times 3$ 的小积木块,如图(3). 接着切去第四块积木,剩下一个由 5 个木块组成的"L"形,如图(4),最后再切去第五块积木,为了保证剩下的积木是一个整体,只能从"L"形的一端切去一个 $1×1×1$ 的积木块,于是剩下的图形只能如图(5)所示.

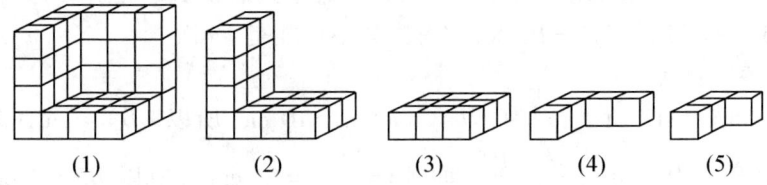

(1)　　　(2)　　　(3)　　　(4)　　　(5)

13. 答案:(D).

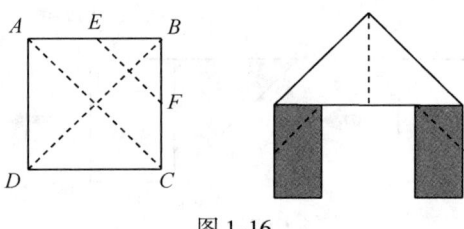

图 1-16

解　显然在六块图形中,两个最大的三角形面积总和占整个木片的一半,而在拼得的图中(图 1-16),仅有这两个三角形没有加上阴影,因此阴影部分的面积应等于整个木片面积的一半,即 $\frac{1}{2}×40^2=800(\text{cm}^2)$.

14. 答案:(E).

解　设某个日期为 x,且 $24>x>7$,则同一竖行上与其相邻的上下两个日期分别可以表示为 $x-7$ 和 $x+7$.则三个数的和为 $x-7+x+x+7=3x>21$,即三个数的和应为 3 的倍数且大于 21,而圈出 11、18、25 即可得 54,故选 E.

15. 答案:(B).

解　设小正方体的棱长为 a cm,则 $6a^2×8-(2a)^2×6=216$,$24a^2=216$,故可得 $a=3(\text{cm})$.

评注　因每个小正方体只有三个面显露出来,另外三个面隐藏在内部,8 个小正方体共隐藏 $8×3=24$ 个面,正好是减少的表面积,设小正方体的棱长为 a cm,则 $24a^2=216$,解得 $a=3(\text{cm})$.

16. 答案:(A).

解　由题意该球员经由两分球与三分球共拿下 39 分,由于这个分数是奇

15

数,故该球员投中三分球的次数是奇数,因此他可能命中 1 个三分球和 18 个两分球;或者 3 个三分球与 15 个两分球;或者 5 个三分球与 12 个两分球;或者 7 个三分球与 9 个两分球(若三分球大于或等于 9 个,则两分球的命中次数比三分球少,不合题意),因此他两分球和三分球命中的总次数可能是 $1+18=19$、$3+15=18$、$5+12=17$ 或 $7+9=16$ 次,故总次数不可能是 15 次.

17. 答案:(A).

解 如图 1-17 所示,因为 $AD=6$ cm、$AB=10$ cm,所以 $BD=4$ cm,那么最右图中由于 $BC//DE$,可得 $\frac{AB}{AD}=\frac{BF}{DE}$,而 $AB=6-4=2$(cm),所以 $BF=2$ cm,那么 $S_{\triangle ABF}=\frac{1}{2}AB\times BF=2\text{cm}^2$.

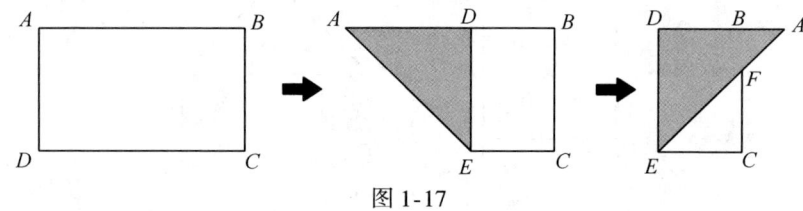

图 1-17

18. 答案:(C).

解 遥控车所走的路线构成一个正多边形,且它的每个外角为 30°,根据多边形的外角和为 360°可知边数为 12,则遥控车共走了 12 m.

19. 答案:(E).

解 假设这个凸多边形的边数为 n,因它的每个内角都大于 100°小于 140°,故知 $100n<(n-2)180<140n$,即 $4.5<n<9$. 故这个多边形的边数不可能是 9.

20. 答案:(D).

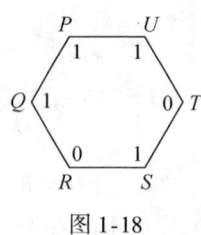

图 1-18

解 由于 $3+7+15+31+63=119<180$,故可知乘以 127 的那个数必须是 1,又因为 $63+127>180$,所以乘以 63 的那个数必须是 0,因此乘以 63 的那个数所在的顶点为 R 或 T. 由此可以推算出小明必须从 P 点或者 T 点开始. 若从 P 点开始,则得到的整数为 168,不是 180;若从 T 点开始,则得到的整数为 $0\times3+1\times7+1\times15+1\times31+0\times63+1\times127=180$,因此他是从 T 点开始的(图 1-18).

21. 答案:20m.

解 由题目条件知醉汉的第 1、3、5、7 次行走都是东西方向,第 2、4、6 次行走都是朝南北方向,因此他在东西方向上最多可移动 $1+3+5+7=16$ m,在南北

16

方向上最多可移动 $2+4+6=12(\mathrm{m})$,由勾股定理可得知他与出发点最多可能相距 $\sqrt{16^2+12^2}=20(\mathrm{m})$.

22. 答案:4.

解 如图 1-19 所示,设线段 CF 的长度为 x,由 $BG//CF$ 及 E 是 BC 的中点,易知 $\triangle BEG\cong\triangle CEF$,故 $BG=CF=x$.

由于 $\angle AFE=\angle CFE=\angle AGE$,故 $AG=AF$.

而 $AG=AB+BG=25+x$,因此 $AF=25+x$. 又 $AD=20$、$DF=25-x$,在直角三角形 ADF 中利用勾股定理得 $(25+x)^2=(25-x)^2+20^2$,整理得 $100x=400$,故 $x=4$.

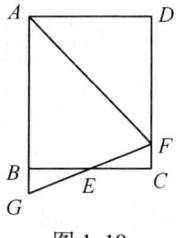

图 1-19

23. 答案:198.

解 整数部分是一位数的有 $5\times4\times3\times2\times1=120$ 个,这也是序列中的前 120 个数. 再看整数部分是两位数的,一旦整数部分确定,那么小数部分的三个数字还有 $3\times2\times1=6$ 种排列. 两位整数部分从小到大依次是 12、13、14、15、21、23、⋯. 因此第 145 个数是 21.345、第 150 个数是 21.543,两数相差 0.198,它的 1000 倍为 198.

24. 答案:8 种.

解 使用逆推法,考虑每次操作前的状态.

当操作后出现一颗白子时,则操作前为两颗同色的棋子,即:

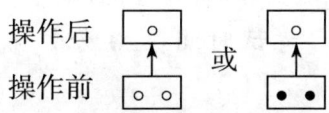

当操作后出现一颗黑子时,则操作前为两颗异色的棋子,即:

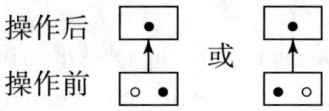

依此逐步向前推导,即可得:

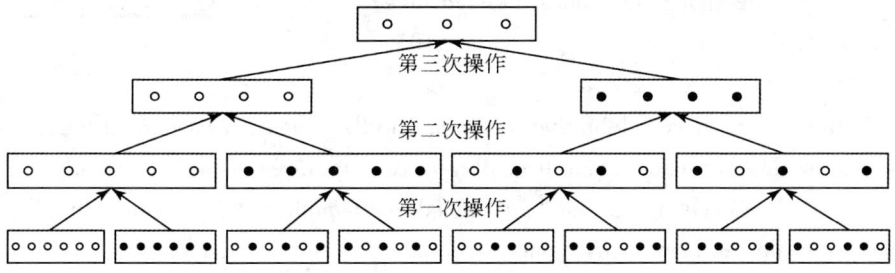

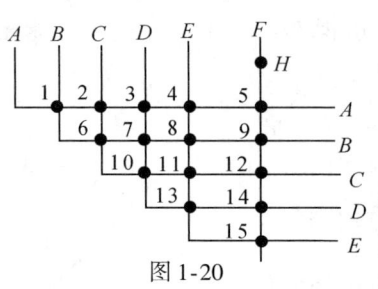

图 1-20

故开始 6 枚棋子的颜色共有 8 种不同的可能性.

25. 答案:18 次.

解 如图 1-20 所示,注意到每条线路上有 5 个换乘车站,而每乘坐一次该线路,最多游历其中 2 个车站,因此小明必须在每条线路上都乘坐至少 3 次. 而对于经过他家的线路,他则需要乘坐 4 次(因为第一次开始和最后一次结束是在他家的地铁站上下车,无法换乘). 因此小明至少要乘坐 $3\times5+4=19$ 次地铁,也就是说至少要进行 18 次换乘. 如图 1-20 的 A、B、C、D、E、F 六条线路,共有编号 1 到 15 的转乘车站,小明从 H 站出发,可利用以下 18 次转乘路线回到 H 站:$H\to15\to4\to1\to9\to14\to3\to2\to12\to5\to4\to13\to10\to6\to8\to11\to10\to7\to9\to H$.

第 1 届国际中小学生数学能力检测
2011 初中组第二轮检测试题

考试时间:120 分钟

1.4 第二轮英文试题

1. The diagram shows a neon-light sign by the river representing the number "2012" for the New Year Party of a certain city celebrating the arrival of 2012. Looking at the reflection off the water from the opposite shore, how does the sign look?

(A)2102　　(B)5015　　(C)5105
(D)5012　　(E)2015

2. In the centenary celebration of China Middle School, a basketball tournament was organized. After each team had played exactly three games, six teams were eliminated. The surviving teams then played one another exactly once. In all, 33 games were played. How many teams participated in this tournament?

(A)16　　　(B)23　　　(C)24　　　(D)12　　　(E)26

3. There are four kids. If we compute the total ages of three of them at a time, the sums are 22, 20, 17 and 25 respectively. What is the difference in age between the oldest and the youngest among these four kids?

(A)4　　　(B)5　　　(C)6
(D)7　　　(E)8

4. The diagram shows a point E on the extension of the side DC of a rectangle $ABCD$. The segment AE intersects the side BC at F. Three ants, X, Y and Z, all start from A. X crawls along the path A–B–F–C, Y along A–F–E–C–D and Z along A–F–C–D. All three crawl at the same constant speed. What is their order of finish to their respective destinations? List them from the one which finishes soonest to the one which finishes latest.

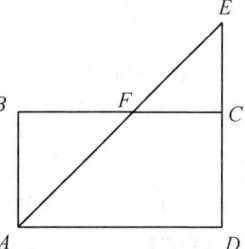

(A)XYZ　　(B)XZY　　(C)YXZ　　(D)YZX　　(E)ZXY

5. The currency of a certain country consists of bills of denominations $1, $5, $10, $20, $50 and $100. One day, two customers came to Mr. Wong's confectionery shop. Each bought a box of chocolate which cost $15. The first customer had two $10 bills and the second one a $20 bill and a $5 bill. Having no money in the tilt, Mr. Wong was unable to give change when the customer paid separately. However, the first customer could pay the second customer with his two $10 bills and receive the $5 bill as change, and then the second customer could pay Mr. Wong the $20 bill and one $10 bill for both boxes. On another day, two customers came, and each bought a box of caramel. Once again, the tilt was empty, and the correct change could only be made if the two customers paid together. Among the following prices, which could have been that of a box of caramel?

(A) $2　　(B) $5　　(C) $6　　(D) $7　　(E) $8

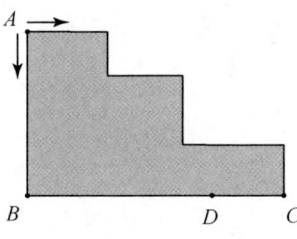

6. The diagram shows a city block (shaded). Peter starts from A and moves to the east while Toney starts from A and moves to the south. They both follow the perimeter of the city block, and eventually meet at the point D on the side BC, 2 km from C. If the constant speed of the Toney is $\frac{3}{4}$ of the constant

speed of the Peter, what is the length of the zig-zag line from A to C?

7. A Youth Hostel has twenty-one rooms numbered from 1 to 21. To conceal their identifies from outsiders but not from the staff, the keys are assigned two-digit codes. The first digit is the remainder when the room number is divided by 3, and the second digit is the remainder when the room number is divided by 7. For instance, the key to room 8 has the code 21. Which room has the key with the code 12?

8. The diagram shows a 3×3 table in which three squares have been filled with numbers. The remaining squares are also to be filled with numbers so that the sum of each row, each column and each of the two diagonals are the same. What number goes into the square marked A?

9. The diagram shows a rubber band tightly wrapped around three identical solid cylinders (shaded). The base radius of each cylinder is 10 cm. What is the total area, in cm^2, of the unshaded regions within the rubber band? Give the answer in terms of π.

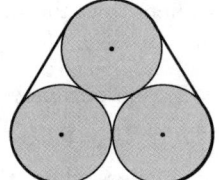

10. A magic number is a positive integer with distinct digits such that the difference between the number obtained by writing its digits in descending order and the number obtained by writing its digits in ascending order is equal to the positive integer itself. For example, 495 is a magic number since 954−459=495. Find all four-digit magic numbers.

11. The diagram shows how a regular pentagon $ABCDE$ may be constructed by tying a knot in a rectangular piece of paper. If the dimensions of the original rectangle is 17.2 cm by 2.5 cm, and $CN+DP=CD$, what is the area, in cm^2, of the quadrilateral $ACDE$?

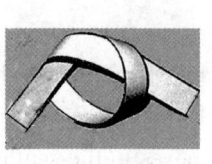 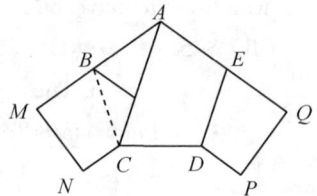

Figure(1)   Figure(2)

12. The integers $a_1, a_2, b_1, b_2, c_1, c_2$ and M satisfy
$$(a_1x+b_1y+c_1)(a_2x+b_2y+c_2) = 2x^2+10xy+My^2+7x+18y+6$$

for any numbers x and y. What is the value of M?

13. As shown in the diagram, there are five pieces used in the video game Tetris. We have four identical copies of each piece. From the twenty copies, we choose four and try to use them to form a 4×4 square. The copies may be turned or flipped. How many different choices are there?

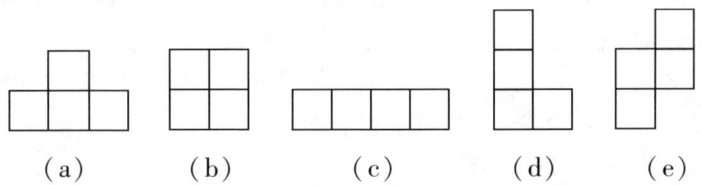

(a)　　(b)　　(c)　　(d)　　(e)

14. Given an arbitrary rectangle $ABCD$, find a point E on the side BC such that the total length of the segments AE and DE is as large as possible. Justify your answer.

15. As shown in the diagram, Leon has a 5×5 sheet of stamps. He cuts out the 5 stamps marked X. In doing so, he satisfies the following three conditions.

(1) No stamps on the edge or at a corner can be cut.

(2) If two stamps share a common edge, they cannot both be cut.

(3) After cutting, the remaining part of the sheet is still in one connected piece.

As it turns out, 5 is the maximum number of stamps that can be cut. Now Leon has a 9×9 sheet of stamps. What is the maximum number of stamps that can be cut if the same three conditions must be satisfied? Give a method for cutting that many stamps, and a proof that no larger number of stamps can be cut.

1.5　第二轮中文试题

答题指引：
- 请勿翻开此页，直到听到答题指令为止．
- 请在本页的对应位置填写您的姓名及准考证号码．
- 第二轮试题包括三个部分，总分100分．

- 第1~5题为选择题,只需在空格内填写英文字母答案,以其他文字书写一律不计分,不须计算过程.题目只有一个答案,答对才给分.每题4分,答错不倒扣分.
- 第6~13题为填空题,只需在空格内填写阿拉伯数字答案,以其他文字书写一律不计分,不须计算过程,若题目有不止一个答案,则全部答对才给分.每题5分,答错不倒扣分.
- 第14、15题为详答题,必须填写详细计算过程或证明,每题20分,根据答题情况给予部分分数,答错不倒扣分.
- 不得使用任何电子计算器具.
- 可使用铅笔、蓝色或黑色圆珠笔作答.
- 答题结束后,监试人员会将所有纸张收回.

1-5题,每题4分

1. 2012年元旦某城市举办新年庆祝晚会,江边一座宣传霓虹灯上的"2012"如图1-21所示.从对岸看,请问它在水中倒影所显示的数是什么?

图1-21
（A）2102　（B）5015　（C）5105
（D）5012　（E）2015

2. 中华中学在100年校庆时举办班际篮球比赛.假设在这次比赛中,每支队伍都先进行了3场比赛后,淘汰6支队伍,剩下的队伍再进行单循环赛.所有的参赛队伍共进行了33场比赛.请问总共有多少支队伍参加这次比赛?
（A）16　（B）23　（C）24　（D）12　（E）26

3. 有四位小朋友,其中每三位小朋友的岁数之和分别为22、20、17、25,请问这四位小朋友中年龄最大的比年龄最小的大多少岁?
（A）4　（B）5　（C）6　（D）7　（E）8

4. 有一个矩形$ABCD$,点E在DC的延长线上,点F是BC与AE的交点,如图1-22所示.有甲、乙、丙三只蚂蚁都从A点出发,甲蚂蚁沿着A-B-F-C的路径爬行,乙蚂蚁沿着A-F-E-C-D的路径爬行,丙蚂蚁沿着A-F-C-D的路径爬行.假设三只蚂蚁爬行的速度都相同,请问它们到达各自的目的地的先后顺序(由先至后)是什么?
（A）甲乙丙　（B）甲丙乙　（C）乙甲丙　（D）乙丙甲　（E）丙甲乙

5. 某国流通的纸币面值有 1 元、5 元、10 元、20 元、50 元和 100 元. 老王开了一家杂货店,这天有两位顾客各买了价格 15 元的巧克力糖,其中一人以两张 10 元的纸币付款,另一人以一张 20 元和一张 5 元的纸币付款. 两人独自付账时,老王都没有零钱找给他们,但两人一起付账时,老王只需将第一人的一张 10 元找给第二个人,将第二个人的 5 元找给第一个人即可. 有一天,又有两位顾客来购买口香糖,也发生了两人独自付账时,老王都没有零钱找给他们,但两人一起付账时,老王只需将第一人支付的某些纸币找给第二个人,将第二个人支付的某些纸币找给第一个人即可. 请问下列哪一项是口香糖可能的价格?

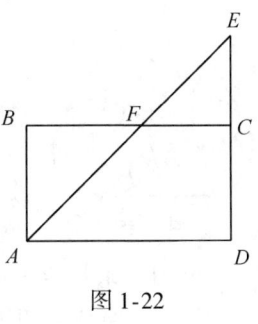

图 1-22

(A)2 元　　　(B)5 元　　　(C)6 元　　　(D)7 元　　　(E)8 元

6—13 题,每题 5 分

6. 图 1-23 为一个小镇的街道图,小王和小李同时从点 A 出发,小王沿 $A \to B \to D$ 的路线行走,小李沿折线 $A \to C \to D$ 的路线行走,结果两人在距离 C 点 2 km 的 D 点处相遇. 已知小王行走速度是小李行走速度的 $\frac{3}{4}$,请问折线 AC 的长度是多少 km?

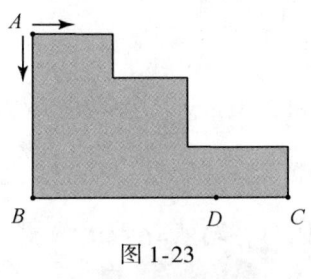

图 1-23

7. 青年旅馆有编号为 1~21 的 21 间房间. 他们在每间房间的钥匙上刻上两位数码,为使旅馆员工很容易辨认是哪一间房间的钥匙,而使局外人不容易猜到,他们依以下规则在每把钥匙上刻数码:第一位的数码是这把钥匙的房号除以 3 所得的余数;第二位的数码是这把钥匙的房号除以 7 所得的余数. 例如:8 号房间的钥匙上所刻的两位数码是 21. 如果有一把钥匙上所刻的两位数码为 12,请问这是几号房间的钥匙?

8. 在 3×3 方格表的每个小方格内,各填入一个正整数,使得每行、每列与两条主对角上三个数之和均相等. 在方格表内如图 1-24 所示已填入三个数,请问标记 A 处小方格内所填入的数是什么?

A		7
	10	3

图 1-24

9. 用一条绷紧的橡皮筋捆住三个大小一样的实心圆柱,其截面如图 1-25 所示,已知每个圆柱的底面半径为 10 cm,请问图中橡皮筋内部

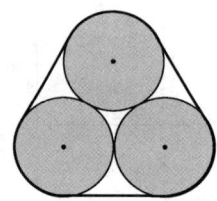

图 1-25

空隙部分的面积是多少 cm²？（圆周率用 π）

10. 我们将满足以下条件的正整数称为"魔术数"：该整数的每个数码都不为零且互不相同，并且将其各位数码从大到小排列与从小到大排列得到的两个新的数之差正好等于它本身．例如：495 是个"魔术数"，因为 954−459 = 495．请找出所有四位数的"魔术数"．

11. 用一条长方形的纸条，如图 1-26 所示的方法打一个结，然后轻轻拉紧、压平，就可以得到如图 1-27 所示的正五边形 ABCDE．

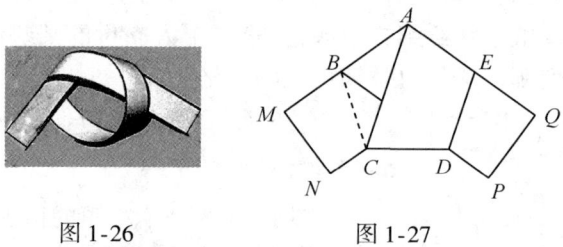

图 1-26　　　　　　图 1-27

已知原来长方形纸条的长和宽分别为 17.2cm 和 2.5cm，且 $CN+DP=CD$，请问四边形 ACDE 的面积为多少 cm²？

12. 设整数 a_1、a_2、b_1、b_2、c_1、c_2 和 M 满足恒等式

$$(a_1x+b_1y+c_1)(a_2x+b_2y+c_2) = 2x^2+10xy+My^2+7x+18y+6,$$

请问整数 M 的值是多少？

13. 俄罗斯方块游戏有以下五种方块：

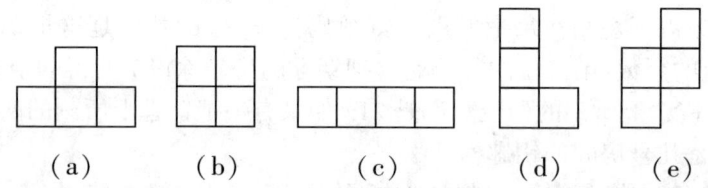

(a)　　(b)　　(c)　　(d)　　(e)

现有这五个品种的方块各 4 片，相同品种的方块完全相同，欲从这 20 片方块中任意挑选出 4 片拼成一个 4×4 的正方形，这些方块可以旋转或翻转．请问共有多少种不同挑选方块的方法？

14、15 题，必须填写详细计算过程或证明，每题 20 分

14. 任意给定一个矩形 ABCD，请在 BC 边上找出一点 E，使得线段 AE 与 DE 的长度之和最大，并证明您的结果．

15. 小亮有一大张正方形邮票,他要从中剪下几张小正方形邮票,但剪邮票时要满足以下三个条件:
(1)不能剪边上或角落上的邮票;
(2)剪掉的任意两张邮票不能有公共边;
(3)剪掉这些邮票后,剩下的邮票依然是一个整体.
例如:如果小亮原有的邮票是 5×5 的大正方形,则他最多可以剪下 5 张邮票(标记 X 的位置),如图 1-28 所示.

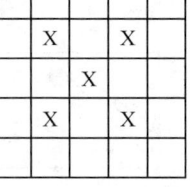

图 1-28

如果小亮原有的邮票是 9×9 的大正方形,请问最多可以剪下多少张邮票?请给出您的答案的一种剪法并且证明剪下的张数不能再多.

1.6　第二轮试题解答与评注

1. 答案:(B).

解　在水中倒影下,各个数字的顺序不变,但每个数位均上下颠倒,这样 0 和 1 没有变化,而 2 变成了 5,故水中倒影所显示的数为 5015. 故选 B.

2. 答案:(D).

解　设总共有 n 支队伍,则有 $\dfrac{3n}{2}+\dfrac{(n-6)(n-7)}{2}=33$,得 $n=12$ 或 $n=-2$(舍去). 故选 D.

3. 答案:(E).

解　设四位小朋友的岁数之总和为 x,那么四个小朋友的岁数分别可以表示为 $x-22$、$x-20$、$x-17$、$x-25$. 则 $(x-22)+(x-20)+(x-17)+(x-25)=x$,解得 $x=28$. 由此可知四个小朋友的岁数分别为 6,8,11,3;年龄最大的为 11 岁,最小的为 3 岁,所以年龄最大的比最小的大 8 岁.

评注　设四位小朋友的岁数之总和为 x,那么四个小朋友的岁数分别可以表示为 $x-22$、$x-20$、$x-17$、$x-25$. 可知年龄最大者为 $x-17$ 岁,年龄最小者为 $x-25$ 岁,则年龄最大的比最小的大 $(x-17)-(x-25)=8$ 岁,故选 E.

4. 答案:(B).

解　如图 1-29 所示,设蚂蚁甲、乙、丙爬过的路程分别为 x,y,z. 首先比较 x 和 z,由于 $x=AB+BC=CD+BF+CF$,$z=AF+FC+CD$,故只需比较 AF 与 BF 的长度. 由于斜边大于直角边,故 $AF>BF$,因此 $x<z$. 再比较 y 和 z,由于 $y=AF+EF+EC+CD$,故只需比较 CF 与 $EF+EC$ 的长度. 由于两点之间线段最短,故 $CF<EF+EC$,即 $z<y$. 因此 $x<z<y$,则路程越长到达终点所用的时间越长,它们到达各自

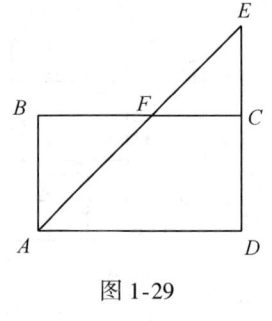

图 1-29

的目的地的先后顺序(由先至后)为甲丙乙,故选 B.

5. 答案:(E).

解 若口香糖的价格为 2 元,则两个人付给老王的钱一共是 4 元,这 4 元为四张 1 元,由此可见其中一个人至少有两张 1 元,这样他可以单独付账,矛盾.

若口香糖的价格为 5 元,则两个人付给老王的钱一共是 10 元,这 10 元为十张 1 元,或五张 1 元一张 5 元,或两张 5 元,或一张 10 元,无论是哪种情况,肯定有一个人持有 5 元,这样他可以单独付账,矛盾.

若口香糖的价格为 6 元,则两个人付给老王的钱一共是 12 元,这 12 元中有两张为 1 元,这时持有 1 元的人不能持有 5 元,否则他可以单独付账,所以他只能持有 1 元(1 元的张数不能大于 5)和 10 元(大于 10 元的面值不用考虑,因为它都可以用 10 元代替),若他持有 11 元,必须给他找回 5 元,这 5 元是另一个人给他的,这时无论他给另一个人的钱是 1 元还是 10 元,都会得到另一个人原先可以单独付账. 同样可以证明他不能持有 12、13、14、15 元. 所以口香糖的价格不能为 6 元.

若口香糖的价格为 7 元,则两个人付给老王的钱一共是 14 元,这 14 元中有四张为 1 元,由此可见其中一个人至少有两张 1 元,这个人不能持有 5 元,否则他可以单独付账. 同上面的讨论可得口香糖的价格不能为 7 元.

若口香糖的价格为 8 元,此时若其中一人带有一张 10 元和三张 1 元的纸币,另一人带有两张 5 元的纸币,因口香糖的价格为 8 元,可以将第一个人的两张 1 元找给第二个人,第二个人的一张 5 元找给第一个人,故选 E.

6. 答案:14 km.

解 设折线 AC 的长度为 x,小李的速度为 v,则小王的速度为 $\frac{3}{4}v$,根据题意有 $\frac{x+2}{v} = \frac{x-2}{\frac{3}{4}v}$,解得 $x = 14$ km.

7. 答案:16 号房间.

解 钥匙上所刻的首位数码为 1 时,所对应的房号可能为 1,4,7,10,13,16,19 号. 钥匙上所刻的第二位数码为 2 时,所对应的房号可能为 2,9,16 号. 故当钥匙上所刻的两位数码为 12 时,所对应的房号为 16.

评注 15 是 3 的倍数且除以 7 余 1,7 是 7 的倍数且除以 3 余 1,所以如果一把钥匙上的数字是 $\overline{ab}$,则它对应的房号为 $a\times7+b\times15$ 除以 $21(=3\times7)$ 所得的余数. 故当钥匙上所刻的两位数码为 12 时,所对应的房号为 $16(1\times7+2\times15=37,37=21\times1+16)$.

8. 答案:9.

解 如图 1-30 所示,设未知位置的数为 A、B、C、D、E、F,因为 $F+10+3=F+D+7$,所以 $D=6$. 又因为 $10+D+B=A+B+7$,所以 $A=3+D=9$.

A	B	7
C	D	E
F	10	3

图 1-30

9. 答案:$600-200\pi+100\sqrt{3}$ cm^2.

解 整个图形的截面可以看成是由三个相同的长方形、三个相同的扇形和一个正三角形组成,如图 1-31 所示.

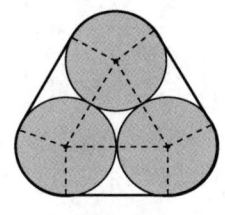

图 1-31

其中每个长方形的长和宽分别为 20 cm 和 10 cm;每个扇形的半径为 10 cm,圆心角为 120°,三个这样的扇形恰好组成一个圆;正三角形的边长为 20 cm. 整个截面积为:$20\times10\times3+10\times10\times\pi+100\sqrt{3}$ cm^2,减去三个圆的面积等于空隙部分的面积 $600-200\pi+100\sqrt{3}$ cm^2.

10. 答案:6174.

解 假设 N 是一个四位数的"魔术数",且 N 的四个数码从大到小的依次为 $a>b>c>d$. 由题目的条件可知,$\overline{abcd}-\overline{dcba}=N$. 根据 a、b、c、d 的大小关系,我们得到 N 的个位数为 $10+d-a$,N 的十位数为 $9+c-b$,N 的百位数为 $b-c-1$,N 的千位数为 $a-d$. 又由题目的条件可知,
$$a+b+c+d=(10+d-a)+(9+c-b)+(b-c-1)+(a-d)=18.$$
又因为 $a-d>b-c-1$,$9+c-b>10+d-a$,而且 $a-d<a$,由此可得
$$9+c-b=a. \qquad(1-1)$$

如果 $10+d-a=b$,则 $10+d=a+b$,由(1-1)可得 $9+c=10+d$,所以 $c=d+1$. 这时 $a-d=c$、$b-c-1=d$,得到 $b=2d+2$、$a=2d+1$,即 $a<b$,矛盾. 所以 $a-d=b$. 而 $10+d-a>d$,所以 $10+d-a=c$、$b-c-1=d$. 由此可得 $b+c=(a-d)+(10+d-a)=10$,$a+d=8$. 因为 $a>b>c>d$,所以 $a\geqslant d+3$,从而 d 最大能取 2:

当 $d=1$ 时,可得 $a=8-d=7$,$b=a-d=6$,$c=10-b=4$;

当 $d=2$ 时,可得 $a=8-d=6$,$b=a-d=4$,$c=10-b=6$,与 $b>c$ 矛盾.

因此只有 $d=1$,$c=4$,$b=6$,$a=7$ 满足要求. 所以四位数的"魔术数"只有 $7641-1467=6174$.

11. 答案:8.6cm².

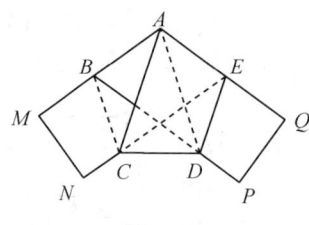

图 1-32

解 如图 1-32 所示,由于 ABCDE 是正五边形,且 CN+DP=CD,所以可将四边形 MNCB 和四边形 PQED 以 MN、PQ 边重合而使 B、E 共线以及 C、D 共线,合并起来而构成一个与四边形 ACDE 全等的四边形. 再由折叠的方式可知组成正五边形 ABCDE 的纸条是由四个相同的四边形纸条 ABCE、ACDE、ABCD、ABDE 所构成,因此原来纸条长方形的面积等于四边形 ACDE 的面积的 5 倍,所以四边形 ACDE 的面积为 17.2×2.5÷5=8.6(cm²).

12. 答案:12.

解 条件中未知量众多,无法一次求出,先退而求其次,注意到
$$(a_1x+c_1)(a_2x+c_2)=2x^2+7x+6=(x+2)(2x+3),$$
故可设 $a_1=1$、$c_1=2$、$a_2=2$ 及 $c_2=3$(有可能会相差一个倍数,但不影响结论). 下面考虑 xy 项和 y 项的系数知 $(2x+3)b_1+(x+2)b_2=10x+18$,求解二元一次方程组得 $b_1=2$、$b_2=6$,故 $M=b_1b_2=12$.

13. 答案:12 种.

解 根据正方形的对称性,方块(b)在 4×4 的正方形中有以下三种摆放方式,其中第三种方式不能再放下方块(a),在另外两种方式中,如果再放一个方块(a),都会导致有一个空白区域不能放任方块. 由此可知方块(a)与(b)不能同时选出. 同样可知方块(b)与(e)不能同时选出(图 1-33).

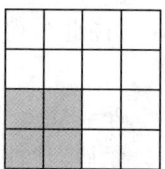 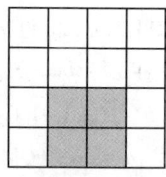 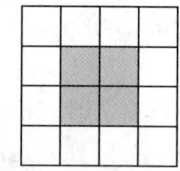

图 1-33

根据正方形的对称性,方块(e)在 4×4 的正方形中有以下两种摆放方式,由此可见方块(e)单独重复不能拼成一个 4×4 的正方形,并且如果选出方块(e),必须同时选出方块(d)(图 1-34).

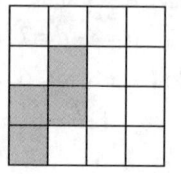 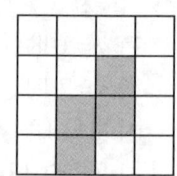

图 1-34

(1)选一种:前面四种方块单独重复使用都可以拼成一个 4×4 的正方形,所以这种情况共有 4 种选择方法.

(2)选两种:方块(a)不能与其他任何一种方块一起拼成一个 4×4 的正方形.方块(e)只能和方块(d)一起拼成一个 4×4 的正方形.在剩下的 3 种方块中,任何两种一起都可以拼成一个 4×4 的正方形.所以这种情况有 4 种选择方法.

(3)选三种:由于方块(a)与(b)不能同时选出,方块(b)与(e)也不能同时选出,这种情况有 4 种选择方法,分别是(a)(c)(d)、(a)(d)(e)、(b)(c)(d)、(c)(d)(e).它们的拼法如图 1-35 所示.

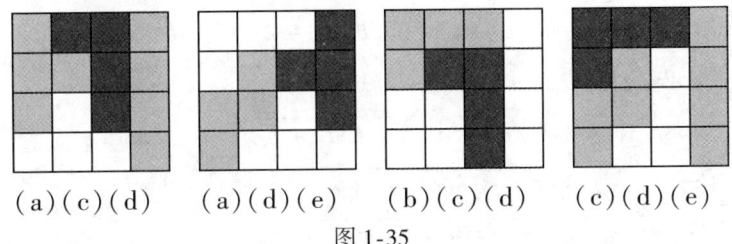

图 1-35

(4)选四种:由于方块(a)与(b)不能同时选出,方块(b)与(e)也不能同时选出,而(a)(c)(d)(e)不能拼成一个 4×4 的正方形.所以这种情况不存在.

因此共有 12 种可能.

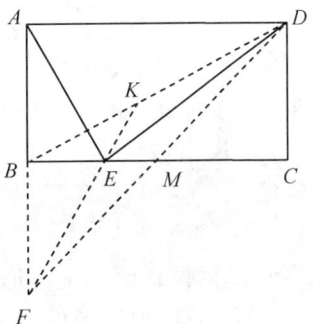

图 1-36

14. **解** 如图 1-36 所示,记 BC 的中点为 M,由对称性不妨设 E 点在线段 BM 上.延长 AB 到 F,使得 $BF=AB$. 显然 F、M、D 三点共线,连接 FE 和 BD,并设 FE 的延长线与 BD 相交于点 K.

由于 $BF=BA$、$BE=BE$、$\angle FBE=\angle ABE=90°$,故 $\triangle FBE \cong \triangle ABE$,即 $FE=AE$.

若 E 不与 B、M 重合,则由三角形三边关系定理得:
$$AE+DE=FE+DE<FE+EK+KD=FK+KD$$
$$<FB+BK+KD=FB+BD=AB+BD.$$

若 E 与 M 重合,则 $AE+DE=AM+DM=FM+DM=FD$;

若 E 与 B 重合,则 $AE+DE=AB+BD$.

因此 AE 与 DE 的长度之和的最大值为 $AB+BD$,所求的 E 点即为 B 点(由对称性,C 点亦可).

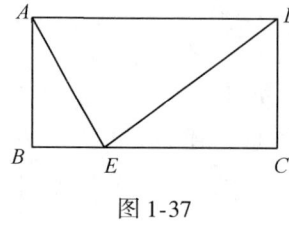

图 1-37

评注 下面证明当点 E 与点 B(或点 C)重合时,线段 AE 与 DE 的长度之和最大. 设 E 为 BC 边上任一点(除点 B 和点 C 外),令设 $AB=a$,$BC=b$,$BE=x$,$CE=b-x$. 由勾股定理可得 $AE=\sqrt{a^2+x^2}$,$DE=\sqrt{a^2+(b-x)^2}$(图 1-37).

下面只需证明:当 $0<x<b$ 时,

$$\sqrt{a^2+x^2}+\sqrt{a^2+(b-x)^2}<a+\sqrt{a^2+b^2}$$
$$\Leftrightarrow \sqrt{a^2+(b-x)^2}-a<\sqrt{a^2+b^2}-\sqrt{a^2+x^2}$$
$$\Leftrightarrow -2a\sqrt{a^2+(b-x)^2}-2bx<-2\sqrt{a^2+b^2}\sqrt{a^2+x^2}$$
$$\Leftrightarrow 2\sqrt{a^2+b^2}\sqrt{a^2+x^2}-2bx<2a\sqrt{a^2+(b-x)^2}$$
$$\Leftrightarrow 8b^2x^2-8bx\sqrt{a^4+a^2x^2+b^2a^2+b^2x^2}<-8ba^2x$$
$$\Leftrightarrow 8b^2x^2+8ba^2x<8bx\sqrt{a^4+a^2x^2+b^2a^2+b^2x^2}$$
$$\Leftrightarrow bx+a^2<\sqrt{a^4+a^2x^2+b^2a^2+b^2x^2}$$
$$\Leftrightarrow 2ba^2x<a^2x^2+b^2a^2$$
$$\Leftrightarrow 2bx<x^2+b^2$$
$$\Leftrightarrow 0<(x-b)^2.$$

15. **答案**:21 张.

解 最多可以剪下 21 张邮票,如图 1-38 所示.

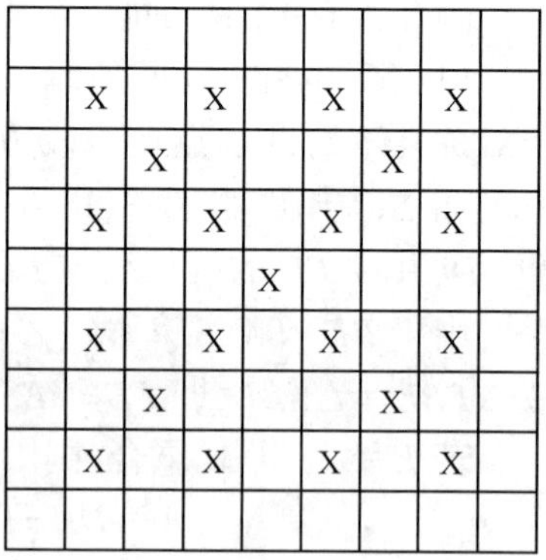

假设每张邮票小正方形之边长为 1,若他共剪下 x 张邮票,根据条件(1)和(2),剩下的邮票的周长为 $36+4x$;另一方面,我们可以将剪剩下的邮票看成是在外框一圈邮票的基础上,再将其他邮票逐一"黏回去"而得到的. 已知外框邮票的周长为 $(7+9)\times 4=64$,还要粘回去 $7^2-x=49-x$ 张邮票,每粘回一张邮票,总周长最多增加 2,因此剩下邮票的周长最多为 $64+2(49-x)=162-2x$.

因此 $36+4x\leqslant 162-2x$,故 $x\leqslant 21$,即最多可以剪下 21 张邮票.

图 1-38

1.7　第1届国际中小学生数学能力检测样题

初中第1轮

1. (代数)用甲乙两种原料按照 $x:y$ (重量比)混合配制成一种新饮料,原来两种原料成本是:甲每500克5元,乙每500克4元. 现甲的成本上升10%,乙的成本下降10%,而新饮料成本恰好保持不变,请问 $x:y$ 的值为多少?
   (A)1:2　　(B)2:3　　(C)2:5　　(D)3:4　　(E)4:5
   答案:(E).

   解　由 $5x+4y=5.5x+3.6y$, $5x=4y$, $x:y=4:5$.

2. (代数)两条纸带,较长的一条为23 cm,较短的一条为15 cm. 把两条纸带剪下同样长的一段后,剩下的两条纸带中,要求较长的纸带的长度不少于较短的纸带长度的两倍,请问剪下的长度至少是多少?
   (A)6 cm　　(B)7 cm　　(C)8 cm　　(D)9 cm　　(E)10 cm
   答案:(B).

   解　设剪下的长度为 x cm,则
   $$23-x \geqslant 2(15-x),$$
   解得 $x \geqslant 7$. 因此,剪下的长度至少为 7 cm.

3. (组合)要在10个盒子中放乒乓球,球的个数彼此不同,不能少于11个,不能是13个,个数也不能是5的倍数,请问至少需要多少个乒乓球?
   (A)150　　(B)155　　(C)162　　(D)173　　(E)186
   答案:(D).

   解　至少需要 $11+12+14+16+17+18+19+21+22+23=173$(个).

4. (数论)在一条3000 m长的新公路的一侧,从一端开始等距离立电线杆,按原设计,电线杆间隔50 m,已挖好了坑. 若间隔距离改为60 m,请问需要重新挖多少个坑?
   (A)11　　(B)40　　(C)50　　(D)60　　(E)61
   答案:(B).

   解　原来挖好坑的个数为 $\dfrac{3000}{50}+1=61$(个).

   现需 $\dfrac{3000}{60}+1=51$(个),而50与60的最小公倍数为300,即每隔300 m处的

坑应该保留,共有 $\frac{3000}{300}+1=11$ 个坑被保留,故还需要挖 $51-11=40$ 个坑.

5.(数论)在下面五个数中:
1234554321、 1234554321^2、 123454321、 123454321^2、 123454321
$\times 1234554321$,

请问 2009 的倍数有多少个?
(A)0　　　(B)1　　　(C)2　　　(D)3　　　(E)4

答案:(B).

解　我们知道: $2009=7^2\times 41$,$111111=7\times 11\times 13\times 111$,$11111=41\times 271$,
$1234554321=11111\times 111111$ 是 41 和 7 的倍数但不是 7^2 的倍数;
$123454321=11111\times 11111$ 不是 7 的倍数,所以仅有 1234554321^2 是 2009 的倍数.

6.(几何)直角坐标平面上的每个整点 (x,y)(x、y 都是整数的点)处放一盏灯.当时刻 $t=0$ 时,仅原点处有一盏灯亮着.当 $t=1,2,\cdots$ 时,满足下列条件的灯被打开:至少与一盏亮着的灯的距离为 5.请问直角坐标平面上永远不能打开的灯有多少盏(图 1-39)?
(A)0　　　(B)4　　　(C)8　　　(D)12　　　(E)无穷多

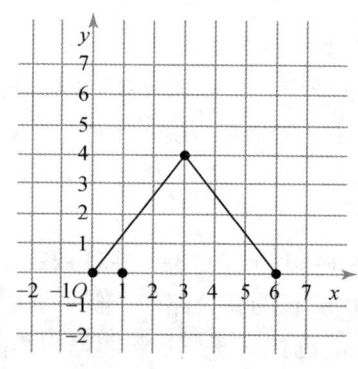

图 1-39

答案:(A).

解　所有的灯都能被打开.下面是依次被打开的灯的坐标(相邻两点距离都为 5):$(0,0)\to(3,4)\to(6,0)\to(1,0)$.这说明与原点距离为 1 的整点放置的灯能被打开,于是所有的灯都能被打开.

7.(几何)如图 1-40 所示的立体图形由 9 个棱长为 1cm 的立方块搭成,请问这个立体图形的表面积为多少?

答案:32.

解 从上、下、前、后、左、右看到的这个立体图形的表面的面积分别为 5 cm², 5 cm², 5 cm², 5 cm², 6 cm², 6 cm²,总和为 32 cm².

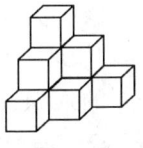

图 1-40

8.(组合)在 2000, 2001, 2002, $\cdots$, 2011 这 12 个数中,请问不能表示成两个完全平方数的差的数有多少个?

答案:3.

解法 1 如果数 a 是奇数,则

$$a = \left(\frac{a+1}{2}\right)^2 - \left(\frac{a-1}{2}\right)^2.$$

如果 a 是 4 的倍数,则

$$a = \left(\frac{a}{4}+1\right)^2 - \left(\frac{a}{4}-1\right)^2.$$

一个偶数如果能表示成两个平方数的差,则这两个数一定同时为奇数或者偶数. 而两个奇数(偶数)的平方差一定是 4 的倍数,因为 2002, 2006, 2010 不是 4 的倍数,故不能表示成两个完全平方数的差.

解法 2 一个完全平方数被 4 除的余数为 0 或 1,故两个数的平方差被 4 除的余数一定不为 2,故 2002, 2006, 2010 不能表示成两个完全平方数的差.

而 1. $a^2 - b^2 = (a-b)(a+b) = 2000$,其中一解为 $a=501, b=499$.

2. $a^2 - b^2 = (a-b)(a+b) = 2001$,其中一解为 $a=335, b=332$.

3. $a^2 - b^2 = (a-b)(a+b) = 2003$,其中一解为 $a=1002, b=1001$.

4. $a^2 - b^2 = (a-b)(a+b) = 2004$,其中一解为 $a=502, b=500$.

5. $a^2 - b^2 = (a-b)(a+b) = 2005$,其中一解为 $a=1003, b=1002$.

6. $a^2 - b^2 = (a-b)(a+b) = 2007$,其中一解为 $a=1004, b=1003$.

7. $a^2 - b^2 = (a-b)(a+b) = 2008$,其中一解为 $a=503, b=501$.

8. $a^2 - b^2 = (a-b)(a+b) = 2009$,其中一解为 $a=1005, b=1004$.

9. $a^2 - b^2 = (a-b)(a+b) = 2011$,其中一解为 $a=1006, b=1005$.

1.8 第 1 届国际中小学生数学能力检测样题

初中第 2 轮

1.(数论)请问恰有 20 个因数的最小正整数是什么?

(A)120　　(B)240　　(C)360　　(D)432　　(E)1536

答案:(B).

解 因为 $20=2\times 10=4\times 5=2\times 2\times 5$,因此,具有 20 个因数的最小正整数可能是 3 与 9 个 2 的乘积,即 $3\times 2\times 2\times 2\times 2\times 2\times 2\times 2\times 2\times 2=1536$;也可能是 3 个 3 与 4 个 2 的乘积,即 $3\times 3\times 3\times 2\times 2\times 2\times 2=432$;也可能是 3,5 与 4 个 2 的乘积,即 $3\times 5\times 2\times 2\times 2\times 2=240$,经比较知最小的正整数为 240.

2.(数论)已知 m,n 是正整数,下列命题中恰好有一个是错误的,请问哪个选项是错误的命题?

(A)$m+n$ 能被 3 整除　　　　(B)$m+1$ 能被 n 整除

(C)$m+7n$ 是一个素数　　　　(D)$m=2n+5$

(E)mn 是一个偶数

答案:(A).

解 若(A)是正确的,则 $m+7n=(m+n)+6n$ 大于 3 且能被 3 整除,不是素数,故(C)是错的;(D)也是错的,若不然,$m=2n+5$,则由(A)正确知:$m+n=(2n+5)+n=3n+5$ 应能被 3 整除,但 $3n+5$ 不能被 3 整除,故(D)也是错的.以上与(A)、(B)、(C)、(D)、(E)中恰好有一个错误矛盾.从而(A)是错误的.事实上,可取 $m=17,n=6.$ 或 $m=9,n=2.$

3.(代数)已知 -2 和 2 对应的点将数轴分成 3 段,如果数轴上任意 n 个不同的点中至少有 3 个在其中一段之中,请问 n 的最小值是多少(图 1-41)?

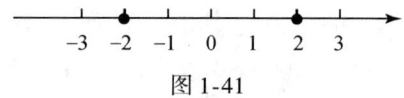

图 1-41

(A)4　　　(B)5　　　(C)6　　　(D)7　　　(E)8

答案:(D).

解 数轴的三段包含了所有数对应的点,再由抽屉原理得出 D 是对的.

4.(代数)某手表每小时比准确时间慢 3 分钟,若在清晨 4 点 30 分与准确时间对准,则在当天上午手表指示时间为 10 点 50 分时,请问准确时间应该是几点几分?

答案:11 点 10 分.

解 设所求的准确时间为 x 小时,由题意得:

$$\frac{1}{20}\left(x-4\frac{1}{2}\right)=\left(x-10\frac{5}{6}\right).$$

解之得:$x=11\frac{1}{6}$(小时)$=11$ 小时 10 分.

5. (组合)如图 1-42,A 是邮局,$B,C,D,E,$ F 是 5 户人家. 相邻两家的路程如图所标示. 邮递员从邮局出发要给这 5 户人家送信(每家都有信),要求最后把信送到 D 户,但不须返回邮局. 请问邮递员走的最短路程是多少 m?

答案:500 m.

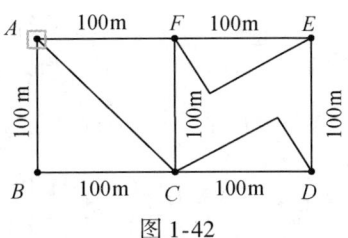

图 1-42

解 $A \xrightarrow{100} B \xrightarrow{100} C \xrightarrow{100} F \xrightarrow{100} E \xrightarrow{100} D.$

6. (几何)如图 1-43 所示,某风景区的沿湖公路 $AB=3$ km,$BC=4$ km,$CD=12$ km,$AD=13$ km,其中 $AB\perp BC$,图中阴影是草地,其余是水面. 乘游艇由点 C 出发,行进速度为每小时 10 km,请问到达对岸 AD 最少要用多少小时?

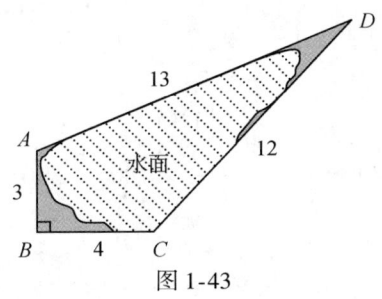

图 1-43

答案:$\dfrac{6}{13}$.

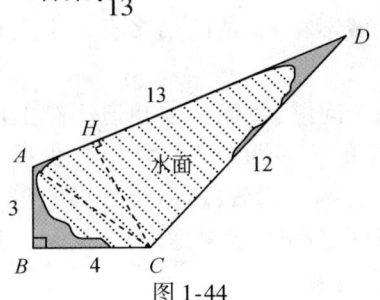

图 1-44

解 连接 AC(图 1-44). 由勾股定理容易求得 $AC=5$ km. 又因为 $5^2+12^2=13^2$,所以三角形 ACD 是直角三角形,$\angle ACD=90°$. 要乘游艇由点 C 出发,行进速度为每小时 10 km,到达对岸 AD 所用时间最少,游艇行进路线必须最短,即为点 C 到 AD 的距离,也就是直角三角形 ACD 中斜边 AD 上的高线,

这个高线 $=\dfrac{AC\times CD}{AD}=\dfrac{5\times 12}{13}=\dfrac{60}{13}$(km).

所以游艇行进最少时间为

$$\dfrac{60}{13}\div 10=\dfrac{6}{13}(\text{小时}).$$

7.（几何）一个正 m 边形恰好被 m 个正 n 边形包围（图 1-45 是 $m=4$ 和 $n=8$ 的情况）．当 $m=10$ 时，请问 n 等于多少？

解 如图 1-45 所示，正 m 边形的内角的大小为 $\frac{(m-2)\times 180°}{m}$，所以正 10 边形的内角（$m=10$）为 $\frac{(10-2)\times 180°}{10}=144°$．在正 m 边形的每个顶点都有两个正 n 边形恰好外接，所以正 m 边形的内角加上于正 n 边形的内角的两倍等于 $360°$，从而

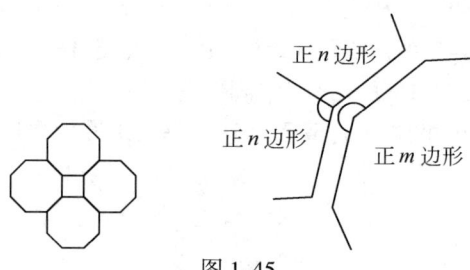

图 1-45

$$144° + 2\times \frac{n-2}{n}\times 180° = 360°,$$

所以 $n=5$．

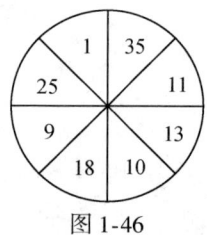

图 1-46

8.（组合）有一群人向下图 1-46 所示的靶掷飞镖，靶上的数表示飞镖掷到该区域的得分．每个人掷 4 把飞镖，且每个人总分都是 62 分．如果每两个人的得分区域至少有一区域不相同，请问最多有多少人玩这个游戏？

解 为了解决这个问题，我们必须知道用靶上的数 0（未中目标），1,9,10,11,13,18,25 和 35 中的至多四个之和能以多少种不同方式表示 62，和式中的数可以重复．这里只有两个偶数，所以得分可能包含 18,18，或 10,18，或 10,10，或都是奇数．这帮助我们缩小了考虑的范围，从而我们找到四个飞镖都击中目标且得分为 62 的情况有 8 种．

$$\begin{aligned}
62 &= 35 + 25 + 1 + 1 \\
&= 35 + 13 + 13 + 1 \\
&= 35 + 9 + 9 + 9 \\
&= 25 + 25 + 11 + 1 \\
&= 25 + 18 + 18 + 1 \\
&= 25 + 18 + 10 + 9
\end{aligned}$$

$$= 25 + 13 + 13 + 11$$
$$= 18 + 18 + 13 + 13.$$

3个飞镖击中目标的情况有一种$\{35,18,9\}$.

靶上的两个最大数之和为$25+35=60$,故不可能只有2个飞镖击中目标.

这说明最多有9个人玩这个游戏.

第2章 第2届国际中小学生数学能力检测(IMAS)(初中组)

2.1 第一轮英文试题

考试时间:75分钟

Questions 1–10, 3 marks each

1. What is the value of $2012^0+(-1)^2+|-2012|$?
   (A)-2010　(B)1　(C)2012　(D)2013　(E)2014

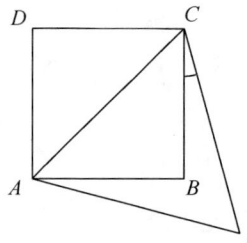

2. In the diagram below, $ABCD$ is a square and ACE is an equilateral triangle. What is the measure, in degrees, of $\angle BCE$?
   (A)15　(B)20　(C)25
   (D)30　(E)cannot be determined

3. The smallest interior angle of a triangle is $50°$. Which of the following statements about this triangle is correct?

(A) It must be isosceles.
(B) It must be right angled.
(C) It must be acute angled.
(D) It must be obtuse angled.
(E) None of these is correct.

4. The diagram to the below shows three squares $EFGH$, $KLMN$ and $PQRS$ inside a rectangle $ABCD$. The areas of the three squares are 1 cm^2, 9 cm^2 and 4 cm^2 respectively. What is the sum of areas of the shaded regions in cm^2?
   (A)3　(B)4　(C)5　(D)6　(E)7

第 2 章 第 2 届国际中小学生数学能力检测(IMAS)(初中组)

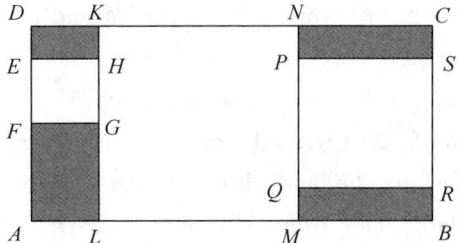

5. A triangle is formed with 10 matchsticks of equal length connected end to end. No matchsticks are bent or broken. How many different triangles can be formed?

(A)2　　　　(B)3　　　　(C)4　　　　(D)5　　　　(E)6

6. A piece of paper in the shape of parallelogram is folded into two with the crease bisecting the area of parallelogram. How many different kinds of origami methods are possible?

(A)0　　　　　　　　(B)1　　　　　　　　(C)2

(D)3　　　　　　　　(E)infinitely many

7. A TV company plans to broadcast a series with 48 episodes. One episode is aired each day except on Saturday and Sunday. If the first episode is aired on Thursday, on what day of the week will the last episode be aired?

(A)Monday　　　　　(B)Tuesday　　　　　(C)Wednesday

(D)Thursday　　　　(E)Friday

8. Cups labelled 1, 2, 3, 4 and 5 with mouth upwards line in row, as shown below. Initially a ball is put into cup #3. In each move, the ball is transferred to an adjacent cup. If the ball is in cup #1, it can only be moved to cup #2. If the ball is in cup #5, it can only be moved to cup #4. After $2^{10}+3^8$ moves, which of the following statements about the ball is correct?

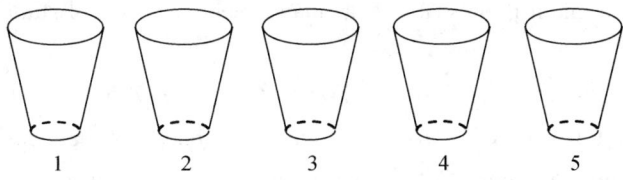

(A) It cannot be in cup #3, cannot be in cup #4 and cannot be in cup #5

(B) It cannot be in cup #2, cannot be in cup #4 and cannot be in cup #5

39

(C) It cannot be in cup #1, cannot be in cup #4 and cannot be in cup #5

(D) It cannot be in cup #1, cannot be in cup #3 and cannot be in cup #5

(E) It cannot be in cup #2 and cannot be in cup #4

9. During the holidays, Dick worked part-time washing bowls in a restaurant. He got paid 3 dollars for washing one bowl. If he broke a bowl, he got no pay for washing it, and must pay 9 dollars to the owner. In one week, Dick washed 500 bowls and earned 1368 dollars. How many bowls did he break?

(A) 7　　　(B) 8　　　(C) 9　　　(D) 10　　　(E) 11

10. The diagram below shows four squares with numbers which exhibit a certain pattern. What number should be inside the fourth box?

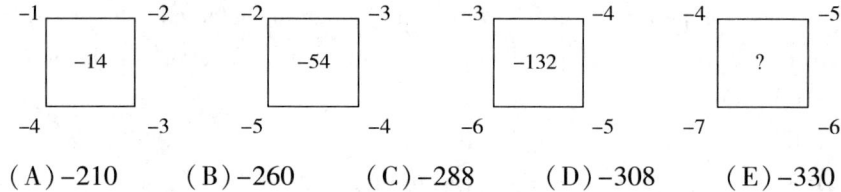

(A) −210　　　(B) −260　　　(C) −288　　　(D) −308　　　(E) −330

Questions 11−20, 4 marks each

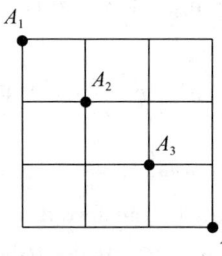

11. The diagram below shows a square network of roads, A_1, A_2, A_3 and A_4 are four intersections on the same diagonal. We want to go from A_1 to A_4 by going only to the east or to the south, without passing through A_3. How many different paths are there?

(A) 8　　　(B) 10　　　(C) 20

(D) 15　　　(E) 12

12. Each row in a cinema has 80 seats, and row 13 to row 24 are reserved for students from a secondary school. There are 15 empty seats in these rows when all the students have taken their seats. How many secondary school students went to the cinema?

(A) 945　　　(B) 875　　　(C) 865　　　(D) 775　　　(E) 765

13. The total weight of 3 apples is equal to that of 4 bananas, and the total weight of 5 bananas is equal to that of 6 oranges. How many apples have the same total weight as 16 oranges?

(A) 6　　　(B) 7　　　(C) 8　　　(D) 9　　　(E) 10

14. The diagram below shows a cube with three of its faces labelled A, B and C, and a 3×3 square with six of its squares labelled 1, 2, 3, 4, 5 and 6. The cube is tipped over so that face C lies on square 1, tipped over again so that face B lies on square 2, and so on until the cube lies on square 6. What is the sum of the numbers of the squares on which the cube has laid with face B on top?

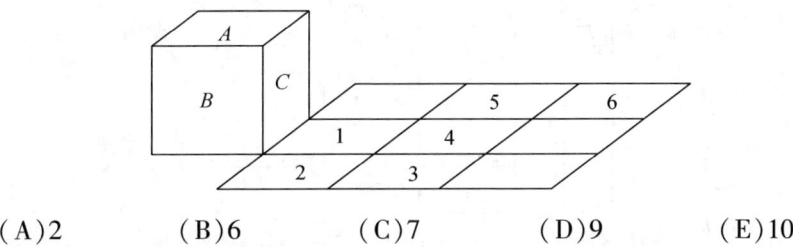

(A)2   (B)6   (C)7   (D)9   (E)10

15. A deck of 54 cards has 2 jokers, and 13 cards of each of spades, hearts, clubs and diamonds. At least how many cards should be drawn at random so that there are at least 4 cards of the same suit?

(A)54   (B)14   (C)15   (D)16   (E)17

16. The number $5^n + 7^n$ is divided by 100 where n is any non-negative integer. How many different values of the remainder are there?

(A)4   (B)6   (C)8   (D)10   (E)15

17. For any positive integers a and b, define a new operation $a \odot b$ which yields the remainder when the larger of a and b is divided by the smaller one. For example, $5 \odot 12 = 12 \odot 5 = 2$. Given that $(19 \odot x) \odot 19 = 5$, what value below is not possible for x?

(A)12   (B)26   (C)33   (D)39   (E)45

18. What is the total number of positive integers consisting of three different digits in which the tens digit is equal to the units digit of the sum of the other two digits?

(A)36   (B)60   (C)72   (D)90   (E)108

19. The diagram below shows seven squares resting on a straight line. The areas of three tilted squares are 1, 2 and 3. What is the total area of the other four squares?

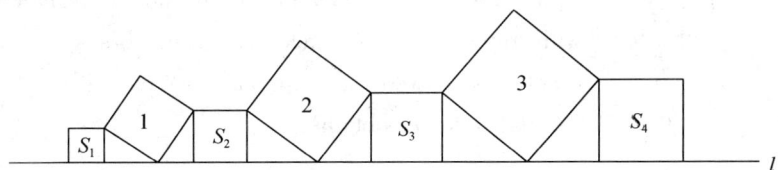

(A)4　　(B)5　　(C)6　　(D)7　　(E)8

20. On a 4×4 chessboard shown in the diagram below on the left, we wish to place a minimum number of copies of the shape shown in the diagram below on the right, so that no more copies of this shape can be placed. Copies may be rotated. What is this minimum number of copies?

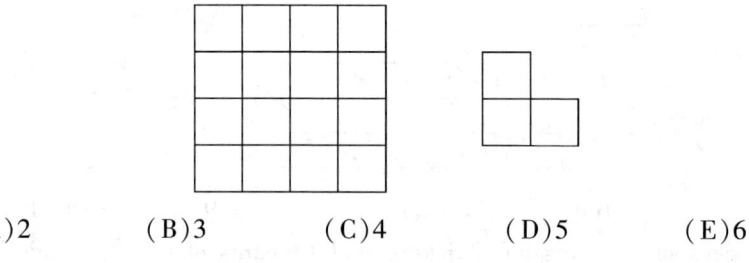

(A)2　　(B)3　　(C)4　　(D)5　　(E)6

Questions 21–25, 6 marks each

21. We place 100 table tennis balls inside n boxes so that the number of balls in each box contains the digit 8, such as 8 balls, 18 balls, 83 balls and 88 balls. When $n=3$, the number of table tennis balls in the boxes are 8, 8 and 84 respectively. If $n=5$, and two of the boxes have the same number of balls while other boxes have different number of balls, what is the largest total number of balls in two boxes?

22. Let a,b,c and d be positive integers less than 10, and x be an integer such that $ax^3-bx^2-cx-d=0$. What is maximum value of x?

23. Let a,b and c be real numbers such that $a+b+c=0$ and $abc=-15$. What is the value of $a^2(b+c)+b^2(c+a)+c^2(a+b)$?

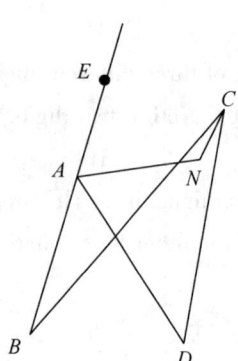

24. The diagram below shows four line segments AB, BC, CD and DA on the plane where $\angle ABC=24°$ and $\angle ADC=42°$. Point E is on the extension of line BA, and the angle bisectors of $\angle DAE$ and $\angle BCD$ intersects at point N. What is the measure, in degrees, of $\angle ANC$?

25. In the expression 6□7□8□9, an arithmetic sign (plus, minus, multiplication or division sign, can be used with repetition) is placed in each bracket □. Open bracket is allowed (it is optional). What will be the largest 3-digit number obtained?

第2章 第2届国际中小学生数学能力检测(IMAS)(初中组)

2.2 第一轮中文试题

1–10题,每题3分

1. 请问算式 $2012^0 + (-1)^2 + |-2012|$ 之值为何?

(A)-2010　　(B)1　　(C)2012　　(D)2013　　(E)2014

2. 如图2-1,四边形 ABCD 是正方形,三角形 ACE 是正三角形. 请问∠BCE 等于多少度?

(A)15　　(B)20　　(C)25　　(D)30　　(E)无法确定

3. 有一个三角形最小的内角为50°,请问关于这个三角形的描述以下哪一项一定是对的?

(A)必定是等腰三角形　　(B)必定是直角三角形

(C)必定是锐角三角形　　(D)必定是钝角三角形

(E)以上都不对

4. 长方形 ABCD 内有三个相邻的正方形 EFGH、KLMN、PQRS,如图所示. 已知它们的面积分别为 $1\ cm^2$,$9\ cm^2$,$4\ cm^2$,请问图2-2中阴影部分的面积总和为多少 cm^2?

(A)3　　(B)4　　(C)5　　(D)6　　(E)7

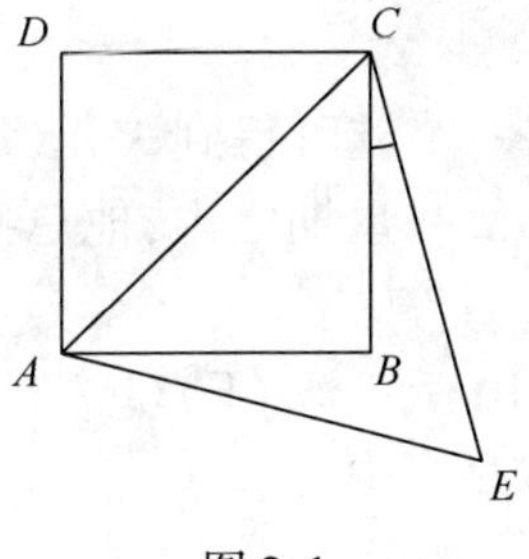

图2-1 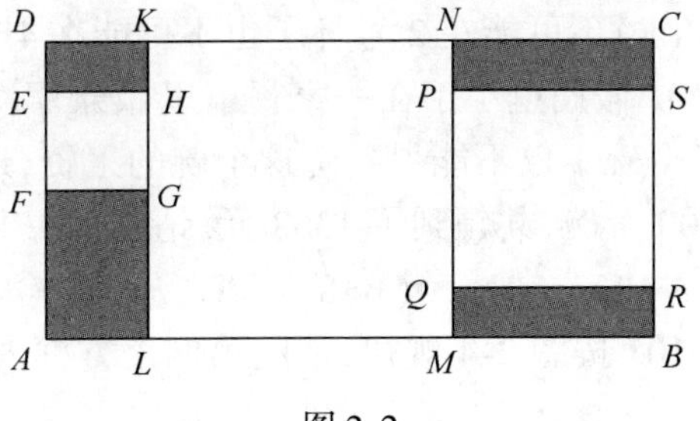　　　　　　　　　图2-2

5. 用10根长度相同的火柴棒首尾依次连接构成一个三角形,火柴棒不可以折断,请问能连接成多少种不同形状的三角形?

(A)2　　(B)3　　(C)4　　(D)5　　(E)6

6. 将一张平行四边形的纸片沿一条直线折一次,使得折痕平分该平行四边形的面积. 请问共有多少种不同的折法?

(A)0　　(B)1　　(C)2　　(D)3　　(E)无穷多

7. 某电视台计划播出一部 48 集的电视连续剧,每星期一、二、三、四、五各播出一集.请问如果第一集是在某个星期四播出的,那么最后一集是星期几播出的?

(A)一 (B)二 (C)三 (D)四 (E)五

8. 如图 2-3 所示,编号为 1、2、3、4、5 的五个杯子排成一排,起初 3 号杯子中有一个小球.现按以下方式操作,每次操作必须将小球移动到与它所在杯子相邻的杯子中(1 号杯子中的球只能移动至 2 号杯、5 号杯子中的球只能移动至 4 号杯).请问经过 $2^{10}+3^8$ 次操作后,请问下列哪一项是关于小球的正确描述?

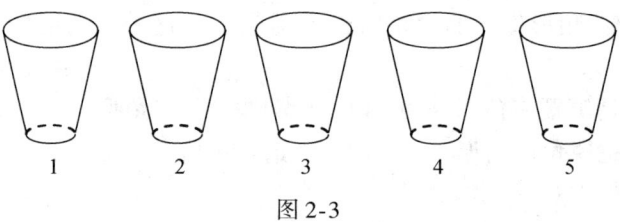

图 2-3

(A)不可能在 3 号杯子、不可能在 4 号杯子也不可能在 5 号杯子
(B)不可能在 2 号杯子、不可能在 4 号杯子也不可能在 5 号杯子
(C)不可能在 1 号杯子、不可能在 4 号杯子也不可能在 5 号杯子
(D)不可能在 1 号杯子、不可能在 3 号杯子也不可能在 5 号杯子
(E)不可能在 2 号杯子也不可能在 4 号杯子

9. 假期里小丁在一家餐馆里做兼职洗碗.每洗好一个碗可得到 3 元,每打破一个碗不仅不能得到洗这个碗的工资,还要另赔 9 元.一星期之内,他总共洗了 500 个碗,共领到了 1368 元.请问他一共打破了多少个碗?

(A)7 (B)8 (C)9 (D)10 (E)11

10. 按图 2-4 规律,请问第四个方框内应填入的数是多少?

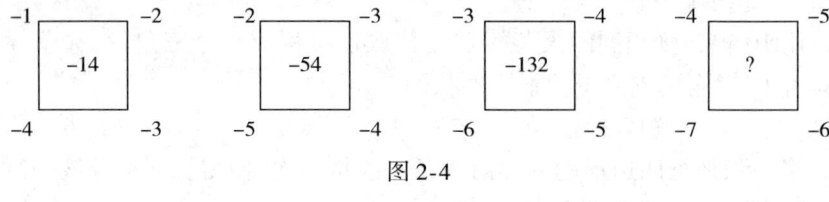

图 2-4

(A)−210 (B)−260 (C)−288 (D)−308 (E)−330

11–20题,每题4分

11. 如图2-5所示,点A_1、A_2、A_3、A_4是某市正方形道路网的部分交汇点,且它们都位于同一条对角线上. A_3处因修路不通,请问某人从点A_1出发,不经过A_3到达点A_4的走法共有多少种?(规定只能向右或向下行走)

(A)8　　(B)10　　(C)20　　(D)15　　(E)12

12. 电影院每排有80个座位,把第13排到第24排的座位留给某中学的学生,学生入座后在这些排中还剩15个空座位.请问该学校进场看电影的学生有多少人?

(A)945　　(B)875　　(C)865　　(D)775　　(E)765

13. 已知三个苹果与四根香蕉的重量相同,五根香蕉与六个橘子的重量相同,请问十六个橘子与几个苹果的重量相同?

(A)6　　(B)7　　(C)8　　(D)9　　(E)10

14. 如图2-6所示,一个正方体有三个分别标记为A,B,C的表面与一个$3×3$方格表有六个分别标记为1、2、3、4、5、6的小方格.将这个正方体翻转,使得C面与标记为1的小方格吻合,再翻转正方体使得B面与标记为2的小方格吻合;依序继续将正方体翻转,直到第6格为止.请问此翻转过程中使得正方体朝上一面为字母B的所有小方格上的数之和是多少?

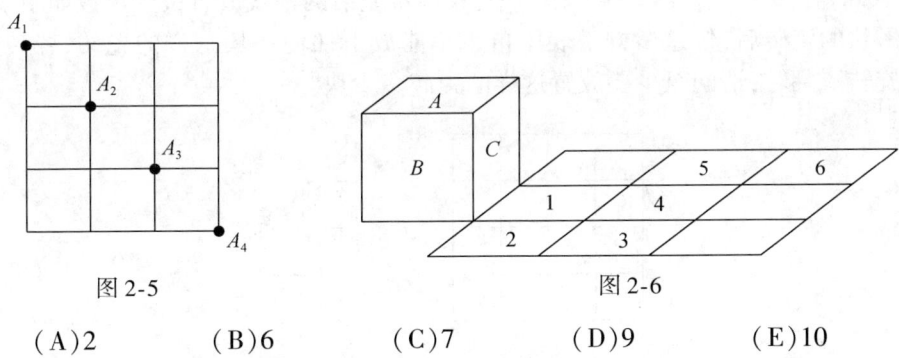

图2-5　　　　　　　图2-6

(A)2　　(B)6　　(C)7　　(D)9　　(E)10

15. 一副扑克牌共54张,由两张鬼牌与黑桃、红心、梅花、方块四门花色各13张牌组成.请问至少要从中任意抽出多少张牌,才能保证有一门花色至少有4张牌?

(A)54　　(B)14　　(C)15　　(D)16　　(E)17

16. 将数5^n+7^n除以100,其中n为非负整数,请问共可能得到多少种不同的余数?

(A) 4 　　(B) 6 　　(C) 8 　　(D) 10 　　(E) 15

17. 定义新运算：$a \odot b$ 表示正整数 a、b 中较大的数除以较小的数后所得的余数，例如 $5 \odot 12 = 2$、$12 \odot 5 = 2$。已知 $(19 \odot x) \odot 19 = 5$，请问 x 不可能是下列哪一项？

(A) 12 　　(B) 26 　　(C) 33 　　(D) 39 　　(E) 45

18. 请问共有多少个三位数，它的数码互不相同且十位上的数码等于其他两个数码之和的末位数？

(A) 36 　　(B) 60 　　(C) 72 　　(D) 90 　　(E) 108

19. 如图 2-7 所示，在直线 l 上依次摆放着七个正方形。已知斜放置的三个正方形的面积分别是 1、2、3，请问其他四个正方形的面积总和是多少？

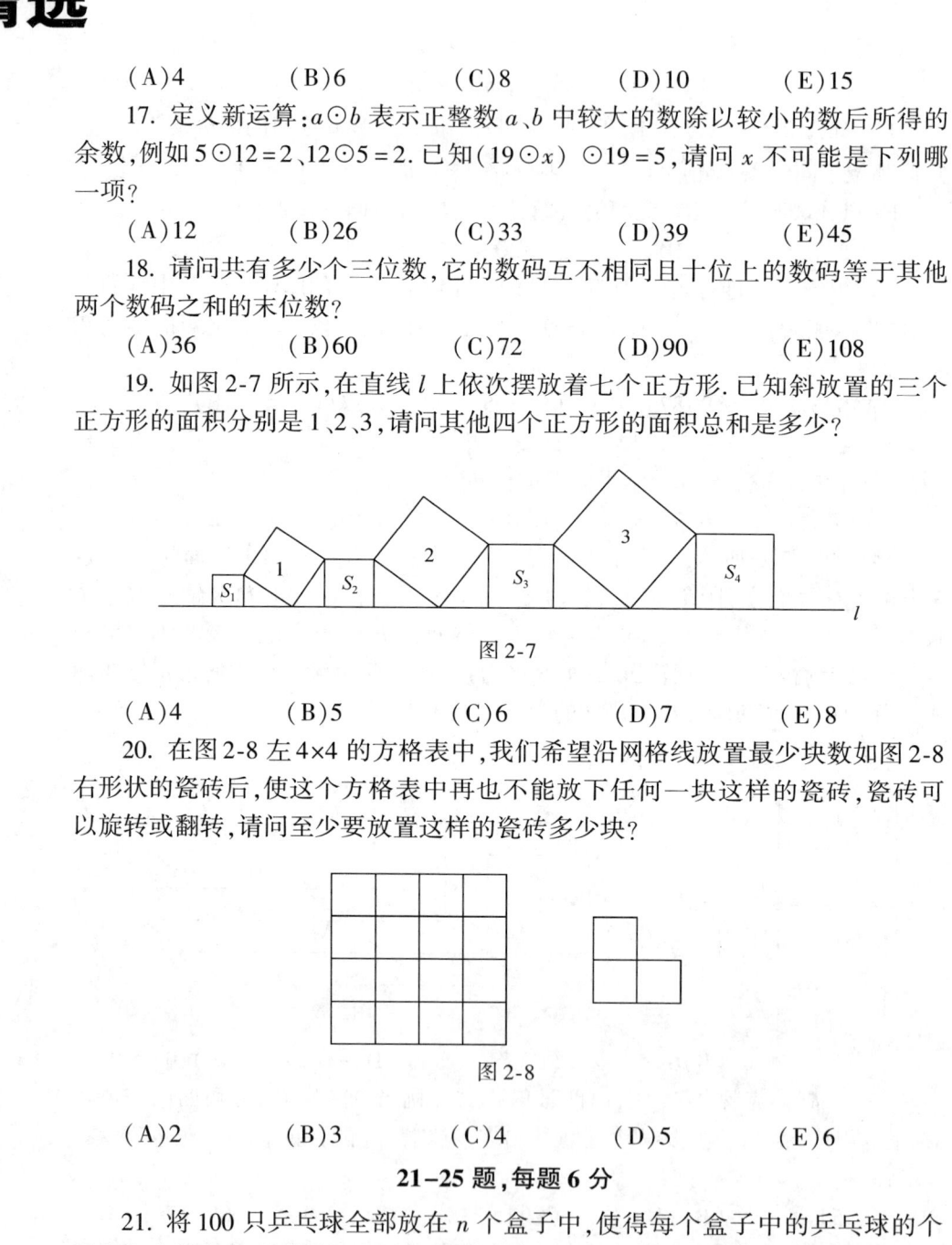

图 2-7

(A) 4 　　(B) 5 　　(C) 6 　　(D) 7 　　(E) 8

20. 在图 2-8 左 4×4 的方格表中，我们希望沿网格线放置最少块数如图 2-8 右形状的瓷砖后，使这个方格表中再也不能放下任何一块这样的瓷砖，瓷砖可以旋转或翻转，请问至少要放置这样的瓷砖多少块？

图 2-8

(A) 2 　　(B) 3 　　(C) 4 　　(D) 5 　　(E) 6

21—25 题，每题 6 分

21. 将 100 只乒乓球全部放在 n 个盒子中，使得每个盒子中的乒乓球的个数都含有数码"8"，例如：8、18、83、88；当 $n = 3$ 时，盒子中的乒乓球的数目可以分别为 8、8、84；若 $n = 5$，且恰有两个盒子中的乒乓球个数相同，其余盒子中的乒乒乓球个数彼此不同,在此情况下,请问乒乓球数最多的两个盒子中的乒乓球数之总和是多少?

22. 设 a、b、c、d 都是小于 10 的正整数,整数 x 满足 $ax^3-bx^2-cx-d=0$,请问 x 的最大可能值是多少?

23. 已知实数 a、b、c 满足 $a+b+c=0$ 且 $abc=-15$.

请问代数式 $a^2(b+c)+b^2(c+a)+c^2(a+b)$ 的值是多少?

24. 如图 2-9,平面上四条线段 AB、BC、CD、DA,$\angle ABC=24°$、$\angle ADC=42°$,点 E 在 BA 的延长线上,$\angle DAE$ 的平分线和 $\angle BCD$ 的平分线交于点 N,请问 $\angle ANC$ 是多少度?

25. 在算式 $6\square 7\square 8\square 9$ 中的每一个 $\square$ 处放入一个四则运算符号(加号、减号、乘号或除号,可重复挑选),然后仅允许在算式中添加一些括号(也可以不添加),请问所能得到的最大的三位数是多少?

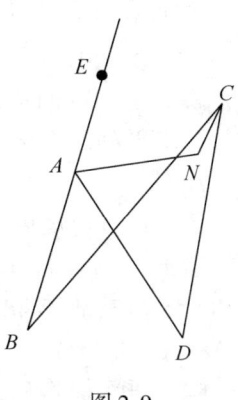

图 2-9

2.3 第一轮试题解答与评注

1. 答案:(E).

解 由于 $2012^0=1$、$(-1)^2=1$、$|-2012|=2012$,因此代数式的值为 $1+1+2012=2014$,故选(E).

2. 答案:(A).

解 由于 $ABCD$ 是正方形,故 ABC 是等腰直角三角形,因此 $\angle ACB=45°$. 又因为 ACE 是正三角形,故 $\angle ACE=60°$,因此 $\angle BCE=60°-45°=15°$,故选(A).

3. 答案:(C).

解 注意到最小的一个内角为 $50°$,因此第二小的内角至少为 $50°$,故最大的内角不超过 $180°-50°-50°=80°$,这说明此三角形一定为锐角三角形. 另外,当三个内角分别为 $50°$、$60°$ 和 $70°$ 时,此三角形并非是等腰三角形,直角三角形或钝角三角形,可排除其余选项,故选(C).

4. 答案:(B).

解 已知三个正方形的边长依次为 $1cm$、$3cm$、$2cm$,故 $AB=1+3+2=6cm$,因此矩形 $ABCD$ 的面积为 $6×3=18cm^2$,故阴影部分的面积总和为 $18-(1+9+4)=4cm^2$,故选(B).

5. 答案:(A).

解 设每根火柴棒长度为1,则三角形的三边长度均需为整数,且周长为10.由三角形三边关系定理(或两点之间直线最短)知任意一条边的长度不能大于或等于5,因此三条边长均只能在1、2、3、4中选择,显然只有 $2+4+4=3+3+4=10$,因此仅能接成2个不同形状的三角形,故选(A).

6. 答案:(E).

解 由平行四边形的中心对称性可知,只要折痕经过平行四边形的中心,它就一定平分该平行四边形的面积,故有无穷多种折纸的方法,故选(E).

7. 答案:(A).

解 逐步递推可知第2集在星期五播出、第3集在星期一播出、第4集在星期二播出、第5集在星期三播出、第6集又在星期四播出、每5集为一个循环.由于 $48=5×9+3$,故第48集(最后一集)是在星期一播出,故选(A).

8. 答案:(D).

解 每次操作后,球所在杯子序号的奇偶性均发生改变,由于进行了 $2^{10}+3^8$ 次操作,操作次数是一个奇数,故最终球所在杯子序号的奇偶性与最初时不同,球起初在3号杯子中,即最终球所在杯子序号必为偶数,即球不可能在1号杯子、不可能在3号杯子也不可能在5号杯子,故选(D).

9. 答案:(E).

解法1 设小明打破了 x 个碗,则他洗好了 $500-x$ 个碗,由题意得 $3×(500-x)-9x=1368$,解得 $x=11$,故选(E).

解法2 洗500个碗,应该领到 $3×500=1500$ 元,但是小丁只领到了1368元,少领了 $1500-1368=132$ 元,那么原因是小明打破了一些碗,洗一个碗,应得3元,但打破一个,需要赔偿9元,也就是说打破一个碗实际减少12元工资,故小丁共打破 $132÷12=11$ 个碗,故选(E).

10. 答案:(B).

解 观察图2-4,可发现其中规律:方框中所填数等于其左下角与右下角的数之和再乘上左上角与右上角的数之积.因此第四个方框内应填入 $(-4)×(-5)×((-6)+(-7))=-260$,故选(B).

11. 答案:(A).

解 如图2-10,每一点旁的数代表从 A_1 走到该点的走法数.则可知从 A_1 出发不经过 A_3 到达 A_4 的方法数为8种,故选(A).

评注 从 A_1 走到 A_4 需要向右和向下各三次,如果不考虑不能经过 A_3 这一条件,行走的方法数应为 $C_6^3=20$ 种.而从 A_1 经过 A_3 到达 A_4 的方法数为 $C_4^2×C_2^1$

=12 种,因此从 A_1 出发不经过 A_3 到达 A_4 的方法数为 20-12=8 种,故选(A).

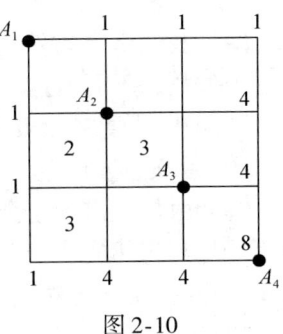

图 2-10

12. 答案:(A).

解 从第 13 排到第 24 排共有 24-13+1=12 排,每排 80 个座位,共计 $80\times12=960$ 个座位,由于全部入座后有 15 个空位,故该校学生总数为 960-15=945,故选(A).

13. 答案:(E).

解 由题意知,一根香蕉与 $\frac{3}{4}$ 个苹果等重,一个橘子与 $\frac{5}{6}$ 根香蕉等重,因此 16 个橘子与 $16\times\frac{5}{6}\times\frac{3}{4}=10$ 个苹果等重,故选(E).

14. 答案:(B).

解 正方体翻到第 1 格时,正面为字母 B;正方体翻到第 2 格时,底面为字母 B;正方体翻到第 3 格时,左侧面为字母 B;正方体翻到第 4 和 5 格时,不改变左侧面,仍为字母 B;正方体翻到第 6 格时,朝上一面为字母 B.所以使得正方体朝上一面为字母 B 的所有格子中的数之和是 6.故选(B).

15. 答案:(C).

解 考虑最坏情况,抽出了两张鬼牌与每种花色各 3 张,总计 14 张牌,无法找到一门花色至少有 4 张牌.另外,若抽取 15 张牌,则至少有 13 张不是鬼牌,由抽屉原理知存在 4 张牌花色相同,因此答案为 15 张,故选(C).

16. 答案:(B).

解 当 $n=0$ 时,5^n+7^n 之值为 2,即除以 100 所得之余数为 2;当 $n=1$ 时,5^n+7^n 之值为 12,即除以 100 所得之余数为 12;而当 $n\geq 2$ 时,5^n 除以 100 所得之余数恒为 25,7^n 除以 100 所得之余数必为 1、7、49、43 之一,因此两者之和除以 100 所得之余数为 26、32、74、68 之一,所以共有 6 种不同的可能,故选(B).

17. 答案:(D).

解 若 $x=12$,则 $(19\odot 12)\odot 19=7\odot 19=5$;若 $x=26$,则 $(19\odot 26)\odot 19=7\odot 19=5$;若 $x=33$,则 $(19\odot 33)\odot 19=14\odot 19=5$;若 $x=39$,则 $(19\odot 39)\odot 19=1\odot 19=0$;若 $x=45$,则 $(19\odot 45)\odot 19=7\odot 19=5$.其中只有 39 不满足题目条件,故选(D).

18. 答案:(C).

解 我们满足条件的三位数称为"快乐"数.由条件知"快乐"数的百位数码与个位数码不同,且都不能为0,在此条件不存在唯一的十位数码满足题目条件,故"快乐"数共有 $9\times8=72$ 个,故选(C).

19. 答案:(A).

解 由勾股定理与全等三角形的性质不难推出,每个斜放置的正方形的面积等于与其相邻的两个正放置的正方形的面积之和,故四个正放置的正方形的面积之和为 $1+3=4$,故选(A).

20. 答案:(B).

解 将 4×4 的正方形划分成 4 个 2×2 的部分,若要图 2-11 中无法再放下"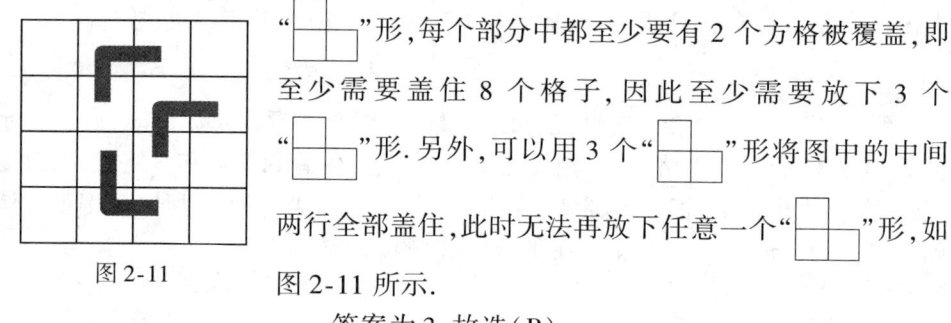"形,每个部分中都至少要有 2 个方格被覆盖,即至少需要盖住 8 个格子,因此至少需要放下 3 个"形.另外,可以用 3 个"形将图中的中间两行全部盖住,此时无法再放下任意一个"形,如图 2-11 所示.

图 2-11

答案为 3,故选(B).

21. 答案:66.

解 首先,每个盒子内的乒乓球数至少为8,故任意一个盒子内的乒乓球个数不会多于 $100-8\times4=68$,这说明每个盒子内球数含有的数字8都在个位上.其次,由于恰有两个盒子中乒乓球个数相同,故所有盒子内的乒乓球个数之和最少为 $8+8+18+28+38=100$,故仅可能为这一种情况,而乒乓球数最多的两个盒子中的乒乓球数之总和为 $28+38=66$.

22. 答案:9.

解 若 $x\geq10$,则
$$x^3\geq10x^2\geq(b+1)x^2=bx^2+x^2\geq bx^2+10x$$
$$\geq bx^2+(c+1)x\geq bx^2+cx+10>bx^2+cx+d.$$
故 x 必须小于10.另外,当 $a=1$、$b=c=8$、$d=9$ 时,$x=9$ 满足条件.因此所求 x 的最大可能值为9.

23. 答案:45.

解 $a^2(b+c)+b^2(c+a)+c^2(a+b) = a^2b+a^2c+b^2c+b^2a+c^2a+c^2b$
$= ab(a+b)+bc(b+c)+ca(a+c)$
$= ab(-c)+bc(-a)+ca(-b)$
$= -3abc$
$= 45.$

24. 答案:123.

解 如图 2-12,设 AD 与 BC 相交于点 O,延长 AN 交 CD 于点 F,根据三角形外角性质,得

$\angle BOD = \angle BCD + \angle CDO = \angle BCD + 42°,$

从而 $\angle BAD = \angle BOD - \angle ABO = \angle BCD + 18°.$

因此 $\angle EAD = 180° - \angle BAD = 162° - \angle BCD.$

因为 N 是两条角平分线的交点,所以

$\angle DAN = \frac{1}{2} \angle EAD = 81° - \frac{1}{2} \angle BCD 、 \angle NCD = \frac{1}{2} \angle BCD,$

延长 AN 交 CD 于点 F,则

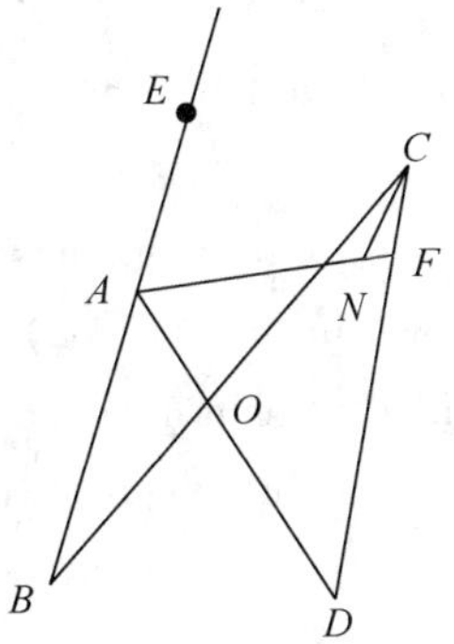

$\angle ANC = \angle NCF + \angle NFC = \angle NCD + \angle DAN + \angle ADC = \frac{1}{2} \angle BCD + 81° - \frac{1}{2} \angle BCD + 42°$

$= 123°.$

图 2-12

25. 答案:936.

解 将四个数相乘得到的结果必然大于 1000,因此稍小一点的答案应该由其中两个数相加,再乘以剩下的两个数得到。经计算知 $(6+7) \times 8 \times 9 = 936$、$6 \times (7+8) \times 9 = 810$、$6 \times 7 \times (8+9) = 714$,其中 936 为最大的三位数。

2.4 第二轮英文试题

考试时间:120 分钟

Questions 1–5,4 marks each

1. In a promotional sale, anyone who buys a cup of juice at the regular price of 7 dollars can get a second cup of juice by paying 1 more dollar. What is the minimum number of dollars a party of 9 people must pay if each of them wants a cup of juice?

(A)32　　(B)36　　(C)39　　(D)40　　(E)63

2. Into the expression $y = \dfrac{x^2}{1+x^2}$, we substitute for x the numbers $\dfrac{1}{2012}$, $\dfrac{1}{2008}$, $\dfrac{1}{2004}$, $\cdots$, $\dfrac{1}{4}$, $4, 8, 12, \cdots, 2012$. What is the sum of all the y values?

(A)1　　　(B)16　　　(C)251.5　　　(D)503　　　(E)2012

3. In a flower shop, each Carnation sells for \$3 and each Rose sells for \$4. A bouquet is a combination of these two kinds of flowers. How many different bouquets selling for \$60 are there?

(A)4　　　(B)5　　　(C)6　　　(D)7　　　(E)8

4. A rectangular strip, 30 cm in length and 3 cm wide, is folded in a pattern shown in diagram (2), producing a right angle $\angle ACB$. After the strip is completely folded as shown in diagrams (3) and (4), the lengths of AM and GM are equal. What is the length of AC in diagram (1)?

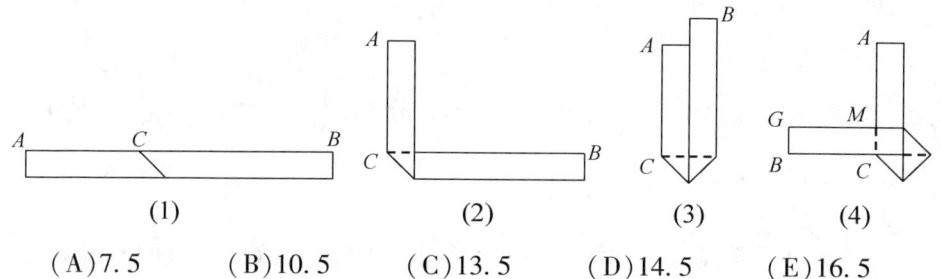

(1)　　　　　(2)　　　　　(3)　　　　　(4)

(A)7.5　　　(B)10.5　　　(C)13.5　　　(D)14.5　　　(E)16.5

5. Let a, b, c be rational numbers such that $c = -\dfrac{ab}{a+b}$. Which of the following expressions is correct?

(A) $a+b+c = a^3+b^3+c^3$

(B) $(a+b+c)^2 = a^2+b^2+c^2$

(C) $(a+b+2c)^2 = a^2+b^2-4c^2$

(D) $(a+b+c)^3 = a^3+b^3+c^3$

(E) $(a+b+c)(a^2+b^2+c^2) = a^3+b^3+c^3+abc$

Questions 6–13, 5 marks each

6. In an isosceles triangle ABC, $AB = AC$. Point D lies on side AC, so that $AD = DB = BC$. What is the measure of $\angle BAC$?

7. The diagram below shows three overlapping regular hexagons, each with side

length 12 cm^2. One of the vertices of the middle hexagon coincides with the center O_1 of the hexagon on the left, while one of the vertices of the hexagon on the right coincides with the center O_2 of the middle hexagon. What is the total area of the two shaded parts?

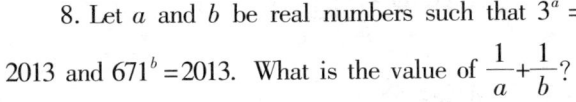

8. Let a and b be real numbers such that $3^a = 2013$ and $671^b = 2013$. What is the value of $\frac{1}{a}+\frac{1}{b}$?

9. In the diagram below, $ABCD$ is a right-angled trapezoid such that $AD//BC$ and E is the midpoint of CD. If $BE = 20$ cm and $AB = AD + BC$, determine the area of trapezoid $ABCD$, in cm^2?

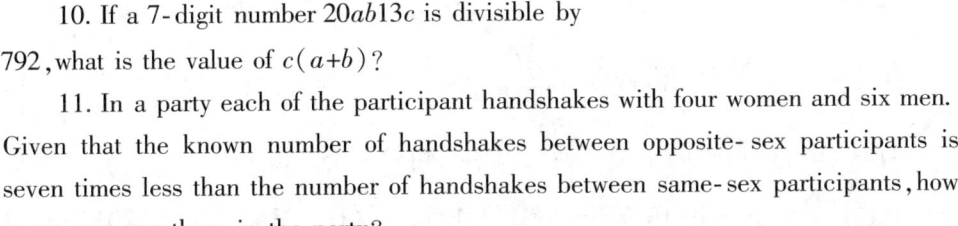

10. If a 7-digit number $\overline{20ab13c}$ is divisible by 792, what is the value of $c(a+b)$?

11. In a party each of the participant handshakes with four women and six men. Given that the known number of handshakes between opposite-sex participants is seven times less than the number of handshakes between same-sex participants, how many men are there in the party?

12. We put 130 identical balls into several identical boxes, such that the number of balls in each box is at least 10 but at most 20. The numbers of balls in the boxes are all different. How many distinct ways of putting these balls in the boxes are there?

13. Let a and b be non-negative integers less than 100. If $a-2b$ is a positive prime number and $2ab$ is a perfect square number, what is maximum value of $a+b$?

Questions 14–15, 20 marks each
Detailed solutions are needed for these two problems

14. Let k be a real number. The product of all the real roots of the equation $x^4 + 2x^3 + (3+k)x^2 + (2+k)x + 2k = 0$ is -2012. Find the sum of the squares of the real roots.

15. A 9×11 chessboard may be covered without overlap with a combination of the following three shapes. What is the minimum number of copies of the piece

consisting of three squares must be used?

2.5 第二轮中文试题

1–5题,每题4分

1. 某饮料店推出优惠活动,买一杯原价7元的橙汁后可以加1元再送同样的一杯橙汁. 现有9名同学一起去买饮料,每个人都要买一杯橙汁. 请问他们至少共需花费多少元?

(A)32   (B)36   (C)39   (D)40   (E)63

答:_____

2. 当 x 分别等于 $\dfrac{1}{2012},\dfrac{1}{2008},\dfrac{1}{2004},\cdots,\dfrac{1}{4}$、$4,8,12,\cdots,2012$ 时,计算代数式 $\dfrac{x^2}{1+x^2}$ 的值. 请问将所得的结果全部加起来之和等于多少?

(A)1   (B)16   (C)251.5   (D)503   (E)2012

答:_____

3. 花店中每支康乃馨之售价为3元,每支玫瑰之售价为4元,若用这两种花搭配制作价值60元的花束(两种花必须都使用),请问共有多少种不同的花束可供选择?

(A)4   (B)5   (C)6   (D)7   (E)8

答:_____

4. 一张长30 cm、宽3 cm 的长方形纸条,按照下图的过程进行折迭,其中图2-13(2) 的 $\angle ACB$ 为直角. 折迭完成后纸条上 AM 与 GM 的长度相等,请问最初折迭时,AC 的长为多少 cm?

(A)7.5   (B)10.5   (C)13.5   (D)14.5   (E)16.5

答:_____

5. 有理数 a、b、c 满足 $c=-\dfrac{ab}{a+b}$,请问下列等式中哪一项一定成立?

(A) $a+b+c=a^3+b^3+c^3$

第 2 章　第 2 届国际中小学生数学能力检测(IMAS)(初中组)

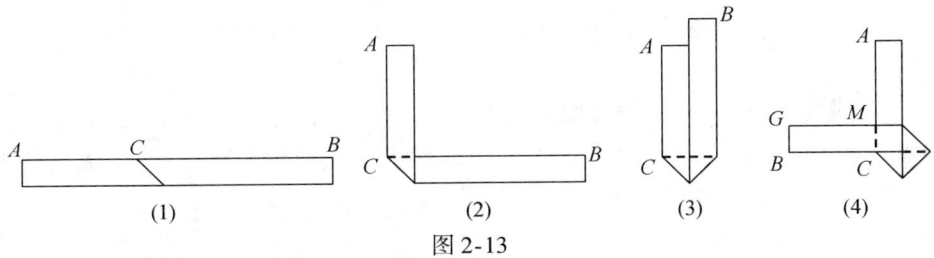

图 2-13

(B) $(a+b+c)^2 = a^2+b^2+c^2$

(C) $(a+b+2c)^2 = a^2+b^2-4c^2$

(D) $(a+b+c)^3 = a^3+b^3+c^3$

(E) $(a+b+c)(a^2+b^2+c^2) = a^3+b^3+c^3+abc$

答：＿＿＿＿＿

6–13 题，每题 5 分

6. 在等腰三角形 ABC 中，$AB = AC$．在边 AC 上有一点 D，满足 $AD = DB = BC$，请问 $\angle BAC$ 等于多少度？

答：＿＿＿＿＿度

7. 三个面积均为 12cm² 的正六边形重叠在一起，中间的正六边形的一个顶点恰好与左侧的正六边形的中心 O_1 重合；右侧的正六边形的一个顶点恰好与中间的正六边形的中心 O_2 重合，如图 2-14 所示．请问阴影部分的面积是多少？

答：＿＿＿＿＿cm²

8. 已知实数 a、b 满足 $3^a = 2013$、$671^b = 2013$．请问 $\dfrac{1}{a} + \dfrac{1}{b}$ 的值是多少？

答：＿＿＿＿＿

9. 如图 2-15，在直角梯形 $ABCD$ 中，$AD//BC$，点 E 是边 CD 的中点，若 $BE = 20$cm 且 $AB = AD + BC$．请问梯形 $ABCD$ 的面积是多少 cm²？

答：＿＿＿＿＿cm²

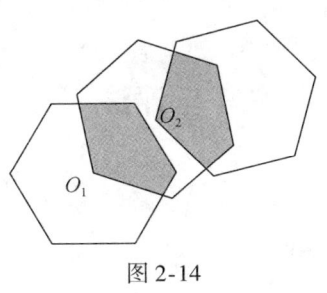

图 2-14

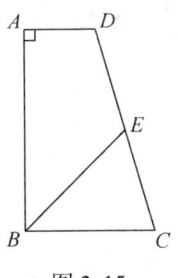

图 2-15

10. 已知七位数 $\overline{20ab13c}$ 能被 792 整除，请问 $c(a+b)$ 之值等于多少？

答：_____

11. 某次宴会上每一位参加者都与 4 位女士和 6 位男士握手，已知异性参加者之间握手的次数比同性参加者之间的握手的次数少 7 次，请问此次宴会总共有多少位男士参加？

答：_____ 位

12. 有 130 个球，放入若干个完全相同的箱子中，一个箱子最少放 10 个，最多放 20 个，且各个箱子的球数均不相同．请问不同的放法有多少种？（不计箱子的排列，即两种放法经过箱子的重新排列后，若箱子内的球数对应相同，就视为同一种放法）

答：_____ 种

13. 已知 a、b 均为小于 100 的非负整数，$a-2b$ 为正质数，且 $2ab$ 为完全平方数，请问 $a+b$ 的最大值是多少？

答：_____

14、15 题，必须填写详细计算过程或证明，每题 20 分

14. 设 k 是一个实数，关于 x 的一元四次方程 $x^4+2x^3+(3+k)x^2+(2+k)x+2k=0$ 有实根，且所有实根之积为 -2012，求所有实根的平方和．

15. 有足够多图 2-16 所示的三种拼板，用它们来覆盖一张 9×11 的棋盘，拼板的边必须与棋盘的网格线重合，且任意两片拼板都互不重叠，请问至少需要三单位正方形的那种拼板多少片？

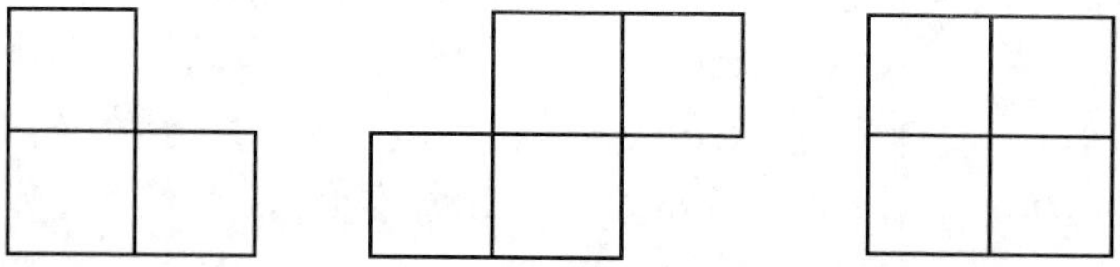

图 2-16

2.6 第二轮试题解答与评注

1. 答案：(C)．

解法 1 由于买一杯饮料加 1 元可再送一杯，所以买 4 杯加 4 元可以得到 8

杯饮料,共有 9 个人,所以还需买一杯,共花费 $4\times7+4+7=39$ 元.

解法 2 可知买一杯 7 元橙汁加 1 元可再送一杯橙汁,故知每两杯橙汁最少需花费 8 元. 现有 9 人,故需 9 杯. 因 $9=2\times4+1$,故知花费最少的方式 $4\times8+1\times7=39$ 元. 所以选(C).

2. 答案:(D).

解 观察可知 $\dfrac{x^2}{1+x^2}+\dfrac{\left(\dfrac{1}{x}\right)^2}{1+\left(\dfrac{1}{x}\right)^2}=\dfrac{x^2}{1+x^2}+\dfrac{1}{1+x^2}=1$,那么

$$\dfrac{4^2}{1+4^2}+\dfrac{\left(\dfrac{1}{4}\right)^2}{1+\left(\dfrac{1}{4}\right)^2}=1\,\text{、}\,\dfrac{8^2}{1+8^2}+\dfrac{\left(\dfrac{1}{8}\right)^2}{1+\left(\dfrac{1}{8}\right)^2}=1\,\text{、}\cdots\text{、}\,\dfrac{2012^2}{1+2012^2}+\dfrac{\left(\dfrac{1}{2012}\right)^2}{1+\left(\dfrac{1}{2012}\right)^2}=1.$$

因此,所求结果为 $1\times503=503$. 所以选(D).

3. 答案:(A).

解 设花束中有 x 支康乃馨,y 支玫瑰,根据题意可得,$3x+4y=60$. 其中,x 和 y 都是正整数,且满足 $0<3x<60$、$0<4y<60$,故 $0<x<20$,$0<y<15$. 方程可变形为 $4y=60-3x$,方程左右两边都能被 4 整除,所以 $3x$ 能被 4 整除,又 3 不能被 4 整除,从而 $4|x$. 因此 $x=4$、$x=8$、$x=12$ 或者 $x=16$;对应的 $y=12$、$y=9$、$y=6$ 或者 $y=3$,所以有 4 种不同的花束. 所以选(A).

4. 答案:(B).

解 将折好的纸条再次展开,折痕应如图 2-17 所示. 由条件知 $AM_1=GM_2$. 由 $CM_1=FM_2=3$ 知 $AC=FG$,因此整个图形关于纸条的中心对称,故 $AC=\dfrac{30}{2}-3-\dfrac{3}{2}=10.5\,\text{cm}$.

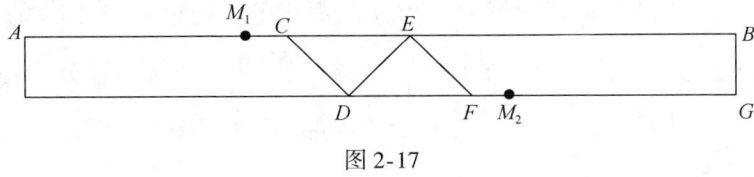

图 2-17

5. 答案:(B).

解 由 $c=-\dfrac{ab}{a+b}$ 去分母再移项得 $ab+bc+ca=0$,五个选项中仅有(B)项的左

右两边之差为 $(a+b+c)^2-(a^2+b^2+c^2)=2(ab+bc+ca)=0$,其余选项的左右两边之差均不一定为0(代入 $a=2$,$b=-1$,$c=2$,选项(A)的左边为3,右边为15;选项(C)的左边为25,右边为-11;选项(D)的左边为27,右边为15;选项(E)的左边为27,右边为11,均不能相等).所以选(B).

6. **解** 设 $\angle BAC=\alpha$,由 $AD=DB$ 得 $\angle ABD=\angle BAC=\alpha$,故 $\angle BDC=2\alpha$(三角形外角定理).

由 $DB=BC$ 得 $\angle BCD=\angle BDC=2\alpha$.

再由 $AB=AC$ 得 $\angle ABC=\angle ACB=2\alpha$.

在三角形 ABC 中,三个内角分别为 α、2α、2α,故 $\alpha+2\alpha+2\alpha=180°$,解得 $\alpha=36°$(图2-18).

7. **答案**:8.

解 我们先求出其中一块阴影部分的面积.如图2-19所示,五边形 O_1MBCN 即为原题中左侧的一块阴影部分.由正六边形的性质知

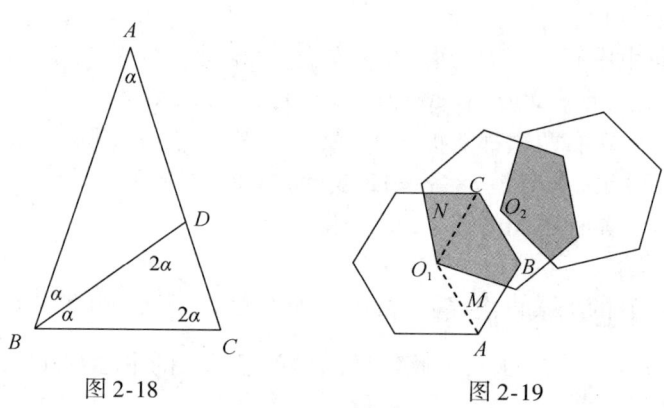

图2-18　　　　　　图2-19

$\angle MO_1N=120°=\angle AO_1C$,去掉公共部分的角度得 $\angle MO_1A=\angle NO_1C$.注意到 $O_1A=O_1C$、$\angle MAO_1=\angle NCO_1=60°$(正六边形的性质),故 $\triangle MO_1A\cong\triangle NO_1C$,因此 $S_{\triangle MO_1A}=S_{\triangle NO_1C}$,也就是说五边形 O_1MBCN 的面积等于四边形 O_1ABC 的面积,而后者恰为正六边形面积的 $\dfrac{1}{3}$,即 $12\times\dfrac{1}{3}=4$,故左侧的一块阴影部分面积为4.同理,右侧的一块阴影部分面积也为4,故阴影部分的总面积为8.

8. **答案**:1.

解 由条件知 $2013^{\frac{1}{a}}=(3^a)^{\frac{1}{a}}=3^{a\cdot\frac{1}{a}}=3$、$2013^{\frac{1}{b}}=(671^b)^{\frac{1}{b}}=671^{b\cdot\frac{1}{b}}=671$,因此 $2013^{\frac{1}{a}+\frac{1}{b}}=3\times671=2013=2013^1$,故 $\dfrac{1}{a}+\dfrac{1}{b}=1$.

9. 答案:400.

解法 1 如图 2-20 所示,连接 AE 并延长交 BC 的延长线于点 F. 由点 E 是边 CD 的中点及 AD//BC 知 △ADE ≌ △FCE,故 AD=CF、AE=FE. 又 AB=AD+BC=CF+BC=BF 以及 AB⊥BF,故 △ABF 是等腰直角三角形,而 BE 为其斜边中线,因此 AE=EF=BE=20 且 BE⊥AF,由此得 △ABF 的面积为 $\frac{1}{2}×20×(20+20)$ = 400.

由于 △ADE ≌ △FCE,故梯形 ABCD 的面积与 △ABF 的面积相等,故所求答案为 400.

解法 2 如图 2-21 所示,延长 AD 至 G,使得 GD=BC;延长 BC 至 H,使得 CH=AD. 连接 GH、EG. 此时可由 AB=AD+BC=AG=BH 以及 AB⊥BF 可知 ABHG 为正方形,且梯形 ABCD 的面积即为正方形 ABHG 的面积的一半. 因 E 为 CD 中点,故可推知 E 为 BG 中点,即正方形 ABHG 的对角线 BG 的长度为 40,故正方形 ABHG 的面积为 20×20÷2=800,因此梯形 ABCD 的面积为 400.

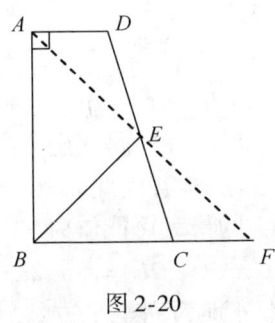

图 2-20

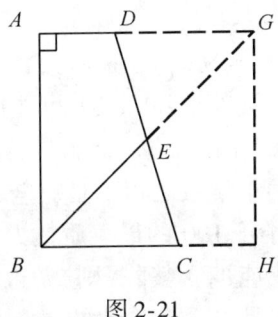

图 2-21

10. 答案:36.

解 注意到 792=8×9×11,且 8、9、11 的最大公因子是 1,故 $\overline{20ab13c}$ 应能被 8、9、11 整除. 由被 8 整除的数的特征知 130+c 能被 8 整除,得 c=6;由被 9 整除的数的特征知 2+0+a+b+1+3+6 能被 9 整除,得 a+b=6 或 a+b=15;由被 11 整除的数的特征知 2-0+a-b+1-3+6 能被 11 整除,得 a-b=5 或 a-b=-6. 注意到 a+b 与 a-b 必须同奇偶,联立 a+b=15 及 a-b=5 解得 a=10、b=5,不合题意,舍去;联立 a+b=6 及 a-b=-6 解得 a=0、b=6. 因此 a=0、b=6、c=6,故 c(a+b) = 36.

11. 答案:21.

解 设此次宴会里有 x 位男士,由于每位男士都与 4 位女士握手,故男士与女士之间握手的次数为 $4x$ 次. 由于每位女士都与 6 位男士握手, 故女士有 $\frac{4x}{6}$ $=\frac{2}{3}x$ 人. 由于每位男士都与 6 位男士握手, 故男士之间的握手次数为 $\frac{1}{2}\times 6x=$ $3x$ 次; 由于每位女士都与 4 位女士握手, 故女士之间的握手次数为 $\frac{1}{2}\times 4\times\frac{2}{3}x=$ $\frac{4}{3}x$ 次. 由题意得 $3x+\frac{4}{3}x-4x=7$, 解得 $x=21$.

12. 答案: 5 种.

解 每个箱子中的球数仅能为 10、11、12、…、20 之一, 我们可以考虑从分别装有 10、11、12、…、20 个球的箱子中拿掉一个或几个箱子, 使剩下的箱子中恰共有 130 个球. 由于 $10+11+12+\cdots+20-130=35$, 故拿掉的箱子中应共有 35 个球. 由 $20\times 1<35<10\times 4$ 知应拿掉 2 个或 3 个箱子. 若拿掉两个箱子, 则箱中球数应为 15、20 或 16、19 或 17、18, 共有 3 种可能; 若拿掉三个箱子, 则箱中球数应为 10、11、14 或 10、12、13, 共有 2 种可能. 因此不同的方法共有 5 种.

13. 答案: 113.

解 设 $a-2b=p$(p 是质数), 分两种情况讨论:

若 a 能被 p 整除, 则 $2b$ 也能被 p 整除, 可设 $2b=p\cdot r$, $a=p\cdot(r+1)$, 其中 r 是非负整数. 因此 $2ab=p^2r(r+1)$ 是完全平方数, 即 $r(r+1)$ 是完全平方数. 由于两个连续的正整数之积不是完全平方数, 故只能有 $r=0$, 因此 $b=0$、$a=p$ 且 $a+b=p$. 由于小于 100 的最大质数为 97, 故此时 $a+b$ 的最大可能值为 97.

若 a 不能被 p 整除, 则 $2b$ 也不能被 p 整除, 故 $(a,2b)=(p,2b)=1$. 由于 $2ab=a\cdot 2b$ 是一个完全平方数, 故 a 和 $2b$ 必然分别为完全平方数. 设 $a=m^2$、$2b=n^2$, 则 $a-2b=m^2-n^2=(m+n)(m-n)$ 是质数, 只能有 $m-n=1$, 即 $m=n+1$, 因此 $m+n=2n+1$ 是质数. 又由于 $2b=n^2<100$, 故 n 是一个不超过 8 的偶数, 因此 n 只能为 2、6、8 之一. 经计算知当 $n=8$ 时, $a=81$, $b=32$, $a+b=113$; 当 $n=6$ 时, $a=49$, $b=18$, $a+b=67$; 又当 $n=2$ 时, $a=9$, $b=2$, $a+b=11$. 故此时 $a+b$ 的最大可能值为 113.

综上所述, $a+b$ 的最大值为 113.

14. 答案: 4025.

解 因 $x^4+2x^3+(3+k)x^2+(2+k)x+2k=(x^2+x+2)(x^2+x+k)$, 而 $x^2+x+2=0$ 显然没有实根, 故 $x^4+2x^3+(3+k)x^2+(2+k)x+2k=0$ 的所有实根就是 $x^2+x+k=0$ 的所有实根. 由条件知 $x^2+x+k=0$ 有实根, 且所有实根乘积为 -2012. 由韦达定

理知 $k=-2012$. 设 $x^2+x-2012=0$ 的两个实根分别为 x_1、x_2, 则 $x_1+x_2=-1$, $x_1x_2=-2012$, 因此
$$x_1^2+x_2^2=(x_1+x_2)^2-2x_1x_2=1^2-2\times(-2012)=4025.$$

15. 答案：21.

解 如图 2-22 所示，将棋盘上位于奇数行奇数列的小正方形涂成灰色，共有 $5\times6=30$ 个灰色正方形.

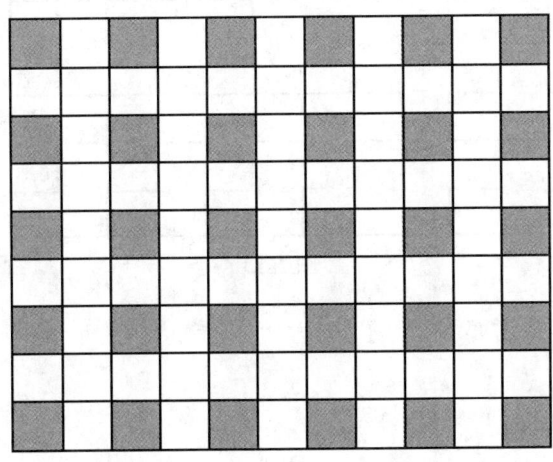

图 2-22

显然，在给定的三种多方块中，每一片多方块至多可以覆盖 1 个红色正方形.因此至少需要 30 片多方块才可以覆盖整张棋盘.如果"L"形三方块使用了 m 片，另两种四方块共享了 n 片，那么
$$m+n\geqslant 30. \tag{2.1}$$
现在，每片"L"形三方块可以覆盖棋盘上 3 个正方形，另外两种四方块每片可以覆盖 4 个正方形，则
$$3m+4n=9\times 11=99. \tag{2.2}$$
根据(2.2)式，可得
$$4n=99-3m,$$
根据(2.1)式，得
$$4m+4n\geqslant 120.$$
因此
$$4m+(99-3m)\geqslant 120,$$
解得 $m\geqslant 21$. 即"L"形方块的数目不能小于 21, 如图 2-23 是恰使用 21 片"L"形

方块的摆放方法.

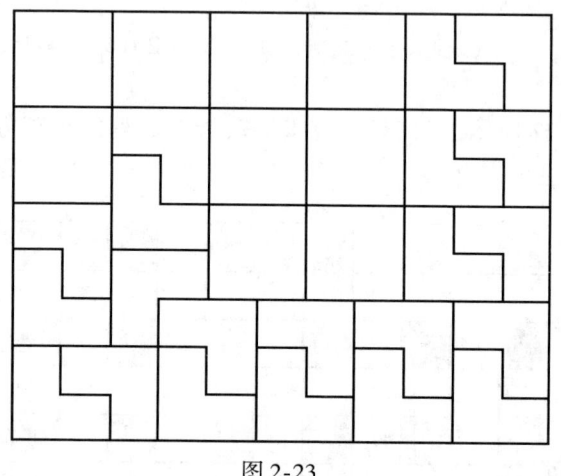

图 2-23

综上所述,至少需要 21 片"L"形方块.

第3章 第3届国际中小学生数学能力检测(IMAS)(初中组)

3.1 第一轮英文试题

考试时间:75分钟

Questions 1–10, 3 marks each

1. What is the value of the expression $|-2013|+2^0+1^3$?
   (A)2014 (B)2015 (C)2016 (D)−2010 (E)−2011

2. Which of the following real numbers has the greatest absolute value?
   (A)$-\pi$ (B)$\sqrt{7}$ (C)3.1 (D)−2 (E)$\frac{23}{8}$

3. Which of the following five numbers is divisible by 6?
   (A)332 (B)363 (C)494 (D)522 (E)586

4. In the diagram, AD is parallel to BC. A point P moves from C to D along the side CD. Which of the following is the accurate description of the change in the area of △ABP during the motion?
   (A) increasing
   (B) decreasing
   (C) increasing then decreasing
   (D) decreasing then increasing
   (E) unchanged

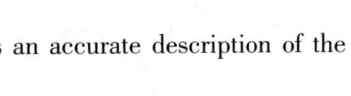

5. If x is a real number, which of the following is an accurate description of the expression $|x|-x$?
   (A) must be positive
   (B) may be positive or zero
   (C) must be negative

(D) may be negative or zero

(E) may be any number

6. In a promotional sale, a store reduces the prices of all merchandises by 40%. If payment is made using a membership card, then there is a further reduction of 10%. What is the combined reduction in using a membership card?

(A) 40% (B) 46% (C) 50% (D) 54% (E) 60%

7. The length of each side of a triangle is a different odd positive integer. What is the minimum perimeter of this triangle?

(A) 9 (B) 11 (C) 13 (D) 15 (E) 21

8. The coordinates of a point in the plane are $(w, 1-w)$, where w is a real number. Which of the following is an accurate description of the position in this point?

(A) cannot be in the fourth quadrant

(B) cannot be in the third quadrant

(C) cannot be in the second quadrant

(D) cannot be in the first quadrant

(E) can be anywhere

9. Mickey accidentally drops a triangular sheet of glass, breaking it into four pieces as shown in the diagram. He wishes to take only one of the pieces to a repair shop so that he can reproduce a triangular sheet of glass. How many different choices of this piece does he have?

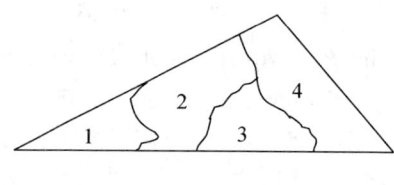

(A) 4 (B) 3 (C) 2 (D) 1 (E) 0

10. In the diagram, $ABCD$ is a square. The common part of $ABCD$ and triangle EFG is shaded. Its area is $\frac{4}{5}$ of that of EFG and $\frac{1}{2}$ of that of $ABCD$. If the area of triangle EFG is 40cm^2, what is the length of a side of $ABCD$, in cm?

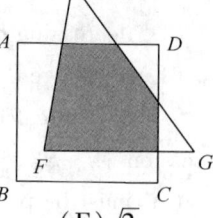

(A) 4 (B) 5 (C) 8 (D) 10 (E) $\sqrt{2}$

Questions 11–20, 4 marks each

11. What is the simplified value of $\dfrac{3^{2013}-3^{2011}}{3^{2013}+3^{2012}}$?

(A) $\dfrac{2}{3}$ (B) $\dfrac{4}{5}$ (C) $\dfrac{3}{2}$ (D) $\dfrac{1}{2}$ (E) $\dfrac{3}{4}$

12. Linda cuts out a shape as shown in the diagram. *AB* is parallel to *CD* and the measure of angle *AFE* is 40°. What, in degrees, is the total measure of angles *BAF*, *FED* and *EDC*?

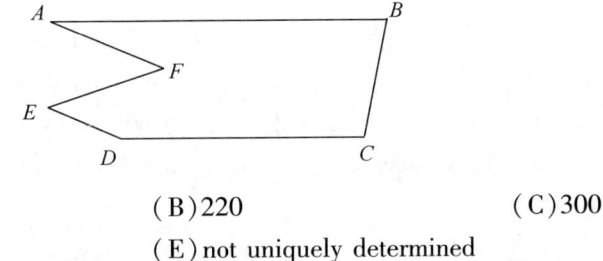

(A) 200   (B) 220   (C) 300

(D) 320   (E) not uniquely determined

13. May and Cherry bought the same kind of colored pens from a stationery store. Such a pen costs more than $10. May's total bill has reached $182 while Cherry's total bill is $221. What is the total number of pens which May and Cherry bought?

(A) 13   (B) 14   (C) 30

(D) 31   (E) 32

14. The diagram shows the outcome of a folded piece of triangular paper such that the vertex *C* becomes the point *C′* on the side *AB*. If $AB = AC$ and $C'A = C'D$, what is the measure, in degrees, of angle *A*?

(A) 18   (B) 20

(C) 24

(D) 30   (E) 36

15. Mickey is asked to multiply four positive integers, but he adds them instead. Amazingly, his correct answer is equal to the correct answer for the multiplication problem. What is the sum of these four numbers?

(A)6　　　(B)8　　　(C)9　　　(D)10　　　(E)12

16. Mickey starts working with his report at 7:30 am. By 10:10, he has finished $\frac{2}{3}$ of his report. He takes one-hour break and then continues to work at the same rate. At what time will he finish his report?

(A)10:50　　(B)11:20　　(C)11:40　　(D)12:30　　(E)12:50

17. P is a point inside a triangle whose side lengths are 7 cm, 24 dm and 25 cm. If P is at the same distance from all three sides of the triangle, what is this distance, in cm?

(A)1　　　(B)1.5　　　(C)2　　　(D)2.5　　　(E)3

18. The diagram shows how each of the digits 0 to 9 can be made from matchsticks. In this representation, the number 609 reads the same way upside down as right side up. How many such three-digit numbers can be formed if the first digit may not be 0?

(A)30　　　(B)36　　　(C)42　　　(D)49　　　(E)245

19. The alien clock divides the earth day into 10 of their hours, each of which is divided into 100 of their minutes. If they plan to attack the earth at 6:36 am our time, what is the time indicated on their clock?

(A)1:75　　(B)2:25　　(C)2:75　　(D)3:15　　(E)3:25

20. Fanny, Lily and Sherry all shop at regular intervals, Fanny shops once every 3 days, Lily once every 4 days and Sherry once every 5 days. Yesterday, all three went shopping. How many in the next 100 days, starting from today (today is the first day), will at least two of them be shopping together?

(A)16　　　(B)17　　　(C)18　　　(D)19　　　(E)20

Questions 21-25, 6 marks each

21. The diagram shows a regular pentagon $ABCDE$ with a point M on AB and a

point N on AE. The pentagon is folded along the segment MN so that the vertex A is now inside the original pentagon. What, in degrees, is the total measure of the angles AMB and ANE?

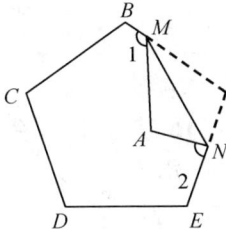

22. Anne arranges some pebbles in the sand forming a pattern of interesting configurations as shown in the diagram. The numbers of pebbles used in the first four configurations are 1, 5, 12 and 22 respectively. What is the number of pebbles used in the tenth configuration of this pattern?

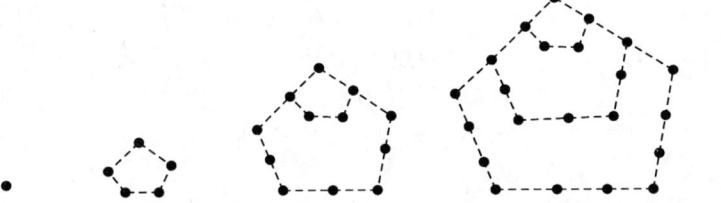

23. The six faces of a cubical die are labeled with six different positive integers. If the numbers on any two adjacent faces, differ by at least 2, what is the minimum value of the sum of these six numbers?

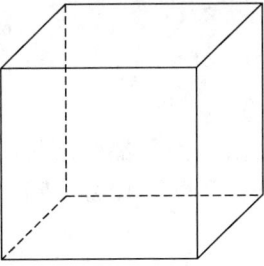

24. The non-zero real numbers x and y satisfies
$$(\sqrt{x^2+2013}-x)(\sqrt{y^2+2013}-y)=2013.$$

What is the value of the expression $\dfrac{2013x+y}{5x+y}$?

25. Determine the least positive integer which has five three-digit divisors?

3.2 第一轮中文试题

1–10题，每题3分

1. 请问算式$|-2013|+2^0+1^3$的值是什么？
(A)2014　　(B)2015　　(C)2016　　(D)-2010　　(E)-2011

2. 请问下列哪一个实数的绝对值最大？
(A)$-\pi$　　(B)$\sqrt{7}$　　(C)3.1　　(D)-2　　(E)$\dfrac{23}{8}$

3. 请问下列哪一项的整数可以被6整除？
(A)332　　(B)363　　(C)494　　(D)522　　(E)586

图3-1

4. 梯形ABCD中，AD平行于BC，它的腰CD上有一个动点P，如图3-1所示. 现将点P从点C的位置移动到点D的位置，在移动过程中，关于△ABP的面积的变化情况，请问下列哪一项叙述是正确的？
(A)变大　　　　　　　(B)变小
(C)先变大再变小　　(D)先变小再变大
(E)不变

5. 若x为实数，关于代数式$|x|-x$的值，请问以下哪一项叙述是正确的？
(A)一定是正数　　　　　(B)可能是正数或0
(C)一定是负数　　　　　(D)可能是负数或0
(E)可能是正数、负数或0

6. 某商场进行促销活动，所有商品都照定价减40%出售，如果在结账时使用会员卡，还可以依照购买金额再减价10%. 请问使用会员卡后，付款金额比原定价便宜了多少？
(A)40%　　(B)46%　　(C)50%　　(D)54%　　(E)60%

7. 一个三角形的三条边长都是奇正整数单位，且两两不相等，请问这个三角形的周长之最小值是多少单位？
(A)9　　(B)11　　(C)13　　(D)15　　(E)21

第3章 第3届国际中小学生数学能力检测(IMAS)(初中组)

8. 设 w 是一个实数,在平面直角坐标系内,关于点 $A(w, 1-w)$ 位置的描述,请问下列哪一项是正确的?

(A)一定不在第四象限 (B)一定不在第三象限

(C)一定不在第二象限 (D)一定不在第一象限

(E)每一个象限都有可能

9. 小明不慎将一块三角形的玻璃桌垫摔碎成如图3-2所示的四块(即图3-2中标记为1、2、3、4的四块),他想选择其中的一块带去玻璃店,以用来复制与原来全等的三角形玻璃.请问他有几种可能的选择?

(A)4种 (B)3种 (C)2种 (D)1种 (E)0种

10. 将正方形 $ABCD$ 与 $\triangle EFG$ 重叠部分涂上阴影,如图3-3所示.已知 $\triangle EFG$ 的面积为 $40 cm^2$,阴影部分的面积占 $\triangle EFG$ 面积的 $\frac{4}{5}$、占正方形 $ABCD$ 面积的一半,请问正方形 $ABCD$ 的边长是多少 cm?

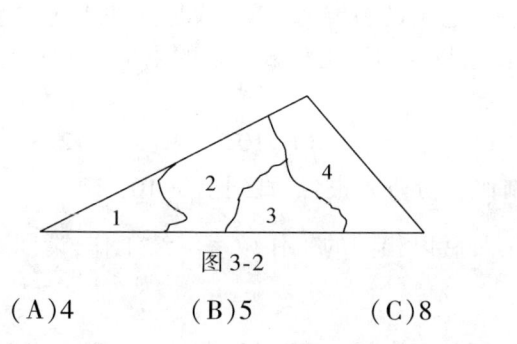

图3-2   图3-3

(A)4 (B)5 (C)8 (D)10 (E)$\sqrt{2}$

11—20题,每题4分

11. 请问算式 $\dfrac{3^{2013}-3^{2011}}{3^{2013}+3^{2012}}$ 的值是什么?

(A)$\dfrac{2}{3}$ (B)$\dfrac{4}{5}$ (C)$\dfrac{3}{2}$ (D)$\dfrac{1}{2}$ (E)$\dfrac{3}{4}$

12. 小玲用剪刀剪出了一个如图3-4的纸片,经过测量得知 $AB // CD$、$\angle AFE = 40°$,请问 $\angle BAF + \angle FED + \angle EDC$ 等于多少度?

(A)200 (B)220 (C)300 (D)320 (E)无确定值

13. 小薇和小翠在文具店买同一种彩色笔,这种笔的单价超过10元.结账时小薇支付了182元,小翠支付了221元.请问两人总共买了多少支彩色笔?

(A) 13　　　(B) 14　　　(C) 30　　　(D) 31　　　(E) 32

14. 如图 3-5 为将三角形纸片 ABC 的边 BC 折起,使点 C 落在边 AB 的点 C′ 上.若 AB=AC 且 C′A=C′D,请问∠A 等于多少度?

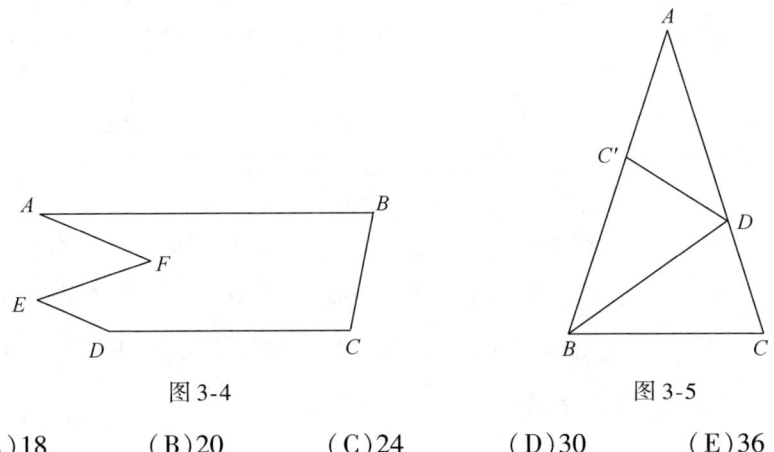

图 3-4　　　　　　　　　　　　图 3-5

(A) 18　　　(B) 20　　　(C) 24　　　(D) 30　　　(E) 36

15. 小明在做一道将四个正整数连乘的习题时,错当成把这四个正整数相加.令人惊奇的是,他所得的结果竟然与这四个正整数连乘的正确答案相同.请问这四个正整数之总和是什么?

(A) 6　　　(B) 8　　　(C) 9　　　(D) 10　　　(E) 12

16. 小明于早上 7:30 开始制作一份研究报告,直到上午 10:10 他完成全部研究报告的 $\frac{2}{3}$,接着他休息一小时后以相同的工作效率继续工作,请问小明在什么时刻可完成这份研究报告?

(A) 10:50　　(B) 11:20　　(C) 11:40　　(D) 12:30　　(E) 12:50

17. 边长为 7cm、24cm、25cm 的三角形内部有一点 P 到三边距离相等,请问这个距离为多少 cm?

(A) 1　　　(B) 1.5　　　(C) 2　　　(D) 2.5　　　(E) 3

18. 如图 3-6 是用火柴棒摆成 0—9 的十个数码的样式.如果用火柴棒摆出 609 这个三位数,那么不论正立着看还是颠倒过来看,都会看到同一个数.请问满足这样性质的三位数(首位数不能是 0)共有多少个?

(A) 30　　　(B) 36　　　(C) 42　　　(D) 49　　　(E) 245

19. 外星人的定时器是将地球上的一天平均分成 10 个"小时",并且它们的每个"小时"有 100"分钟".如果外星人想在地球人类的早上 6 点 36 分展开

第3章 第3届国际中小学生数学能力检测(IMAS)(初中组)

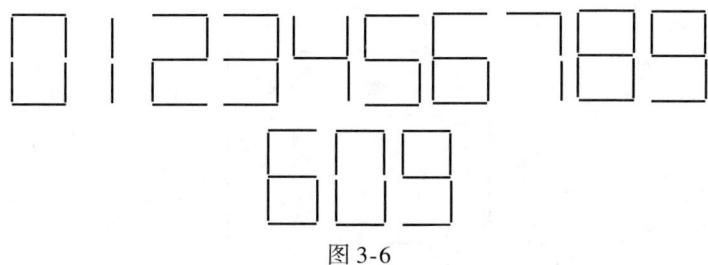

图 3-6

攻击,请问此攻击时刻在它们的定时器上显示的时刻是什么?

(A)1 点 75 分   (B)2 点 25 分   (C)2 点 75 分

(D)3 点 15 分   (E)3 点 25 分

20. 小方、小丽和小雪三人定期去商店购物,小方每 3 天去一次,小丽每 4 天去一次,小雪每 5 天去一次.她们昨天刚好一起去商店.在从今天开始的 100 天内(今天算作第一天),请问她们至少有两人一起去商店的天数是多少?

(A)16   (B)17   (C)18   (D)19   (E)20

21–25 题,每题 6 分

21. 如图 3-7 所示,$ABCDE$ 是一个正五边形,点 M 与点 N 分别在边 AB 与边 AE 上,将顶点 A 沿着 MN 向内折叠,使得点 A 落在正五边形的内部,请问 $\angle AMB + \angle ANE$ 等于多少度?

22. 小恩在沙滩上用小石子排列出一些有趣的图形,如图 3-8 所示,前四个图形所用的小石子数分别是 1、5、12、22. 按此规律继续下去,请问排列第十个图形需要多少颗小石子?

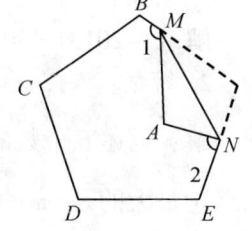

图 3-7

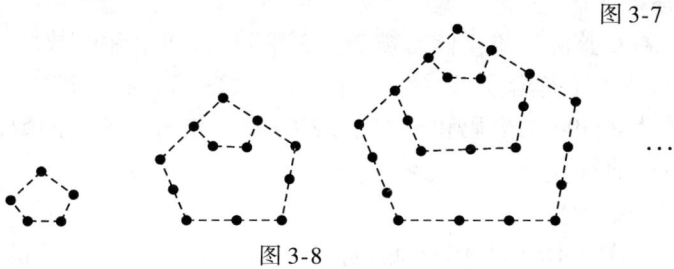

图 3-8

23. 如图 3-9 所示,在一枚正立方体骰子的各面上填写一个互不相同的正整数,使得任意相邻两个面上的数之差至少为 2. 请问这枚骰子六个面上的数之总和的最小值是什么?

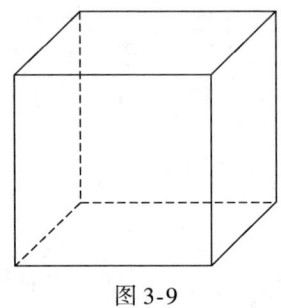

图 3-9

24. 已知 x,y 为非零实数,且满足 $(\sqrt{x^2+2013}-x)(\sqrt{y^2+2013}-y)=2013$,请问代数式 $\dfrac{2013x+y}{5x+y}$ 的值是多少?

25. 请问有 5 个三位数的因子之最小正整数是什么?

3.3 第一轮试题解答与评注

1. 答案:(B).

   解 $|-2013|=2013$,$2^0=1^3=1$,所以算式的值为 $2013+1+1=2015$.

2. 答案:(A).

   解 题述五个数的绝对值分别为 $\pi\approx3.1416$、$\sqrt{7}<\sqrt{9}=3$、3.1、2 及 $\dfrac{23}{8}<\dfrac{24}{8}=3$,其中最大的是 $-\pi$ 的绝对值.

3. 答案:(D).

   解 被 6 整除等价于同时被 2 和 3 整除.被 2 整除的数之末位数必须是偶数,故(B)选项不符合要求.被 3 整除的数之数码和必须被 3 整除,经检验 332 的数码和为 8、494 的数码和为 17、522 的数码和为 9、586 的数码和为 19,因此只有(D)选项符合要求.

4. 答案:(B).

   解 考虑 $\triangle ABP$ 以 AB 为底,将点 P 从点 C 移动到点 D 的过程中,点 P 到 AB 边的距离不断变小,所以 $\triangle ABP$ 的面积不断变小,故选(B).

5. 答案:(B).

   解 若 $x\geq 0$,则 $|x|-x=x-x=0$;若 $x<0$,则 $|x|-x=-x-x=-2x>0$,故其值可

第3章　第3届国际中小学生数学能力检测(IMAS)(初中组)

能为正数或0.

6. 答案:(B).

解　实际的付款金额是原价的 $60\% \times 90\% = 54\%$,故便宜了 $1-54\% = 46\%$.

7. 答案:(D).

解　较长的两条边至少相差2单位,由三角形三边关系定理知最短边至少为3单位,故三角形的三边长最小的可能是3、5、7单位,周长为 $3+5+7=15$ 单位.

8. 答案:(B).

解　点 A 的两个坐标之和为1,故两个坐标不可能都是负数,即它一定不在第三象限.

9. 答案:(D).

解　带第4块去玻璃店,玻璃店可以量出三角形玻璃的一条边长及其两个角的度数,由ASA定理,这样的三角形是唯一确定的.带其余几块均不能得到足够的信息确定这个三角形的形状和大小,故只有1种可能的选择.

10. 答案:(C).

解　阴影部分的面积占 $\triangle EFG$ 面积的 $\dfrac{4}{5}$,故阴影部分的面积为 $40 \times \dfrac{4}{5} = 32 \text{cm}^2$.阴影部分的面积占正方形 $ABCD$ 面积的一半,因此正方形的面积为 $32 \times 2 = 64 \text{cm}^2$,即其边长为8cm.

11. 答案:(A).

解　分子与分母同时除以 3^{2011},算式可化简为 $\dfrac{3^2-1}{3^2+3} = \dfrac{8}{12} = \dfrac{2}{3}$.

12. 答案:(B).

解法1　如图3-10所示,作与 AB 平行的辅助线 FG、EH.

则 $\angle FAB + \angle AFG = 180°$、$\angle GFE + \angle FEH = 180°$、$\angle HED + \angle EDC = 180°$.三式相加再减去 $\angle AFG + \angle GFE = 360° - 40° = 320°$,得到 $\angle BAF + \angle FED + \angle EDC = 220°$.

答案:(B).

解法2　如图3-11所示,作与 AB 平行的辅助线 FG、EH.

则
$$\angle FAB = \angle AFG, \angle GFE = \angle FEH,$$
$$\angle HED + \angle EDC = 180° \text{ 且 } \angle AFG + \angle GFE = \angle AFE = 40°.$$

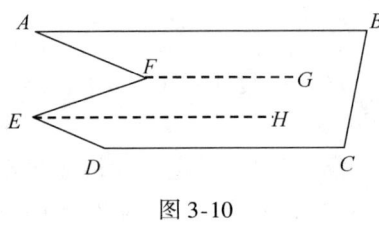

图 3-10

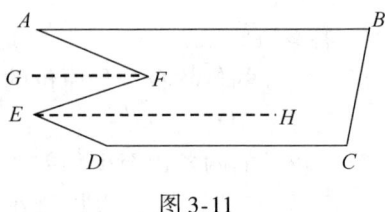

图 3-11

因此

$$\angle BAF + \angle FED + \angle EDC$$
$$= \angle BAF + (\angle FEH + \angle HED) + \angle EDC$$
$$= \angle AFG + \angle GFE + \angle HED + \angle EDC$$
$$= \angle AFE + 180°$$
$$= 220°.$$

13. 答案:(D).

解 由于 $182 = 2 \times 7 \times 13$、$221 = 13 \times 17$,她们买的彩色笔价格相同且超过 10 元,所以彩色笔的单价必为 13 元,故两人总共买了 $2 \times 7 + 17 = 31$ 支彩色笔.

14. 答案:(E).

解法 1 由 $C'A = C'D$ 可假设 $\angle A = \angle ADC' = x°$,而 $\angle BC'D$ 是 $\triangle AC'D$ 的外角,故 $\angle BC'D = 2x°$. 再因为 $\triangle BC'D$ 是 $\triangle BCD$ 折起来的部分,故知两个三角形全等,即有 $\angle BC'D = \angle BCD$;又因 $AB = AC$,故知 $\angle ABC = \angle ACB = \angle BC'D = 2x°$. 最后由三角形的内角和可得知

$$\angle ABC + \angle ACB + \angle A = 180°$$
$$2x° + 2x° + x° = 180°$$
$$x = 36.$$

解法 2 因 $\triangle BC'D$ 是 $\triangle BCD$ 折起来的部分,故两个三角形全等,即有 $\angle BC'D = \angle BCD$. 而由 $C'A = C'D$ 可假设 $\angle A = \angle ADC' = x°$,即有

$$\angle BCD = \frac{180° - \angle A}{2} = \frac{180° - x°}{2} = 90° - \frac{x°}{2};$$

而 $\angle BC'D$ 是 $\triangle AC'D$ 的外角,故有 $90° - \frac{x°}{2} = x° + x°$,即 $x = 36$.

15. 答案:(B).

解 设这四个正整数分别为 $a、b、c、d$,且 $a \leq b \leq c \leq d$. 若 $a = b = c = d$,则 $a^4 = 4a$,即 $a^3 = 4$,不合,故这四个正整数不可能全相等,因此四个数的和应大于 d 且小于 $4d$,即 $d < abcd < 4d$. 所以 $abc = 2$ 或 $abc = 3$.

若 $abc=2$,则 $a+b+c=1+1+2=4$,我们有 $4+d=2d$,解得 $d=4$,此时乘积为 8;

若 $abc=3$,则 $a+b+c=1+1+3=5$,我们有 $5+d=3d$,解得 d 不是整数,不合.

故这四个正整数之总和为 8.

16. 答案:(D).

解 早上 7:30 到 10:10 分小明共工作了 2 小时 40 分钟,且完成全部研究报告的 $\dfrac{2}{3}$,因此他还有 $\dfrac{1}{3}$ 的研究报告需完成,因此还需要工作 2 小时 40 分钟的一半,即 1 小时 20 分钟,再加上他休息的一小时,他应在 12:30 可完成这份研究报告.

17. 答案:(E).

解法 1 令此三角形为 $\triangle ABC$. 由 $7^2+24^2=25^2$,知 $\triangle ABC$ 是直角三角形,其面积为 $\dfrac{1}{2}\times 7\times 24=84\text{cm}^2$. 设点 P 到 $\triangle ABC$ 三边的距离都为 x cm,则由 $\triangle ABC$ 面积等于 $\triangle APB$、$\triangle BPC$、$\triangle CPA$ 面积之和得 $84=S_{APB}+S_{BPC}+S_{CPA}=(7+24+25)\times\dfrac{x}{2}$,解得 $x=3$.

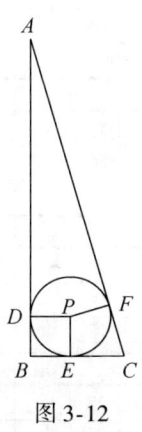

图 3-12

解法 2 令此三角形为 $\triangle ABC$. 因点 P 到 $\triangle ABC$ 三边的距离相等,故知点 P 为 $\triangle ABC$ 的内心,即内切圆圆心,而点 P 到 $\triangle ABC$ 三边的距离即为内切圆之半径. 如图 3-12,由切线 $AD=AF$、$BD=BE$、$CF=CE$ 可得 $PD=PE=DB=BE=\dfrac{AB+BC-AC}{2}=\dfrac{7+24-25}{2}=3$ (cm).

18. 答案:(A).

解 倒过来看还是一个数码的数码仅有 0、1、2、5、6、8 和 9,其中 0、1、2、5、8 倒过来还是自身,而 6 倒过来是 9、9 倒过来是 6. 因此三位数的百位有 1、2、5、6、8、9 共六种选择,当百位选好后个位也定下来了,而十位有 0、1、2、5、8 共五种选择,故共有 $6\times 5=30$ 个这样的三位数.

19. 答案:(C).

解 可知外星人的定时器每小时为地球人类时间一天的 10%、每分钟为地球人类时间一天的 0.1%,而从地球的零点到 6 点 36 分共经过了地球时间的 396 分钟,而一天有 $60\times 24=1440$ 分钟,故此时过了一天的 $\dfrac{396}{1440}=27.5\%$,因此在攻击时刻外星人的定时器上显示的时刻为 2 点 75 分.

20. 答案:(B).

解法1 小方和小丽每 $3\times4=12$ 天就会重新一起去商店一次,而 $100=12\times8+4$,故 100 天内她们一起去了 8 次.同理,100 天内小方和小雪一起去了 6 次、小丽和小雪一起去了 5 次.然而,每 $3\times4\times5=60$ 天她们三人就要一起去一次,即 100 天内有 1 次,因此一共有 $(8-1)+(6-1)+(5-1)+1=17$ 天是至少两人一起去商店.

解法2 因 3、4、5 的最小公倍数为 60,故知三人去商店的情况每 60 天就会循环一次,先观察前 60 天的情形(图 3-13):

	1	2	3	4	5	6	7	8	9	10	11	12	13	14	15
小方			◎			◎			◎			◎			◎
小丽				◎				◎				◎			
小雪					◎					◎					◎
	16	17	18	19	20	21	22	23	24	25	26	27	28	29	30
小方			◎			◎			◎			◎			◎
小丽	◎				◎				◎				◎		
小雪					◎					◎					◎
	31	32	33	34	35	36	37	38	39	40	41	42	43	44	45
小方			◎			◎			◎			◎			◎
小丽		◎				◎				◎				◎	
小雪					◎					◎					◎
	46	47	48	49	50	51	52	53	54	55	56	57	58	59	60
小方			◎			◎			◎			◎			◎
小丽			◎				◎				◎				◎
小雪					◎					◎					◎

图 3-13

可知前 60 天中,第 12、15、20、24、30、36、40、45、48、60 天等 10 天是至少两人一起去商店;而第 61 天至第 100 天会与前 40 天相同,因此第 61 天至第 100 天,第 72、75、80、84、90、96、100 天等 7 天是至少两人一起去商店.所以 100 天内共有 $10+7=17$ 天是至少两人一起去商店.

21. 答案:216.

解 正五边形的每个内角均为 $108°$,故 $\angle AMN+\angle ANM=72°$,因此
$$\angle AMB+\angle ANE=(180°-2\angle AMN)+(180°-2\angle ANM)$$
$$=360°-2\times72°=216°.$$

22. **答案**:145.

解 观察可知,每一个图形比前一个图形多的石子数依次为4、7、10,即第n个图形比第$n-1$个图形多$3n-2$个石子,因此按此规律下去,第五个图形比第四个图形多13颗石子、第六个图形比第五个图形多16颗石子、第七个图形比第六个图形多19颗石子、第八个图形比第七个图形多22颗石子、第九个图形比第八个图形多25颗石子、第十个图形比第九个图形多28颗石子、因此第十个图形需要22+13+16+19+22+25+28=145颗小石子.

评注 第n个图形需要$\frac{n(3n-1)}{2}$个石子.

23. **答案**:27.

解 首先证明不可能有三个面上的整数是三个连续的正整数.若不然,不妨设某三个面上的整数分别为$n,n+1,n+2$,那么由于写有$n+1$的面只有一个相对的面,它必然与写有n或$n+2$的两个面之一相邻,与题设矛盾.因此这六个面上的点数最小的可能值由小到大依次为1、2、4、5、7、8.而当1的对面是2、4的对面是5、7的对面是8时恰好符合题设.故六面点数之和最小是1+2+4+5+7+8=27.

24. **答案**:503.

解 注意到
$$2013=(\sqrt{y^2+2013}-y)(\sqrt{y^2+2013}+y),$$
两边同时除以$\sqrt{y^2+2013}-y$,得$\sqrt{x^2+2013}-x=\sqrt{y^2+2013}+y$,即
$$x+y=\sqrt{x^2+2013}-\sqrt{y^2+2013}.$$
同理,$x+y=\sqrt{y^2+2013}-\sqrt{x^2+2013}$,所以$x+y=0$,即$y=-x$,因此
$$\frac{2013x+y}{5x+y}=\frac{2013x-x}{5x-x}=\frac{2012x}{4x}=503.$$

25. **答案**:540.

解 令这个最小正整数为X.若X的前五个最大的因子恰为X、$\frac{X}{2}$、$\frac{X}{3}$、$\frac{X}{4}$、$\frac{X}{5}$且都是三位数,则X应被60整除,且不小于500,而这样的X的最小可能值是540;若X的前五个最大的因子中有一个因子是小于或等于$\frac{X}{6}$且仍是三位数,则可以推得$\frac{X}{6}\geq 100$,我们有$X\geq 600$.因此这个最小正整数为540.

3.4 第二轮英文试题

考试时间:120 分钟

Questions 1–5, 4 marks each

1. When the digits 0, 1, 2, 5, 6, 8 and 9 are rotated 180°, they become 0, 1, 2, 5, 9, 8 and 6 respectively. What does 9105 become when the four-digit number is rotated 180°?

(A) 6150 (B) 6102 (C) 5016 (D) 2019 (E) 2016

Answer: _____

2. What is the value of the expression
$$(a-b)(a+b-c)+(b-c)(b+c-a)+(c-a)(c+a-b)$$
(A) 0 (B) $a^2+b^2+c^2$ (C) $ab+bc+ca$
(D) $a^2+b^2+c^2-ab-bc-ca$ (E) $a^2+b^2+c^2+ab+bc+ca$

Answer: _____

3. We wish to dissect a square into n squares which need not be of the same size. For which of the following values of n is this impossible?

(A) 5 (B) 6 (C) 7 (D) 8 (E) 9

Answer: _____

4. The total number of players on three badminton teams is 29. No two players on the same team play against each other, while every two players on different teams play each other exactly once. What is the maximum number of games played?

(A) 265 (B) 270 (C) 276 (D) 280 (E) 282

Answer: _____

5. Two distinct quadratic polynomials $f(x)$ and $g(x)$ with leading coefficients equal to 1 satisfy $f(1)+f(3)+f(5)=g(1)+g(3)+g(5)$. Find all solutions of $f(x)=g(x)$.

(A) $x \leq 0$ (B) $-2 \leq x \leq 0$ (C) $0 \leq x \leq 1$
(D) $2 \leq x \leq 2$ (E) 3

Answer: _____

第3章 第3届国际中小学生数学能力检测(IMAS)(初中组)

Questions 6–13, 5 marks each

6. The diagram shows a quadrilateral *ABCD* with *AB* parallel to *DC*. *F* is the midpoint of *BC*. If the area of triangle *AFD* is 10cm^2, what is the area, in cm^2, of *ABCD*?

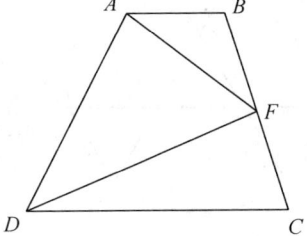

Answer: _____ cm^2

7. Lily has 2014 chocolates. She eats one on the first day. Each day after, she eats twice as many as the day before, until all the chocolates have been eaten. How many chocolates did she eat on the last day?

Answer: _____ chocolates

8. Leon is putting 99 apples into boxes of two different sizes. A large box can hold 12 apples while a small box can hold 5 apples. All boxes must be full. How many boxes will he need if this number must be greater than 10?

Answer: _____ boxes

9. In a convex quadrilateral *ABCD*, *AB* = 3, *BC* = 5, *CD* = 6, *DA* = 10, and the length of the diagonal *AC* is a positive integer. How many different possible shapes can *ABCD* take?

Answer: _____ shapes

10. Divide the ten positive integers from 1 to 10 into two groups so that when the product of the numbers in the first group is divided by the product of the numbers in the second group, the quotient is a positive integer. What is the minimum value of this quotient?

Answer: _____

11. A cardboard windmill with three blades is made from four equilateral triangles of side length 6 cm. Two triangles sharing a common vertex have the corresponding sides lying on the same straight line, as shown in the diagram. The area of the circle swept out by the blades of the windmill is x cm^2. What is the greatest integer less than or equal to x?

Answer: _____

12. Let the real numbers a_1, a_2, a_3, a_4 and a_5 be such that $a_{n+1} = |a_n| - |a_n - 1|$ for $1 \leq n \leq 4$. If $a_5 = \dfrac{1}{2}$ and $a_1 = \dfrac{p}{q}$, where p and q are relatively prime positive

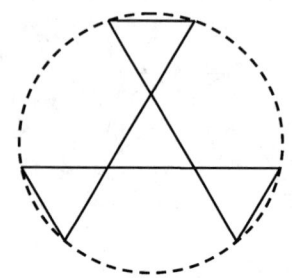

integers, what is the value of $p+q$?

Answer: _____

13. What is the minimum perimeter of a parallelogram which may be partitioned into 462 equilateral triangles of side length 1 cm?

Answer: _____ cm

Questions 14 to 15, 20 marks each
Detailed solutions are needed for these two problems

14. In an acute triangle ABC, $AB=AC$. D is the foot of the perpendicular from B to CA, and E is the foot of the perpendicular from D to BC. If $BC=AB+AD$, prove that $BE=CD$.

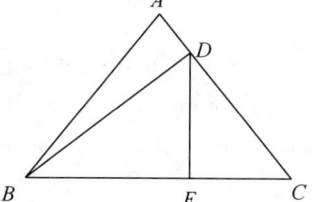

15. A positive integer x with $n \geq 2$ digits is written down twice in a row and the $2n$-digit number so obtained is divisible by x^2. Prove that the first two digits of x are 1 and 4 in that order.

3.5 第二轮中文试题

1–5 题，每题 4 分

1. 将数码 0、1、2、5、6、8、9 旋转 180°，可分别得到数码 0、1、2、5、9、8、6。若将四位数 9105 旋转 180°，请问得到的数是什么？

(A) 6150   (B) 6102   (C) 5016   (D) 2019   (E) 2016

答：_____

2. 代数式 $(a-b)(a+b-c)+(b-c)(b+c-a)+(c-a)(c+a-b)$ 化简后等于什么？

(A) 0   (B) $a^2+b^2+c^2$ (C) $ab+bc+ca$
(D) $a^2+b^2+c^2-ab-bc-ca$ (E) $a^2+b^2+c^2+ab+bc+ca$

答：_____

3. 将一个正方形分割成 n 个小正方形（并不要求小正方形的大小一致），请问 n 不能等于下列哪个数？

(A) 5   (B) 6   (C) 7   (D) 8   (E) 9

答：_____

4. 有29名羽毛球运动员分成三队,每队若干名队员,进行单打比赛,规定同队的运动员之间不比赛,不同队的运动员两两都比赛一场,请问比赛的场数最多为多少场?

(A)265　　(B)270　　(C)276　　(D)280　　(E)282

答:_____

5. 有两个不同的二次多项式 $f(x)$ 与 $g(x)$ 的首项系数都是1,并且满足
$$f(1)+f(3)+f(5)=g(1)+g(3)+g(5).$$
请问 $f(x)=g(x)$ 的所有解是什么?

(A)$x \leqslant 0$　(B)$-2 \leqslant x \leqslant 0$　(C)$0 \leqslant x \leqslant 1$　(D)$-2 \leqslant x \leqslant 2$　(E)3

答:_____

6—13题,每题5分

6. 在梯形 $ABCD$ 中,$AB//DC$,点 F 为 BC 边的中点,如图3-14 所示. 已知 $\triangle AFD$ 的面积为 $10 cm^2$,请问梯形 $ABCD$ 的面积为多少 cm^2?

答:_____ cm^2

7. 小莉和小明轮流每次都从1开始数,数到截至目前尚未被数过的2的第一个次幂为止. 例如从小莉开始,数到1为止,因为1是2的次幂. 接着小明数到2为止,然后小莉数到4为止,按照这种方式继续下去. 所以他们两人数出的前10个数是1;1,2;1,2,3,4;1,2,3. 请问他们两人数出的第2014个数是什么?

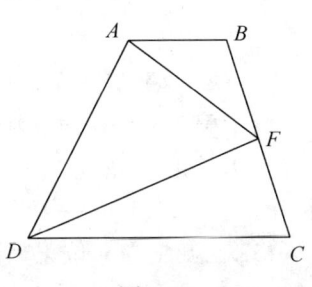

图 3-14

答:_____

8. 小亮要将99颗苹果放入两种规格的盒子中,每个大盒子可装12颗苹果,每个小盒子可装5颗苹果. 若要求使用的盒子数多于10个且每个都盒子必须装满,请问他将苹果正好装完共需多少个盒子?

答:_____个

9. 在凸四边形 $ABCD$ 中,$AB=3$、$BC=5$、$CD=6$、$DA=10$,且对角线 AC 的长度是正整数,请问共有多少个不同的四边形 $ABCD$ 满足上述条件?

答:_____个

10. 把正整数1—10共十个数分为两组,使得第一组数的乘积除以第二组数的乘积所得的商为正整数,请问所得商的最小值是什么?

答:_____

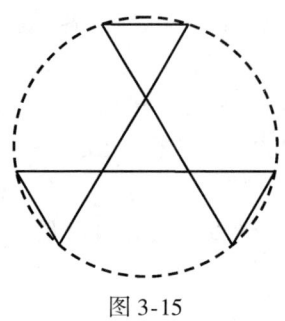

图 3-15

11. 利用四个边长为 6cm 的正三角形纸板可以组成一个纸风车,其中若两个正三角形有共同的顶点时,则其中一个三角形内构成这一个顶点的两边分别与另一个三角形构成这一个顶点的两边各落在一条直线上,如图 3-15 所示. 以中间的正三角形中心为旋转中心,将这个风车旋转一圈,若扫过的面积为 x cm^2,请问不超过 x 的最大整数是什么?

答:_____

12. 已知实数 a_1、a_2、a_3、a_4、a_5 满足 $a_{n+1}=|a_n|-|a_n-1|$,其中 $1 \leqslant n \leqslant 4$. 若 $a_5=\dfrac{1}{2}$,$a_1=\dfrac{p}{q}$(p、q 都为正整数且互质),请问 $p+q$ 的值是什么?

答:_____

13. 若一个平行四边形能被划分成 462 个边长为 1cm 的正三角形,请问这样的平行四边形周长的最小可能值是多少 cm?

答:_____ cm

14、15 题,必须填写详细计算过程或证明,每题 20 分

14. 等腰三角形 ABC 中,顶角 A 是锐角,$AB=AC$ 且 $BD \perp AC$,$DE \perp BC$,如图 3-16 所示. 已知 $BC=AB+AD$,求证:$BE=DC$.

15. 已知 x 为 n 位正整数,其中 $n \geqslant 2$,并且将 x 在一横行上写两遍后得到一个 $2n$ 位数能被 x^2 整除. 请证明所有满足上述条件的 x 的前两位数码依序都必为 1、4.

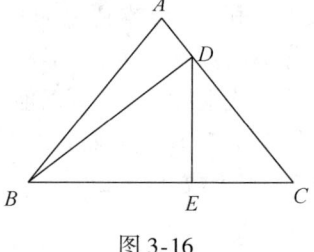

图 3-16

3.6 第二轮试题解答与评注

1. 答案:(C).

解 数码 9 旋转 180° 后得到数码 6;数码 1 旋转 180° 后还是数码 1;数码 0 旋转 180° 后还是数码 0;数码 5 旋转 180° 后还是数码 5.

所以四位数 9105 旋转 180° 后得到数 5016.

2. 答案:(A).

解法 1 计算可知 $(a-b)(a+b-c)=a^2-b^2-ac+bc$;$(b-c)(b+c-a)=b^2-c^2-ab$

$+ac$；$(c-a)(c+a-b)=c^2-a^2-bc+ab$，三式之和为 0.

解法 2 若 $a=b$，则 $(a-b)(a+b-c)+(b-c)(b+c-a)+(c-a)(c+a-b)=0$，所以此代数式可被 $(a-b)$ 整除；同理此代数式亦可被 $(b-c)$ 与 $(c-a)$ 整除，所以此代数式必须是 $(a-b)(b-c)(c-a)$ 倍式，但这个代数式为二次式，故知代数式必为 0.

3. 答案：(A).

解 用如图 3-17 所示之方法分割这个正方形，n 可为 6、7、8、9.

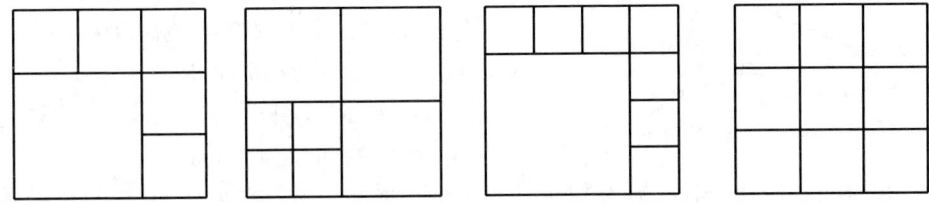

图 3-17

若 n 可为 5，可判断出这 5 个小正方形的大小不会一致. 接着可观察得知大正方形中的每一个顶点都会属于不同的小正方形，令这五个小正方形为 A、B、C、D、E 且其边长分别为 a、b、c、d、e，如图 3-18 所示.

则 $a+b=a+d$、$b+c=a+b$，可得 $b=d$、$a=c$. 又知 $a+e+c=b+e+d$，可得 $2a+e=2b+e$ 即 $a=b$. 从 $a+e+c=a+b$，可得 $e=0$，矛盾. 因此，这个正方形不可能分割为 5 个小正方形.

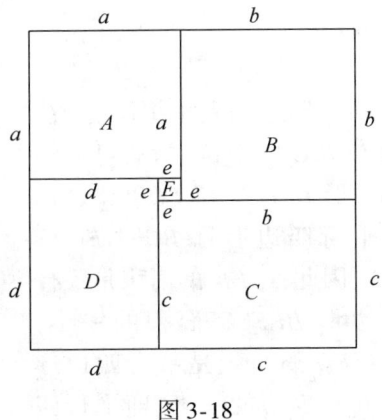

图 3-18

4. 答案：(D).

解 当 A 队比 B 队的人数至少多 2 人时，此时 A 队的队员 X 会与 B 队的每一位队员都比赛一场；若把队员 X 调到 B 队，则队员 X 会与 A 队其余的队员都比赛一场. 可知把队员 X 从 A 队调到 B 队后，比赛的总场数会增加. 所以，当三队运动员人数相等或相差 1 时，比赛总场数最多. 此时，三队运动员人数分别是 10、10、9. 所以，比赛的场数最多为 $10\times10+10\times9+10\times9=280$ 场.

5. 答案：(E).

解 令 $f(x)=x^2+ax+b$ 与 $g(x)=x^2+cx+d$. 则 $f(1)+f(3)+f(5)=35+9a+3b$ 且 $g(1)+g(3)+g(5)=35+9c+3d$.

可得知 $9(a-c)=3(d-b)$.

现有 $0=f(x)-g(x)=(a-c)x+(d-b)$，故 $x=\dfrac{d-b}{a-c}=3$ 是唯一的解.

6. 答案：20cm^2.

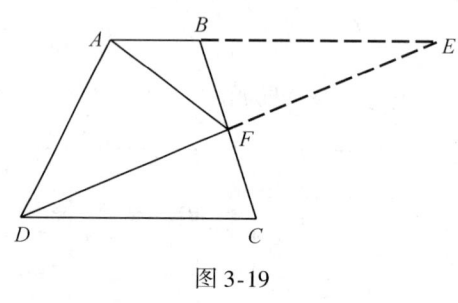

图 3-19

解法 1 如图 3-19，令点 E 为 AB 与 DF 的延长线之交点. 由 $BF=CF$ 且 $AB//DC$ 知 $\triangle BEF$ 与 $\triangle CDF$ 为两全等三角形，因此可以推得 $\triangle BEF$ 与 $\triangle CDF$ 的面积相等且 $EF=DF$.

因 $\triangle AFD$ 的面积为 10cm^2，故知 $\triangle AEF$ 的面积也为 10cm^2，因此梯形 $ABCD$ 的面积为 20cm^2.

解法 2 设 AD 中点为 E 以 E 点为中心，将图形旋转 $180°$ 后得新的梯形 $A'B'C'D'$，以如图 3-20 所示之方式，将 AD 与 $D'A'$ 重合与原图形拼成一个四边形 $BCB'C'$.

可知四边形 $BCB'C'$ 与 $AFDF'$ 都是平行四边形且 FF' 为 $BCB'C'$ 的中位线，故可得知四边形 $BFF'C'$ 与 $FCB'F'$ 也都是平行四边形且 $BC'=FF'=CB'$，因此 $\triangle AFF'$ 的面积是平行四边形 $BFF'C'$ 面积的一半、$\triangle F'FD$ 的面积是平行四边形 $FCB'F'$ 面积的一半，即平行四边形 $AFDF'$ 的面积是平行四边形 $BCB'C'$ 面积的一半.

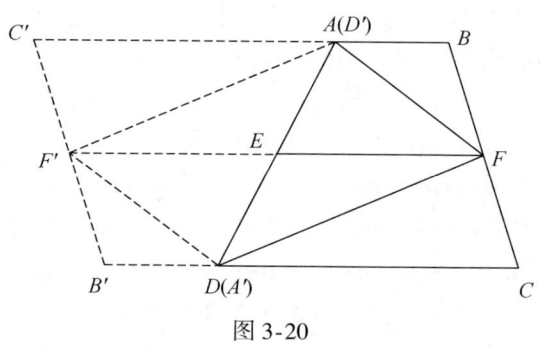

图 3-20

因平行四边形 $AFDF'$ 的面积为 $\triangle AFD$ 的面积的 2 倍，即 $10\times 2=20\text{cm}^2$，故平行四边形 $BCB'C'$ 的面积为 $20\times 2=40\text{cm}^2$，即梯形 $ABCD$ 的面积为 $40\div 2=20\text{cm}^2$.

7. 答案：991.

解 当他们两人数至 2 的 n 次幂时，总共数了 $2^0+2^1+2^2+\cdots+2^n=2^{n+1}-1$ 个数. 而 $2^{10}-1=1023<2014<2047=2^{11}-1$ 个数，因此当他们两人共数完 1023 个数后，还需要再数 $2014-1023=991$ 个数. 他们都从 1 开始数，故他们两人数出的第 2014 个数是 991.

8. 答案:17.

解 因为99是奇数而12是偶数,故可推知小盒子的数量必须是奇数;再因99与12都是3的倍数,故可推知小盒子的数量必须是3的倍数;可判断出小盒子的总数量必小于20个,因此知小盒子的数量为3、9或15:若小盒子的数量为3,此时小盒子共装了15颗苹果,即大盒子共装有84颗苹果,因此需要7个大盒子才能恰好都装完,此时共恰用10个盒子,与题意不合;若小盒子的数量为9,此时小盒子共装了45颗苹果,即大盒子共装有54颗苹果,此时因54不是12的倍数,故知无法用大盒子恰装完54颗苹果,与题意不合;若小盒子的数量为15,此时小盒子共装了75颗苹果,即大盒子共装有24颗苹果,因此需要2个大盒子才能恰好都装完,此时共恰用17个盒子.

9. 答案:3种.

解 利用三角不等式,在△ABC中知 $AC<AB+BC=8$、$AC>BC-AB=2$,而在△ACD中知 $AC<CD+DA=16$、$AC>DA-CD=4$,因此 AC 的可能长度为5、6、7,故共有3种不同的四边形ABCD(图3-21)经检验它们都是凸四边形.

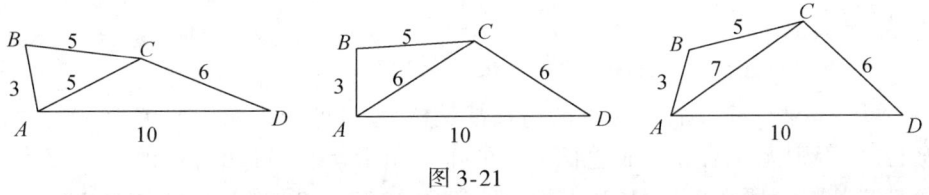

图3-21

10. 答案:7.

解 注意到7只有自己可被7整除,故7必须在被除数上,因此商不小于7. 剩下的数 $1×2×3×4×5×6×8×9×10=2^8×3^4×5^2$,故可以让第二组的乘积等于 $2^4×3^2×5^1$,例如 $\dfrac{3×5×6×7×8}{1×2×4×9×10}=7$,故商的最小值为7.

11. 答案:263.

解 如图3-22所示,令 O 为中间的正三角形中心、A 为其中一个叶片的外围一个顶点,而在中间的正三角形边上取点 H 使 OH 与 AH 垂直,可知 $AH=6+\dfrac{6}{2}=9$ cm.

由 OH 之长度等于正三角形高之 $\dfrac{1}{3}$ 可知

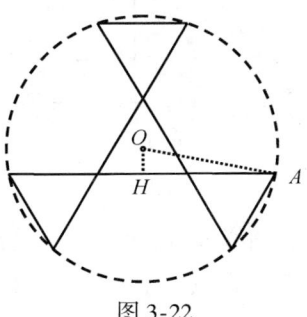

图3-22

$$OH = \frac{1}{3} \times \frac{\sqrt{3}}{2} \times 6 = \sqrt{3}\,\text{cm}^2.$$

再由勾股定理可得：$OA^2 = OH^2 + AH^2 = 3 + 81 = 84\,\text{cm}^2$.

所以风车旋转一周扫过的最大圆的面积为 $\pi \times 84\,\text{cm}^2$.

因 $3.141 < \pi < 3.142$，故 $263.844 < 84\pi < 263.928$，所以不超过 x 的最大整数是 263．

12. 答案：63．

解 可在数在线令点 A 为 0、点 B 为 1、点 P 为 a_4.

可知 $PA - PB = |a_4| - |a_4 - 1| = \frac{1}{2}$，故可判断出点 P 必在 A、B 之间，因此 $\frac{1}{2} = PA - PB = a_4 - (1 - a_4)$，即 $a_4 = \frac{1 + \frac{1}{2}}{2} = \frac{3}{4}$；接着重新令点 P 为 a_3 并满足 $PA - PB = \frac{3}{4}$，同样可推知 $a_3 = \frac{1 + \frac{3}{4}}{2} = \frac{7}{8}$；继续依此方式，可得 $a_2 = \frac{15}{16}$，$a_1 = \frac{31}{32}$，故 $p = 31$、$q = 32$，因此 $p + q = 63$.

13. 答案：64 cm．

解 显然这个平行四边形的边长都是整数，且四个内角中两个为 60°，两个为 120°，否则无法恰好分成边长为 1 的正三角形．设平行四边形的一组邻边长分别为 x 和 y，那么 $2xy = 462$，得到 $xy = 231 = 1 \times 231 = 3 \times 77 = 7 \times 33 = 11 \times 21$. 当 x、y 一个为 11，另一个为 21 时平行四边形的周长 $2(x+y)$ 取到最小值 64 cm．

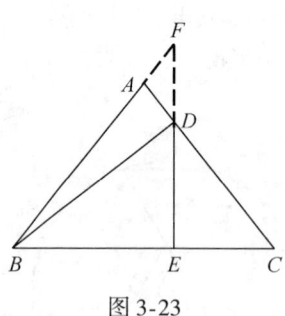

图 3-23

14. **解** 如图 3-23，延长 BA 与 ED，令交点为 F. 可知

$\angle AFD = 90° - \angle ABC = 90° - \angle ACB = \angle CDE = \angle ADF$

因此 $AF = AD$，即 $BC = AB + AD = AF$. 因为 $\angle BDC = 90° = \angle BEF$ 且 $\angle BCD = \angle FBE$，故可知 $\triangle BCD$ 与 $\triangle FBE$ 为两个全等三角形，所以 $CD = BE$.

评注 仅延长 BA 到 F 使得 $BF = BC$，并连接 DF 的，给 5 分．在此基础上证明 F，D，E 三点共线的，给 10 分．

同样地，如果延长 BA，ED 交于 F 并证明 $BF = BC$ 的，也给 10 分．但若仅延长产生交点，则给 0 分．证明思路正确，有瑕疵的，给 15 分．证明完全正确给 20 分．

15. 解 由题目条件知 $(10^n+1)x$ 能被 x^2 整除,故可令 $10^n+1=kx$. 因 x 是 n 位正整数,故 $x>10^{n-1}$,所以 $k\leqslant \dfrac{10^n+1}{10^{n-1}}<11$. 由于 10^n+1 的末位数是 1 且其数码和为 2,故它不能被 2、3 或 5 整除,因此 $k=1$ 或 $k=7$. 若 $k=1$,则 $x=10^n+1$ 不是 n 位数,矛盾;故知 $k=7$. 而当 1000… 这种形式的数被 7 除直到余数为 6 时,可知商至少为 3 位数且前两位数码依序都必为 1、4,即所有这样的 x 的前两位数码依序都必为 1、4.

评注 由题目条件抽象出 $(10^n+1)x$ 能被 x^2 整除,并假设出商数的,给 5 分. 可能有的选手未做假设,但开始考虑商数的值,也给 5 分. 发现商数在 1—10 之间,并去除一些情况的,给 10 分. 证明商数必须为 7 的,给 15 分. 证明完全正确的,给 20 分.

可能有些选手发现只需证明商数为 7,并证明了如果商数为 7,那么 x 的前两位数码依序必为 1、4,此类情况可以给 10 分. 在此基础上如果还排除了商数其他的一些可能情况,基本确定了商数的值,但有 1—2 种情况未排除,则给 15 分.

第4章 第4届国际中小学生数学能力检测(IMAS)(初中组)

4.1 第一轮英文试题

考试时间:75分钟

Questions 1–10, 3 marks each

1. What is the value of $2014 - 1^{204} + \sqrt{(-2014)^2}$?
 (A)1 (B)−1 (C)−2087 (D)4027 (E)4029

2. A compass costs 15.40 dollars and a ruler costs 8.65 dollars. How many more dollars does the compass cost than the ruler?
 (A)7.25 dollars (B)7.75 dollars
 (C)24.05 dollars (D)6.25 dollars
 (E)6.75 dollars

3. The two stars in the diagram represent the same number. The sum of the three numbers in the second row is equal to twice the sum of the three numbers in the first row. What number does each star represent?

5	6	☆		
		☆	19	20

 (A)7 (B)8 (C)13 (D)17 (E)18

4. In a restaurant, one cup of tea and two cups of coffee cost 78 dollars, while three cups of tea and one cup of coffee cost 94 dollars. How many more dollars does a cup of coffee cost than a cup of tea?
 (A)2 (B)4 (C)6 (D)10 (E)12

5. When two numbers are divided by 5, the respective remainders are 4 and 2. What is the remainder when the sum of the two numbers is divided by 5?

(A) 0 (B) 1 (C) 2 (D) 3 (E) 4

6. A circular spinner is divided into eight equal sectors. Two of them are painted red, two black, three white and one yellow. What is the probability for the pointer of the spinner to be pointing at a black sector?

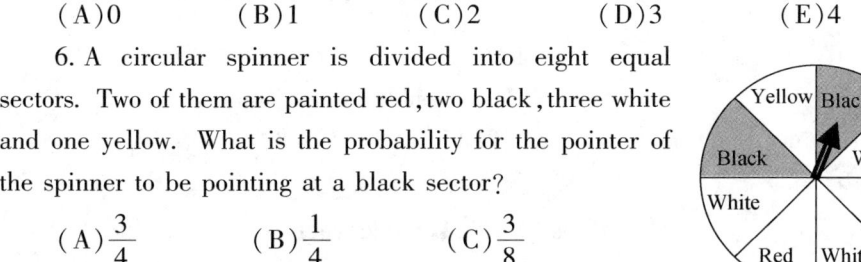

(A) $\dfrac{3}{4}$ (B) $\dfrac{1}{4}$ (C) $\dfrac{3}{8}$

(D) $\dfrac{1}{8}$ (E) $\dfrac{1}{2}$

7. To visit a friend, Rod must take the bus to the nearest Metro station, and this takes 15 minutes. He has to ride the Metro train for 20 stops, each taking 2.5 minutes. He also has to change trains twice, and it takes 3 minutes each time. Finally, after exiting the Metro, he still has to walk another 12 minutes before reaching his friend's place. How many minutes does Rod have to spend traveling to his friend's house?

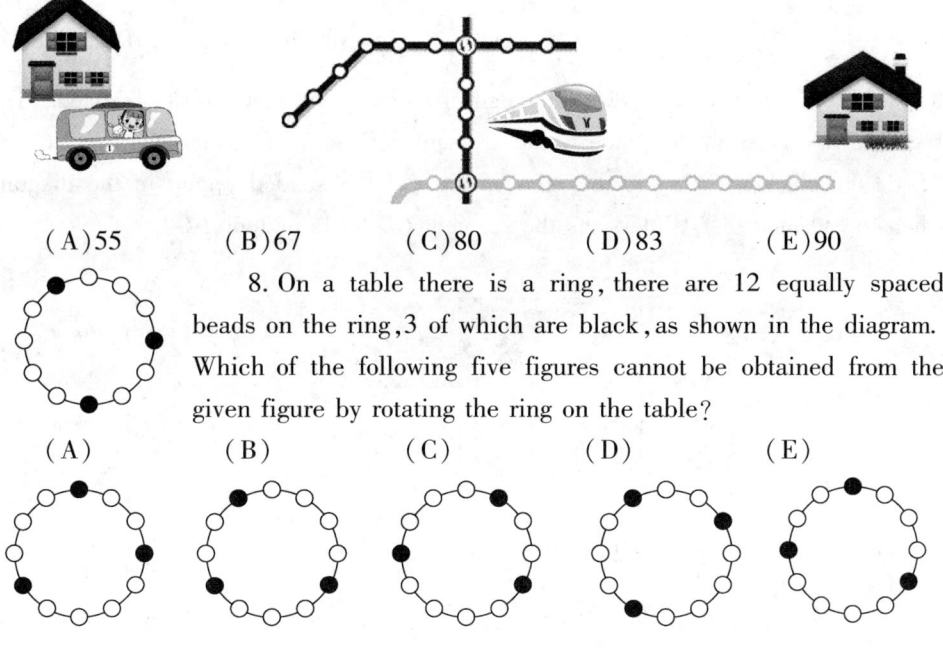

(A) 55 (B) 67 (C) 80 (D) 83 (E) 90

8. On a table there is a ring, there are 12 equally spaced beads on the ring, 3 of which are black, as shown in the diagram. Which of the following five figures cannot be obtained from the given figure by rotating the ring on the table?

(A) (B) (C) (D) (E)

9. If a, x and y are real numbers such that $|2y-12|+\sqrt{ax-y}=0$, what is the

value of the product *axy*?

(A)0 (B)6 (C)12

(D)36 (E)impossible to determine

10. How many integers *a* satisfies $|2a+7|+|2a-1|=8$?

(A)9 (B)8 (C)5 (D)4 (E)infinite

Questions 11–20,4 marks each

11. If *a* and *b* are prime numbers such that $a^2-7b-4=0$, what is the value of *a+b*?

(A)5 (B)8 (C)9 (D)10 (E)13

12. The diagram shows a strip of paper folded along the segment *AB*. If $\angle ACB = 60°$ and the area of triangle *ABC* is $\sqrt{3}$ cm^2, what is the width, in cm, of this strip?

(A)1 (B)$\sqrt{3}$ (C)$\frac{\sqrt{3}}{2}$

(D)$\frac{2\sqrt{3}}{3}$ (E)impossible to determine

13. *ABCD* is a square of side length 10 cm. The segment *BC* is fixed. The segment *AD* moves in the plane to the segment *A'D'* so that the lengths *AB*,*DC* and *AD* do not change. What is the area, in cm^2, of the shaded region in the diagram when the segment *A'D'* intersects the segment *CD* at its midpoint *G*?

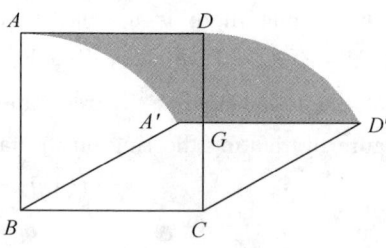

(A)50 (B)$\frac{50\pi}{3}$ (C)60 (D)100 (E)$\frac{100\pi}{3}$

14. We start with an equilateral triangle *ABC* of area 80cm^2. We construct a right isosceles triangle *BCD* using *BC* as the hypotenuse. Then we construct an equilateral triangle using *BD* as a side. This continued alternately, as shown in the

diagram. What is the area, in cm², of the fourth equilateral triangle?

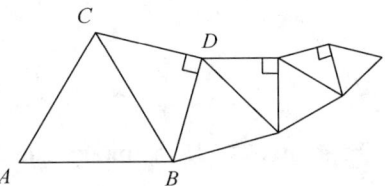

(A)1.25　　(B)5　　(C)6.4　　(D)10　　(E)40

15. We wish to spend 100 dollars to buy 18 stamps, each costing 4 dollars, 8 dollars or 10 dollars. We must buy at least 1 stamp of each of the three kinds. How many different ways can the buying of stamps be possible?

(A)1　　(B)2　　(C)3　　(D)4　　(E)5

16. The sectors MAB and MCD are inside the square $ABCD$ of side length 10 cm, as shown in the diagram. What is the total area, in cm², of these two sectors, correct to 1 decimal place? Take $\pi = 3.14$.

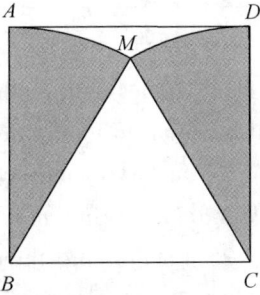

(A)52.3　　(B)78.5　　(C)104.7

(D)157.0　　(E)314.0

17. Three different positive integers m, n and p are such that $(m-3)(n-3)(p-3)=4$. What is the value of $m+n+p$?

(A)5　　(B)6　　(C)8　　(D)14　　(E)15

18. If $x<y<0$ and $x^2+y^2=4xy$, what is the value of $\dfrac{x+y}{x-y}$?

(A)$\sqrt{3}$　　(B)$-\sqrt{3}$　　(C)3　　(D)$\sqrt{6}$　　(E)$-\sqrt{6}$

19. The diagram shows two right triangles OAC and OBD. The lengths of three of the segments AB, AC, CD and DB are 12 cm, 6 cm and 3cm. What is the number of possible lengths, in cm, of the fourth segment?

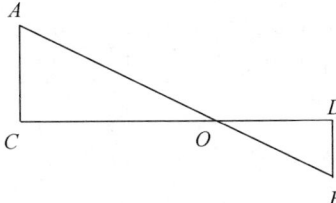

(A)2　　(B)3　　(C)4

(D)5　　(E)6

20. For any real number x, we denote by $[x]$ the greatest integer not greater than x. For

example, $[\pi] = 3$ and $[-\pi] = -4$. How many positive integers n satisfy $\left[\dfrac{\left[\dfrac{100}{n}\right]}{n}\right] = 1$?

(A) 1　　　　(B) 2　　　　(C) 3　　　　(D) 4　　　　(E) 5

Questions 21–25, 6 marks each

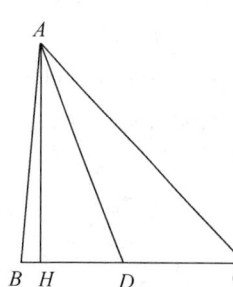

21. In the diagram, AH is perpendicular to BC, $AB = BC < AC$, and AD is the bisector $\angle BAC$. If $\angle DAH = 21°$, what is the measure, in degrees, of $\angle BAC$?

22. How many four-digit numbers are divisible by all of 2, 3, 4, 5, 6, 7 and 8?

23. Each of A, B, C and D has some apples. A has as many apples as the other three together. B has half as many apples as the other three together. C has one-sixth as many apples as the other three together. How many times D's number of apples will be equal to total number of apples of A, B and C?

24. In how many ways can 31 be expressed in the form $a+b+c$ ($a \leq b \leq c$), where a, b and c are prime numbers?

25. Each of the three dimensions of a cuboid of volume a cm³ is an integral number of cm. The cuboid is placed on a table. The total surface area of the five visible faces is a cm². Find the minimum value of a.

4.2　第一轮中文试题

1—10题,每题3分

1. 请问代数式 $2014 - 1^{204} + \sqrt{(-2014)^2}$ 的值等于什么?

(A) 1　　　(B) −1　　　(C) −2087　　　(D) 4027　　　(E) 4029

2. 一把圆规的价格是15.40元,一把直尺的价格是8.65元,请问一把圆规比一把直尺贵多少钱?

(A) 7.25 元　　　　　　(B) 7.75 元　　　　　　(C) 24.05 元

(D) 6.25 元　　　　　　(E) 6.75 元

第4章 第4届国际中小学生数学能力检测(IMAS)(初中组)

3. 在下面两个标有"☆"的方格(图 4-1)内填入相同的数,使得第二行的三个数之和是第一行的三个数之和的两倍.请问填入的数是什么?

5	6	☆		
		☆	19	20

图 4-1

(A)7　　(B)8　　(C)13
(D)17　　(E)18

4. 在某餐馆内,购买一杯红茶和两杯咖啡需 78 元,购买三杯红茶与一杯咖啡需 94 元,请问一杯咖啡比一杯红茶贵几元?

(A)2　　(B)4　　(C)6　　(D)10　　(E)12

5. 若甲数除以 5 余 2,乙数除以 5 余 4,请问甲、乙两数之和除以 5 的余数是什么?

(A)0　　(B)1　　(C)2　　(D)3　　(E)4

6. 把一个圆形转盘平均分成 8 份,依下图方式分别涂上红色、黑色、白色、黄色.随意转动转盘,请问停止后指针停在黑色区域的概率是什么(图 4-2)?

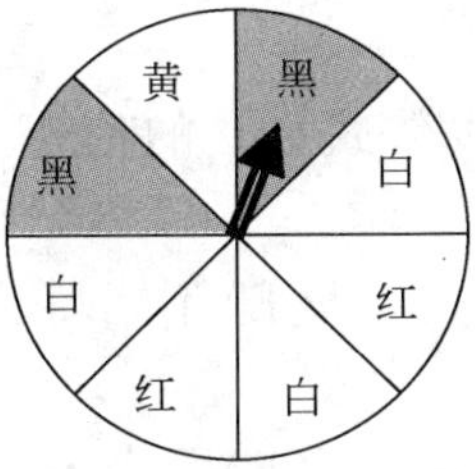

(A)$\frac{3}{4}$　　(B)$\frac{1}{4}$　　(C)$\frac{3}{8}$

(D)$\frac{1}{8}$　　(E)$\frac{1}{2}$

图 4-2

7. 如图 4-3 所示,小罗从家里到朋友家去参加生日派对,最快的方式是乘坐公交车然后转地铁,已知从家里到最近的大南地铁站需要乘坐公交车 15 分钟,然后从大南站到仁和站需要乘坐 20 个站,每个站平均需要 2.5 分钟,中途要转乘 2 次,每次转乘平均需要 3 分钟,不计出入地铁站的时间,从仁和站出去还需要步行 12 分钟才能到朋友家.请问小罗去朋友的家共需费时多少分钟?

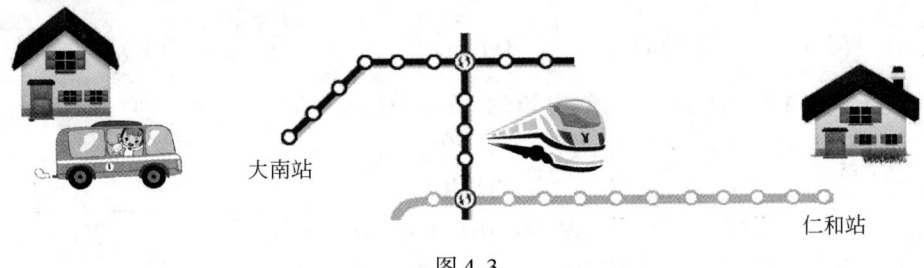

图 4-3

(A)55　　　(B)67　　　(C)80　　　(D)83　　　(E)90

8. 桌面上有一串项链,项链上均匀分布着 12 个小珠子,其中有三个小珠子是黑色的,其他的珠子都是白色的,如图 4-4 所示.

如果只允许项链在桌面上旋转而不可以翻转,请问图 4-5 中哪一项不能得到?

图 4-4

(A)　　　(B)　　　(C)　　　(D)　　　(E)

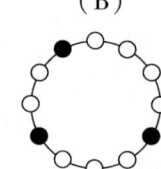
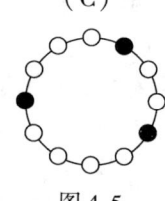
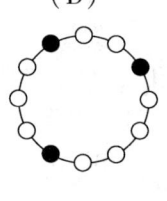
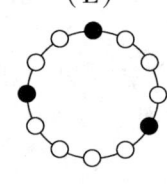

图 4-5

9. 若实数 a、x、y 满足 $|2y-12|+\sqrt{ax-y}=0$,请问代数式 axy 的值等于什么?

(A)0　　　(B)6　　　(C)12　　　(D)36　　　(E)不能确定

10. 请问满足 $|2a+7|+|2a-1|=8$ 的整数 a 有多少个?

(A)9　　　(B)8　　　(C)5　　　(D)4　　　(E)无穷多

11—20 题,每题 4 分

11. 设质数 a、b 满足 $a^2-7b-4=0$,请问 $a+b$ 的值等于什么?

(A)5　　　(B)8　　　(C)9　　　(D)10　　　(E)13

12. 如图 4-6 所示,将一纸条折叠,折痕为 AB,如果 $\angle ACB=60°$,折叠后重叠部分的 $\triangle ABC$ 面积为 $\sqrt{3}$ cm²,请问这张纸条的宽为多少 cm?

(A)1　　　(B)$\sqrt{3}$　　　(C)$\dfrac{\sqrt{3}}{2}$　　　(D)$\dfrac{2\sqrt{3}}{3}$　　　(E)不能确定

13. 平面上 $ABCD$ 是一个边长为 10cm 的正方形,BC 边固定不动,将 AD 边移至 $A'D'$ 的位置,并且在移动过程中 AB、CD 和 AD 边的长度恒不改变.已知 $A'D'$ 与 CD 的交点 G 为 CD 边的中点,如图 4-7 所示.请问在移动过程中 AD 边扫过的面积(即图 4-7 中阴影部分)为多少 cm²?(π 取 3.14)

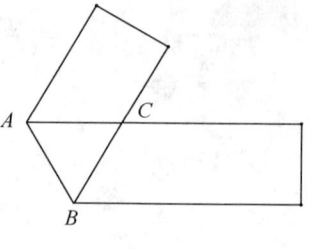

图 4-6

第4章 第4届国际中小学生数学能力检测(IMAS)(初中组)

(A)50　　(B)$\dfrac{50\pi}{3}$　　(C)60　　(D)100　　(E)$\dfrac{100\pi}{3}$

14. 以等边△ABC 的一边为斜边作等腰直角△BCD,再以等腰直角三角形的 BD 边为边作等边三角形,不断地重复此过程,如图 4-8 所示. 如果第一个等边△ABC 的面积为 80cm²,请问第四个等边三角形的面积是多少 cm²?

(A)1.25　　(B)5　　(C)6.4
(D)10　　(E)40

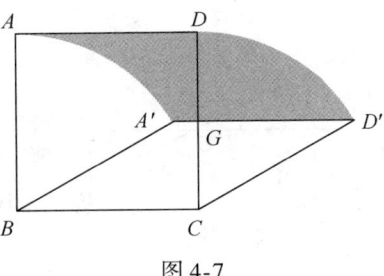

图 4-7

15. 用 100 元购买面值分别为 4 元、8 元、10 元的三种邮票共 18 张,每种邮票至少买一张,请问共有多少种不同的购买方法?

(A)1　　(B)2　　(C)3
(D)4　　(E)5

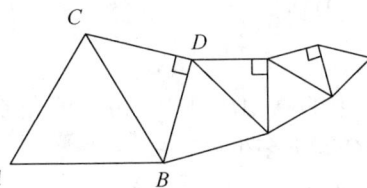

图 4-8

16. 扇形 BMA 与扇形 CDM 在边长为 10 cm 的正方形内,并且只有一个公共点 M,如图 4-9 所示. 请问这两个扇形的面积之和为多少 cm²?(π 取 3.14,结果精确到小数点后 1 位)

(A)52.3　　(B)78.5　　(C)104.7
(D)157.0　　(E)314.0

17. 三个互不相同的正整数 m、n、p 满足 (m-3)(n-3)(p-3)=4,请问 m+n+p 的值等于什么?

(A)5　　(B)6　　(C)8
(D)14　　(E)15

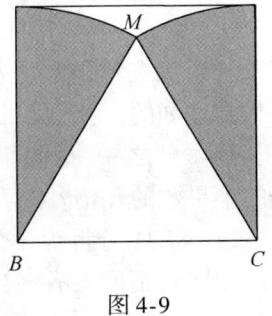

图 4-9

18. 设 $x<y<0$、$x^2+y^2=4xy$,请问 $\dfrac{x+y}{x-y}$ 的值等于什么?

(A)$\sqrt{3}$　　(B)$-\sqrt{3}$　　(C)3　　(D)$\sqrt{6}$　　(E)$-\sqrt{6}$

19. 四条线段的长分别为 x、12、6、3(其中 x 为正实数),用它们拼出两个直角三角形,且 AB 与 CD 是其中的两条线段,如图 4-10 所示. 请问 x 的可取值的个数为多少个?

(A)2 (B)3 (C)4
(D)5 (E)6

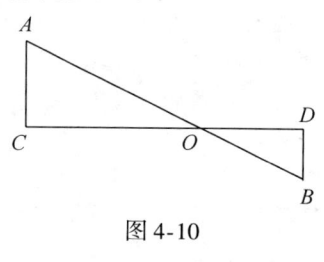

图 4-10

20. 对于实数 x,用 $[x]$ 表示不大于 x 的最大整数,例如,$[\pi]=3$、$[-\pi]=-4$. 现已知 $\dfrac{\left[\dfrac{100}{n}\right]}{n}=1$,其中 n 为正整数,请问 n 共有多少个可能的取值?

(A)1 (B)2 (C)3 (D)4 (E)5

21—25 题,每题 6 分

21. 在 $\triangle ABC$ 中,$AB=BC<AC$,AH 是 BC 边上的高,AD 是 BC 边上的角平分线,如图 4-11 所示. 若 $\angle DAH=21°$,请问 $\angle BAC$ 等于多少度?

22. 在所有的四位数中,请问能同时被 2、3、4、5、6、7、8 整除的整数有多少个?

23. 甲、乙、丙、丁四人各有一些苹果,甲的苹果数等于其余三人苹果数之和,乙的苹果数等于其余三人苹果数之和的一半,丙的苹果数等于其余三人苹果数之和的六分之一,请问甲、乙、丙三人的苹果数之和是丁的苹果数的几倍?

24. 将 31 分拆为 3 个质数之和(不考虑顺序,质数可以相同),请问共有多少种不同的分拆方法?

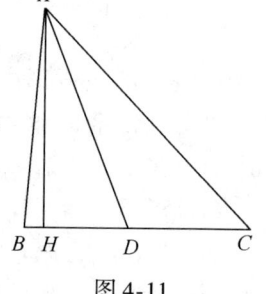

图 4-11

25. 一个长方体的每条棱长都是整数 cm,将它放在桌面上,它露出的五个面的面积之和(单位:cm^2)与它的体积(单位:cm^3)数值相同,请问这个长方体的最小体积是多少 cm^3?

4.3　第一轮试题解答与评注

1. 答案:(D).

    解　原式 $=2014-1+2014=4027$. 故选(D).

2. 答案:(E).

    解　一把圆规比一把直尺贵 $15.40-8.65=6.75$ 元. 故选(E).

第4章 第4届国际中小学生数学能力检测(IMAS)(初中组)

3. 答案:(D).

解 第二行的三个数之和是第一行的三个数之和的两倍,故第二行与第一行的差等于第一行的三个数之和,而第二行与第一行的差是 $19+20-5-6=28$,所以可以得知 ☆ $=28-5-6=17$. 故选(D).

4. 答案:(C).

解 由题设知购买六杯红茶与两杯咖啡需要 $94\times2=188$ 元,因此购买五杯红茶需要 $188-78=110$ 元,即每杯红茶 22 元,又可知每杯咖啡 $94-22\times3=28$ 元,故咖啡比红茶贵 $28-22=6$ 元. 故选(C).

5. 答案:(B).

解 将甲、乙两数余数之和 $2+4=6$,继续除以 5,可得其余数为 1. 故选(B).

6. 答案:(B).

解 8 份中有 2 份是黑色,故指针停在黑色区域的概率为 $\dfrac{2}{8}=\dfrac{1}{4}$. 故选(B).

7. 答案:(D).

解 根据题意,小罗去朋友的家共费时 $15+2.5\times20+3\times2+12=83$ 分钟. 故选(D).

8. 答案:(E).

解 观察白色小珠子的排列方式,按逆时针方向,两个黑色小珠子之间分别有:4 个相连的白色小珠子,接着是 2 个相连的白色小珠子,然后是 3 个相连的白色小珠子. 在五个选项中只有选项(E)不符合这种排列方式. 故选(E).

9. 答案:(D).

解 左边的两项都是非负数,故两项均为 0,因此 $2y-12=0$、$ax-y=0$,故 $ax=y=6$,因此 $axy=36$. 故选(D).

10. 答案:(D).

解 题述等式的左边等于数轴上表示 $2a$ 的点到表示 -7 和 1 的两点距离之和,而 -7 与 1 的距离恰为 8,故表示 $2a$ 的点应在表示 -7 和表示 1 的两点之间,即 $-7\leqslant 2a\leqslant 1$,解得 $-\dfrac{7}{2}\leqslant a\leqslant\dfrac{1}{2}$. 由于 a 是整数,故 a 的取值为 -3、-2、-1、0 共 4 个. 故选(D).

11. 答案:(B).

解法 1 $a=3$ 显然不满足题目条件,故 a 不是 3 的倍数,因此 a^2 被 3 除余 1. 由于 4 也被 3 除余 1,所以 $7b$ 被 3 整除,故 b 是 3 的倍数,即 $b=3$,因此 $a=5$,$a+b=8$. 故选(B).

解法 2 将方程变形为 $(a-2)(a+2)=7b$,显然 $a=2$、3 不符合题意,因此左边的两个因子均大于 1,由于右边是两个质数的乘积,所以左边的两个因子应分别等于这两个质数. 若 $a-2=b$、$a+2=7$,解得 $a=5$、$b=3$,符合题意,此时 $a+b=8$;若 $a-2=7$、$a+2=b$,解得 $a=9$、$b=11$,不合题意. 因此 $a+b=8$. 故选(B).

12. 答案:(B).

解 由折纸的方式及内错角相等可知 $\angle CAB = \angle CBA = \dfrac{180°-60°}{2}=60°$,故 $\triangle ABC$ 是等边三角形. 设 $AC=x$,则三角形的高为 $\dfrac{\sqrt{3}}{2}x$,面积为 $\dfrac{\sqrt{3}}{4}x^2$,故 $\dfrac{\sqrt{3}}{4}x^2=\sqrt{3}$,解得 $x=2$,因此纸条的宽(即 $\triangle ABC$ 的高)为 $2\times\dfrac{\sqrt{3}}{2}=\sqrt{3}$ cm. 故选(B).

13. 答案:(A).

解 连 AA' 与 $D'D$,通过割补方法可知 AD 边扫过的面积等于平行四边形 $AA'D'D$ 的面积,而平行四边形 $AA'D'D$ 的底边 AD 长为 10 cm,高 GD 长为 5 cm,所以面积为 $10\times 5=50$ cm². 故选(A).

14. 答案:(D).

解 勾股定理知,每个等边三角形的边长都是前一个的 $\dfrac{\sqrt{2}}{2}$ 倍,故面积是前一个的一半,因此第四个等边三角形的面积是 $80\times\left(\dfrac{1}{2}\right)^3=10$ cm². 故选(D).

15. 答案:(B).

解 设购买 8 元的邮票 x 张,10 元的邮票 y 张,则 4 元的邮票购买了 $18-x-y$ 张,由题意得 $8x+10y+4(18-x-y)=100$,化简得 $2x+3y=14$,注意到 x、y 都是正整数,故仅有 $x=4$、$y=2$ 和 $x=1$、$y=4$ 两组解,这两组解都满足 $18-x-y$ 是正整数,故有 2 种不同的购买方法. 故选(B).

16. 答案:(A).

解 由题意可知 $\triangle BCM$ 是等边三角形,所以 $\angle ABM=\angle MCD=30°$. 这两个扇形的面积之和为 $3.14\times 10^2\times\dfrac{30}{360}\times 2\approx 52.3$ cm². 故选(A).

17. 答案:(C).

解 由题意,$m-3$、$n-3$、$p-3$ 是三个互不相同的整数,且乘积为 4. 首先由乘积为正数知三个整数必然都是正数或者一正数两负数. 若三个整数都是正数,则乘积至少为 $1\times 2\times 3=6$,不合题意;若为一正数两负数,则不妨设 $m-3<0$、$n-3<$

0、$p-3>0$,由于比 3 小的正整数只有 1 和 2,所以 m、n 必分别为 1 和 2,解得 $p=5$,三者之和为 8. 故选(C).

18. 答案:(A).

解 由 $x<y<0$ 知 $x+y$、$x-y$ 都是负数,故 $\frac{x+y}{x-y}>0$,又

$$\left(\frac{x+y}{x-y}\right)^2=\frac{x^2+y^2+2xy}{x^2+y^2-2xy}=\frac{6xy}{2xy}=3,$$

故 $\frac{x+y}{x-y}=\sqrt{3}$. 故选(A).

19. 答案:(E).

解 显然 AB 是四条线段中最长的,故 $AB=12$ 或 $AB=x$:

(1)若 $AB=12$,当 $CD=x$ 时,$12^2=x^2+(3+6)^2$,$x=3\sqrt{7}$;

当 $CD=6$ 时,$12^2=6^2+(3+x)^2$,$x=6\sqrt{3}-3$;

当 $CD=3$ 时,$12^2=3^2+(6+x)^2$,$x=3\sqrt{15}-6$.

(2)若 $AB=x$,当 $CD=12$ 时,$x^2=12^2+(6+3)^2$,$x=15$;

当 $CD=6$ 时,$x^2=6^2+(12+3)^2$,$x=3\sqrt{29}$;

当 $CD=3$ 时,$x^2=3^2+(12+6)^2$,$x=3\sqrt{37}$.

故 x 可取值的个数为 6 个. 故选(E).

20. 答案:(C).

解 由于 $\sqrt{100}=10$,易知 $\left[\dfrac{\left[\dfrac{100}{n}\right]}{n}\right]$ 随着正整数 n 的增大而减少,故尝试计算 n 取 11、10、9、8、7、6 发现只有 10、9、8 符合题意,故共有 3 个可能取值. 故选(C).

评注 当 m、n 为正整数时有 $\left[\dfrac{\left[\dfrac{x}{m}\right]}{n}\right]=\left[\dfrac{x}{mn}\right]$,故此题等价于 $\left[\dfrac{100}{n^2}\right]=1$,即得

$$1\leqslant\frac{100}{n^2}<2,\text{解得 } n=8、9、10.$$

21. 答案:46.

解 设 $\angle BAC=\alpha$.

由 $AB=BC$ 知 $\angle C=\angle BAC=\alpha$.

由 AD 是 BC 边上的角平分线知 $\angle DAC = \frac{1}{2}\angle BAC = \frac{\alpha}{2}$.

在直角三角形 ACH 中,两个锐角互余,故 $\alpha + \frac{\alpha}{2} + 21° = 90°$,解得 $\alpha = 46°$.

22. 答案:10.

解 2、3、4、5、6、7、8 的最小公倍数是 $3 \times 5 \times 7 \times 8 = 840$,因此共有 840×2、840×3、840×4、$\cdots$、840×11 这 10 个整数符合条件.

23. 答案:41.

解 由题意知,甲的苹果数占四人苹果总数的 $\frac{1}{1+1} = \frac{1}{2}$,乙的苹果数占四人苹果总数的 $\frac{1}{1+2} = \frac{1}{3}$,丙的苹果数占四人苹果总数的 $\frac{1}{1+6} = \frac{1}{7}$,故丁的苹果数占四人苹果总数的 $1 - \left(\frac{1}{2} + \frac{1}{3} + \frac{1}{7}\right) = \frac{1}{42}$,因此甲、乙、丙三人的苹果数之和是丁的苹果数的 $42 - 1 = 41$ 倍.

24. 答案:6.

解 设 $a+b+c=31$ ($a \leqslant b \leqslant c$),其中 a、b、c 都为质数,由 $3a \leqslant 31$ 得 $a \leqslant 10$,故 a 只可能是 2、3、5、7.

若 $a=2$,则 $b+c=29$,无解;
若 $a=3$,则 $b+c=28$,共有 2 个解:$(b,c) = (5,23)$、$(11,17)$;
若 $a=5$,则 $b+c=26$,共有 2 个解:$(b,c) = (7,19)$、$(13,13)$;
若 $a=7$,则 $b+c=24$,共有 2 个解:$(b,c) = (7,17)$、$(11,13)$.
综上所述,共有 $2+2+2=6$ 种不同的拆分方法.

25. 答案:108.

解 设长方体的长、宽、高分别为 x、y、z cm,则由题意得 $xy+2yz+2zx=xyz$.

两边除以 xyz 得 $\frac{1}{z} + \frac{2}{x} + \frac{2}{y} = 1$.

若 $\frac{1}{z} = \frac{2}{x} = \frac{2}{y} = \frac{1}{3}$,则 $x=y=6$、$z=3$,$xyz=108$.

下设 $\frac{1}{z}$、$\frac{2}{x}$、$\frac{2}{y}$ 不全等于 $\frac{1}{3}$,故一定有一个大于 $\frac{1}{3}$.

若 $\frac{1}{z} > \frac{1}{3}$,则 $z<3$,又由 $\frac{1}{z}<1$ 得 $z>1$,故 $z=2$,化简得 $\frac{1}{x} + \frac{1}{y} = \frac{1}{4}$,故 $(x,y)=$

$(5,20)$、$(6,12)$、$(8,8)$、$(12,6)$、$(20,5)$,对应的 $xyz=200$、144、128;

若 $\dfrac{2}{x}>\dfrac{1}{3}$($\dfrac{2}{y}>\dfrac{1}{3}$ 同理),则 $x<6$,又由 $\dfrac{2}{x}<1$ 得 $x>2$,故 $x=3$、4、5.

当 $x=3$ 时,$\dfrac{1}{z}+\dfrac{2}{y}=\dfrac{2}{3}$,解得 $(y,z)=(7,21)$、$(8,12)$、$(9,9)$、$(12,6)$、$(15,5)$、$(24,4)$,对应的 $xyz=441$、288、243、225、216;

当 $x=4$ 时,$\dfrac{1}{z}+\dfrac{2}{y}=\dfrac{1}{2}$,解得 $(y,z)=(5,10)$、$(6,6)$、$(8,4)$、$(12,3)$,对应的 $xyz=200$、144、128;

当 $x=5$ 时,$\dfrac{1}{z}+\dfrac{2}{y}=\dfrac{3}{5}$,解得 $(y,z)=(4,10)$、$(5,5)$、$(20,2)$,对应的 $xyz=200$、125.

综上所述,长方体的最小体积是 $108 cm^3$,当且仅当长和宽为 $6cm$,高为 $3cm$ 时取到.

评注 本题与均值不等式相关.

4.4　第二轮英文试题

考试时间:120 分钟

Questions 1—5,4 marks each

1. Which of the following expressions is equal to
$$(a+1)(b-1)+(b+1)(c-1)+(c+1)(a-1)?$$
(A) $ab+bc+ca-3$
(B) $ab+bc+ca$
(C) $ab+bc+ca+2a+2b+2c+3$
(D) $ab+bc+ca-2a-2b-2c-3$
(E) $ab+bc+ca-2a-2b-2c+3$

Answer:＿＿＿＿＿

2. In triangle ABC, D is the midpoint of BC. E is an arbitrary point on CA, and F is the midpoint of BE. If the area of triangle ABC is $120 cm^2$ and the area of the quadrilateral $AFDC$ is $80 cm^2$, what is the area, in cm^2, of triangle BDF?
(A) $10 cm^2$　　(B) $15 cm^2$　　(C) $17.5 cm^2$　　(D) $20 cm^2$　　(E) $25 cm^2$

Answer:＿＿＿＿＿

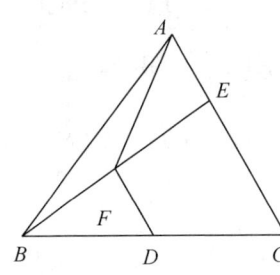

3. Let m be a positive integer such that m^3 can be expressed as a sum of m consecutive odd integers. For instance, $2^3 = 3+5$, $3^3 = 7+9+11$ and $4^3 = 13+15+17+19$. If 999 is one of the consecutive odd integers in the expression for m^3, what is the value of m?

(A) 30　　　(B) 31　　　(C) 32

(D) 33　　　(E) 34

Answer:＿＿＿＿

4. The perimeter of an equilateral triangle is a cm while the perimeter of a square is b cm. If the area of the square is half the area of the triangle, what is the value of $\dfrac{a^2}{b^2}$?

(A) $\dfrac{3\sqrt{3}}{8}$　　(B) $\dfrac{3\sqrt{3}}{4}$　　(C) $\dfrac{3\sqrt{3}}{2}$　　(D) $\dfrac{3\sqrt{3}}{3}$　　(E) $6\sqrt{3}$

Answer:＿＿＿＿

5. Mindy has two boxes, containing 0 and n pieces of candy respectively, where n is a positive integer. She adds 4, 3 and 2 pieces of candy to one of the boxes in that order, always adding to the box containing fewer pieces of candies. If the two boxes have the same number of pieces of candy, then she adds to either of them. In the end, there is 1 more piece of candy in one box than in the other. How many possible values of n are there?

(A) 2　　　(B) 3　　　(C) 4　　　(D) 5　　　(E) 6

Answer:＿＿＿＿

Questions 6 to 13, 5 marks each

6. Let a, b and c be real numbers such that x^2+5x-3 is one of the factors of the polynomial x^3+ax^2+bx+c. What is the numerical value of $a+b+2c$?

Answer:＿＿＿＿

7. How many triples of integers (x, y, z) are such that $|xyz| = 6$?

Answer:＿＿＿＿

8. In triangle ABC, $AB = 7$ cm, $AC = 8$ cm and $BC = 9$ cm. A circle with centre A intersects AB at F and AC at E. The circles with centres B and C and radii BF and CE, respectively, are tangent to each other at a point D on BC. What is the total area,

in cm², of these three circles? (Taking π = 3.14)

Answer: _____ cm²

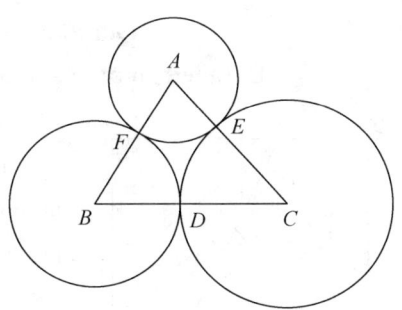

9. There are 2 counters in the first row, and each subsequent row has one more counter than the preceding row. If there are 2015 counters altogether, how many rows of counters are there?

Answer: _____ rows

10. In a book fair, the organizers give a book to each participant. Each male participant gives every other male participant a book, and each female participant gives every other female participant a book. If the total number of books received by the male participants is 31 more than the total number of books received by the female participants, how many participants are there altogether?

Answer: _____ participants

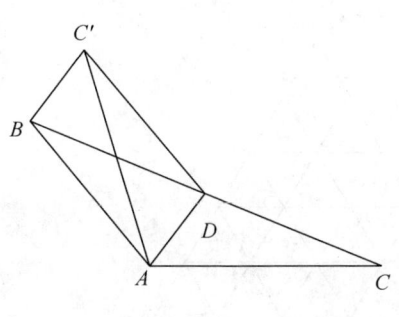

11. D is a point on the side BC of triangle ABC such that $\angle BAD = 76°$. When the point C is reflected across AD to the point C', $ABC'D$ is a parallelogram. What is the measure, in degrees, of $\angle ADC$?

Answer: _____

12. Let k be a non-zero integer such that the equation $x + \dfrac{9k^2 - 81}{x} = 10k$ has two distinct integer roots. What is the difference when the smaller root is subtracted from the larger one?

Answer: _____

13. The integers $1, 2, 3, \cdots, 20$ are divided into two groups. The sum of all the numbers in one group is n, while the product of all the numbers in the other group is also n. What is the maximum value of n?

Answer: _____

Questions 14–15, 20 marks each
Detailed solutions are needed for these two problems

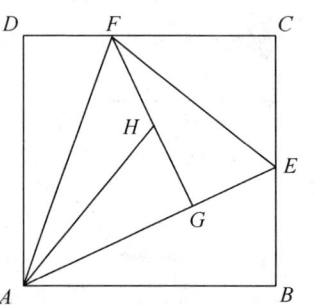

14. E is a point on the side BC and F is a point on the side CD of a square $ABCD$ such that the perimeter of triangle CEF is equal to half the perimeter of $ABCD$. G is the point on AE such that FG is perpendicular to AE, and H is the point on FG such that $AH = EF$. Prove that AH is perpendicular to EF.

15. Each side of an equilateral triangle is divided into 5 equal parts by 4 points, and these points are joined by lines parallel to the sides of the triangle, dividing into 25 small equilateral triangles. A tetriamond is a shape formed of 4 small equilateral triangles joined edge to edge. There are three tetriamonds as shown in the diagram below on the left.

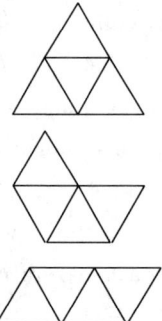
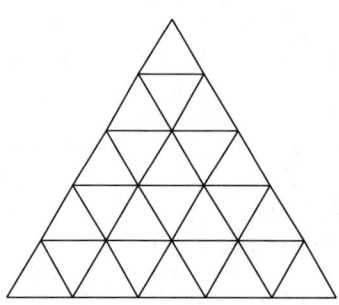

(a) Show that if 7 of the small triangles are painted, then it may be impossible to fit any tetriamond inside the large triangle without covering up any part of the painted small triangles. (4 marks)

(b) Prove that if 6 of the small triangles are painted, then it is always possible to fit a tetriamond inside the large triangle without covering up any part of the painted small triangles. (16 marks)

第4章 第4届国际中小学生数学能力检测(IMAS)(初中组)

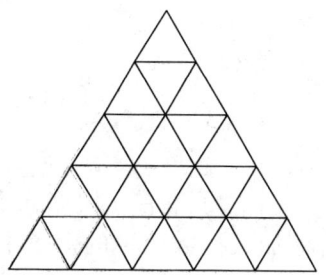
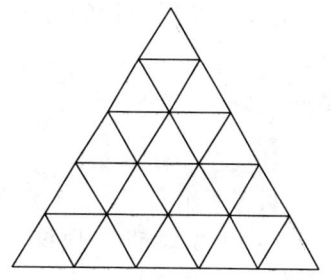

4.5 第二轮中文试题

1-5题,每题4分

1. 代数式$(a+1)(b-1)+(b+1)(c-1)+(c+1)(a-1)$与下面哪一项相等?
 (A)$ab+bc+ca-3$ 　　　　　　　　(B)$ab+bc+ca$
 (C)$ab+bc+ca+2a+2b+2c+3$ 　　(D)$ab+bc+ca-2a-2b-2c-3$
 (E)$ab+bc+ca-2a-2b-2c+3$

 答:_____

2. 在△ABC中,E为AC边上的点,D为BC边的中点,F为线段BE的中点,若△ABC的面积为120cm²且四边形AFDC的面积为80cm²,请问△BDF的面积为多少cm²(图4-12)?
 (A)10cm² 　(B)15cm² 　(C)17.5cm²
 (D)20cm² 　(E)25cm²

 答:_____

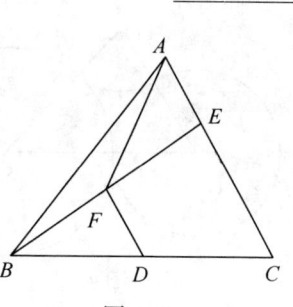

图4-12

3. 已知m为大于1的正整数,m^3可写成m个连续奇数的和,例如,$2^3=3+5$,$3^3=7+9+11$,$4^3=13+15+17+19$,…. 若m^3的表达式的连续奇数中有一个数是999,请问m的值是多少?
 (A)30 　(B)31 　(C)32 　(D)33 　(E)34

 答:_____

4. 已知一个正三角形的周长为a,一个正方形的周长为b,如果此正方形的

105

面积等于此正三角形面积的一半,请问 $\dfrac{a^2}{b^2}$ 的值等于什么?

(A) $\dfrac{3\sqrt{3}}{8}$ (B) $\dfrac{3\sqrt{3}}{4}$ (C) $\dfrac{3\sqrt{3}}{2}$ (D) $\dfrac{3\sqrt{3}}{3}$ (E) $6\sqrt{3}$

答:_____

5. 小明有两个盒子,一个盒子里是空的,另一个盒子里有 n 块糖, n 是正整数. 他以 4 块糖、3 块糖、2 块糖的顺序, 逐次将糖加入糖数较少的盒子中. 如果盒子内的糖数相同, 则他可以任选一个盒子加入糖. 最后, 他发现两个盒子中的糖数恰好相差 1 块, 请问 n 有多少种可能的值?

(A) 2 (B) 3 (C) 4 (D) 5 (E) 6

答:_____

6-13 题,每题 5 分

6. 已知 a、b、c 都是实数, 关于 x 的多项式 x^3+ax^2+bx+c 含有因式 x^2+5x-3, 请问 $a+b+2c$ 的值是多少?

答:_____

7. 请问方程 $|xyz|=6$ 共有多少组整数解?

答:_____

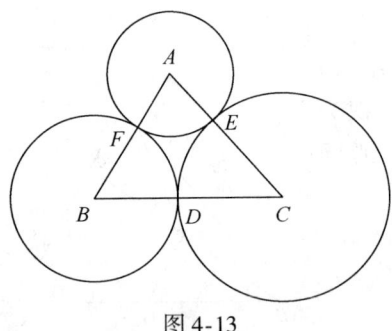

图 4-13

8. 在 $\triangle ABC$ 中, $AB=7\text{cm}$、$AC=8\text{cm}$、$BC=9\text{cm}$. 以 A 为圆心的圆交 AB 于点 F、交 AC 于点 E. 以 B 为圆心、BF 为半径的圆与以 C 为圆心、CE 为半径的圆相切于 BC 上的点 D, 如图 4-13 所示. 请问这三个圆的面积之总和为多少 cm^2? (取 $\pi=3.14$)

答:_____ cm^2

9. 第一行有 2 枚棋子, 接下来的每一行都比前一行多 1 枚棋子. 已知总共有 2015 枚棋子, 请问这些棋子共有多少行?

答:_____ 列

10. 某次读书交流会上, 主办单位赠送每位参加者一本书, 同时每位女性参加者赠送给每位其他的女性参加者一本书, 每位男性参加者也赠送给每位其他的男性参加者一本书. 已知参加者中所有男性收到的赠书之总和比所有女性收到的赠书之总和多 31 本, 请问这次读书交流会总共有多少名参加者?

答:_____ 名

11. 点 D 在 $\triangle ABC$ 的 BC 边上使得 $\angle BAD = 76°$,点 C' 是点 C 关于 AD 的对称点,如图 4-14 所示.已知四边形 $ABC'D$ 是平行四边形,请问 $\angle ADC$ 为多少度?

答：_____

12. 设 k 是非零整数,关于 x 的方程 $x + \dfrac{9k^2 - 81}{x} = 10k$ 有两个不同的整数根,请问较大的根减去较小的根所得的差是什么?

答：_____

13. 将正整数 $1, 2, \cdots, 20$ 分成两组,使得其中一组的所有数之和等于 n,另一组的所有数之积也等于 n,请问 n 的最大值是什么?

图 4-14

答：_____

14、15 题,必须填写详细计算过程或证明,每题 20 分

14. 在正方形 $ABCD$ 中,E、F 分别是 BC、CD 上的点,$\triangle CEF$ 的周长是正方形 $ABCD$ 周长的一半,点 G 为 AE 上的点使得 $FG \perp AE$,点 H 为 FG 上的点使得 $AH = EF$,如图 4-15 所示.证明:$AH \perp EF$.

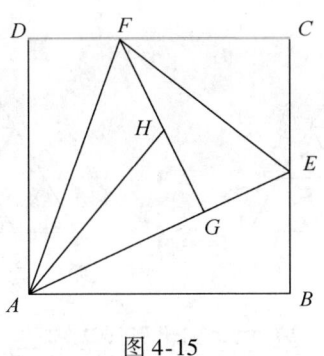

图 4-15

15. 将一个大正三角形的每条边用 4 个点将它 5 等分,然后以平行于三角形各边的直线将这些点相连接,把大正三角形分割为 25 个小正三角形,如图 4-16(b)所示.一片四正三角形块为 4 个小正三角形以边对边连接在一起组成的图形,共有三种不同的四正三角形块,如图 4-16(a)所示.

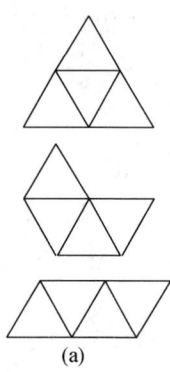
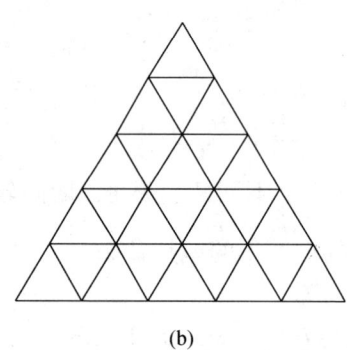

图 4-16

（1）请将 7 个小正三角形涂色，使得无法在此大正三角形内放置任何一片四正三角形块而不盖住任何涂色的小正三角形（图 4-17）.（4 分）

（2）请证明无论如何将 6 个小正三角形涂色，都一定可以在此大正三角形内放置一片四正三角形块而不盖住任何涂色的小正三角形（图 4-18）.（16 分）

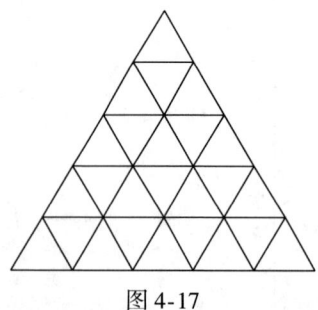
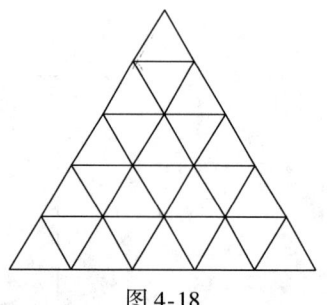

图 4-17　　　　　　　　　　图 4-18

4.6　第二轮试题解答与评注

1. 答案：(A).

解法 1　　$(a+1)(b-1)+(b+1)(c-1)+(c+1)(a-1)$
$= (ab+b-a-1)+(bc+c-b-1)+(ca+a-c-1)$
$= ab+bc+ca-3.$

解法 2　若令 $a=b=c=1$，则原代数式之取值为 0，且有

第4章 第4届国际中小学生数学能力检测(IMAS)(初中组)

(A) $ab+bc+ca-3=1+1+1-3=0$；

(B) $ab+bc+ca=1+1+1=3$；

(C) $ab+bc+ca+2a+2b+2c+3=1+1+1+2+2+2+3=12$；

(D) $ab+bc+ca-2a-2b-2c-3=1+1+1-2-2-2-3=-6$；

(E) $ab+bc+ca-2a-2b-2c+3=1+1+1-2-2-2+3=0$.

即选项中仅(A)与(E)的取值为0.

若令 $a=b=c=-1$，则原代数式之取值为0，且有

(A) $ab+bc+ca-3=1+1+1-3=0$；

(B) $ab+bc+ca=1+1+1=3$；

(C) $ab+bc+ca+2a+2b+2c+3=1+1+1-2-2-2+3=0$；

(D) $ab+bc+ca-2a-2b-2c-3=1+1+1+2+2+2-3=6$；

(E) $ab+bc+ca-2a-2b-2c+3=1+1+1+2+2+2+3=12$.

而选项中仅(A)与(C)的取值为0.

因此只有(A)可能与原代数式相等，故选(A).

2. 答案：(D).

解 连接 FC，由题目条件可知 $S_{\triangle ABF}=S_{\triangle AFE}$、$S_{\triangle BCF}=S_{\triangle FCE}$，即 $S_{\triangle AFC}=\dfrac{1}{2}S_{\triangle ABC}=60\text{cm}^2$. 故 $S_{\triangle BDF}=S_{\triangle FDC}=S_{AFDC}-S_{\triangle AFC}=80-60=20\text{cm}^2$.

3. 答案：(C).

解 将 m^3 写成 m 个连续奇数的和后，若此数列的首项为 $2k+1$，则最末项为 $2k+1+2(m-1)=2k+2m-1$，故知其和为 $\dfrac{(2k+1+2k+2m-1)\times m}{2}=m^3$，即有 $2m^3=4k+2m$，因此 $k=\dfrac{m^2-m}{2}$，所以首项为 $2k+1=m^2-m+1$，末项为 $2k+2m-1=m^2+m-1$，因此 $m^2-m+1\leqslant 999\leqslant m^2+m-1$. 再利用配方法可得

$$m^2-m+1=\left(m-\dfrac{1}{2}\right)^2+\dfrac{3}{4}\leqslant 999\leqslant m^2+m-1=\left(m+\dfrac{1}{2}\right)^2-\dfrac{5}{4}$$

此即

$$\begin{cases}\left(m-\dfrac{1}{2}\right)^2\leqslant 998\dfrac{1}{4}<1024=32^2\\ 961=31^2<1000\dfrac{1}{4}\leqslant\left(m+\dfrac{1}{2}\right)^2\end{cases}$$

因此得到 $m=32$.

4. 答案：(C).

解 正三角形的边长为 $\frac{a}{3}$，用勾股定理求得它的高为 $\frac{a}{3} \cdot \frac{\sqrt{3}}{2} = \frac{\sqrt{3}}{6}a$，故它的面积为 $\frac{1}{2} \cdot \frac{a}{3} \cdot \frac{\sqrt{3}}{6}a = \frac{\sqrt{3}}{36}a^2$；正方形的边长为 $\frac{b}{4}$，故它的面积为 $\left(\frac{b}{4}\right)^2 = \frac{b^2}{16}$，因此得到 $\frac{b^2}{16} = \frac{1}{2} \cdot \frac{\sqrt{3}}{36}a^2$，整理得 $\frac{a^2}{b^2} = \frac{3\sqrt{3}}{2}$.

5. 答案：(D).

解法 1 由操作的过程可列式 $|||n-4|-3|-2| = 1$，先去掉最外层的绝对值符号，得 $||n-4|-3|-2 = 1$ 或 $||n-4|-3|-2 = -1$，故 $||n-4|-3| = 3$ 或 $||n-4|-3| = 1$；再去掉一层绝对值符号，得到 $|n-4|-3 = -3$、-1、1、3，故 $|n-4| = 0$、2、4、6，因此 $n-4$ 等于 -6、-4、-2、0、2、4、6 之一，结合 n 是正整数得到 n 有 2、4、6、8、10 共 5 种可能的值.

解法 2 最终两个盒子中共有 $n+4+3+2 = n+9$ 块糖，由于它们中的糖数恰好相差 1 块，所以两个盒子中糖的总数是奇数，即 n 是偶数；由于原来的空盒子最后至多有 $4+3+2 = 9$ 块糖，而原来有 n 块糖的盒子最终至少有 n 块糖，所以 $n-9 \le 1$，即 $n \le 10$. 不超过 10 的正偶数仅有 2、4、6、8、10 五个，将其逐一代入验证均满足题意，故 n 有 2、4、6、8、10 共 5 种可能的值.

6. 答案：2.

解法 1 x^3+ax^2+bx+c 必为 x^2+5x-3 与一个一次因式的乘积.
设 $x^3+ax^2+bx+c = (x^2+5x-3)(px+q)$，比较 x^3 项的系数得 $p=1$，比较其他项系数得 $a = q+5$、$b = 5q-3$、$c = -3q$，故 $a+b+2c = (q+5)+(5q-3)+2(-3q) = 2$.

解法 2 x^3+ax^2+bx+c 必为 x^2+5x-3 与一个一次因式的乘积. 由 x^3 项的系数得知一次因式的首项系数为 1、由常数项得知末项系数为 $-\frac{c}{3}$，即

$$x^3+ax^2+bx+c = (x^2+5x-3)\left(x-\frac{c}{3}\right)$$
$$= x^3+5x^2-3x-\frac{c}{3}x^2-\frac{5c}{3}x+c$$
$$= x^3+\left(5-\frac{c}{3}\right)x^2-\left(3+\frac{5c}{3}\right)x+c$$

因此 $a = 5-\frac{c}{3}$、$b = -\left(3+\frac{5c}{3}\right)$，故 $a+b+2c = 5-\frac{c}{3}-\left(3+\frac{5c}{3}\right)+2c = 2$.

7. 答案:72.

解 原方程等价于$|x|\cdot|y|\cdot|z|=6$,三个正整数的乘积为6,只能是$1\times1\times6$或$1\times2\times3$的排列.若为一个6两个1,则$|x|$、$|y|$、$|z|$有3种取值方式,若为1、2、3的排列,则$|x|$、$|y|$、$|z|$有6种取值方式,共有9种取值方式.最后x、y、z可以分别取正、负值,故原方程共有$9\times2^3=72$组整数解.

8. 答案:157cm^2.

解 设$AF=AE=x\text{cm}$,则$BF=BD=7-x\text{cm}$、$CE=CD=8-x\text{cm}$,故$(7-x)+(8-x)=9\text{cm}$,解得$x=3\text{cm}$,从而推出三个圆的半径分别为3cm、4cm、5cm,因此三个圆的面积之和为$\pi(3^2+4^2+5^2)=50\pi=157\text{cm}^2$.

9. 答案:62行.

解 假设这些棋子共有n行,则最后一行有$n+1$枚棋子,故$\dfrac{n(2+n+1)}{2}=2015$,解得$n=62$(另一根$n=-65$不合题意,舍去).

评注 本题也可以用估算的方式求出$n=62$.

10. 答案:31名.

解 设这次读书交流会共有m名男参加者,n名女参加者,由题意得$m+m(m-1)=n+n(n-1)+31$,整理得$m^2-n^2=31$,故$(m-n)(m+n)=31$.由$m+n>0$知$m-n>0$,由于31是质数,所以必有$m-n=1$、$m+n=31$,因此共有31名参加者.

11. 答案:$104°$.

解 连接CC'.由题意知$\triangle ADC\cong\triangle ADC'$,故$AC=AC'$,$\angle CAD=\angle C'AD$,由等腰三角形三线合一知$AD\perp CC'$,又$AD//BC'$,故$BC'\perp CC'$.

由于$DC=DC'$,故$\angle DCC'=\angle DC'C$,而$\angle BC'D$是$\angle DC'C$的余角、$\angle C'BD$是$\angle DCC'$的余角,故$\angle BC'D=\angle C'BD$.

由平行四边形的性质知$\angle ADB=\angle C'BD=\angle BC'D=\angle BAD=76°$,

故$\angle ADC=180°-76°=104°$.

12. 答案:82.

解 先将方程整理得$x^2-10k\cdot x+(9k^2-81)=0$,由题意知两个根都是整数,故判别式$\Delta=(10k)^2-4(9k^2-81)$应是一个完全平方数,设$\Delta=m^2$,其中$m$为正整数.整理后可得$m^2=64k^2+324$,因式分解得$(m-8k)(m+8k)=324$.

由m是正整数知$m-8k$、$m+8k$至少有一个为正,故这两个数都是正整数,显然两数不同,但奇偶性相同.由$324=3^4\times2^2$知仅有以下几种情况:

情况1 $m-8k=162$、$m+8k=2$,解得$m=82$、$k=-10$,此时两根分别为-91和-9,符合题意,差为82;

情况 2 $m-8k=54$、$m+8k=6$，解得 $m=30$、$k=-3$，此时两根分别为 -30 和 0，但 0 是增根，不合题意，舍去；

情况 3 $m-8k=6$、$m+8k=54$，与情况 2 相似，出现增根 0，舍去；

情况 4 $m-8k=2$、$m+8k=162$，与情况 1 相似，两根分别为 9 和 91，符合题意，差为 82.

综上所述，两根的差为 82.

13. 答案：192.

解 首先说明 $n=192$ 符合题意，此时令第二组为 4、6、8，第一组为剩余所有数，则第二组三个数的积为 $4\times6\times8=192$，第一组所有数之和为 $(1+2+\cdots+20)-(4+6+8)=192$，符合题意.

下面说明 $n>192$ 不合题意.

当 $n=193$、194、197、199、201、202、203 时，n 分别含有大于 20 的质因子 193、97、197、199、67、101、29，无法成为第二组所有数之积；

当 $n=195$ 时，n 含有质因子 13，故第二组必有 13，但第二组剩余所有数之和为 $(1+2+\cdots+20)-195-13=2$，故第二组必为 2、13，但 $2\times13\ne195$，矛盾；

当 $n=196$ 时，n 含有两个质因子 7，故第二组必有 7 和 14，但这样第一组所有数之和最多为 $(1+2+\cdots+20)-(7+14)=189$，矛盾；

当 $n=198$ 时，n 含有质因子 11，故第二组必有 11，但第二组剩余所有数之和为 $(1+2+\cdots+20)-198-11=1$，故第二组必为 1、11，但 $1\times11\ne198$，矛盾；

当 $n=200$ 时，n 含有两个质因子 5，故第二组必有两个 5 的倍数，但这样第一组所有数之和最多为 $(1+2+\cdots+20)-(5+10)=195$，矛盾；

当 $n\geqslant 204$ 时，第二组所有数之和不超过 $(1+2+\cdots+20)-204=6$，它们的乘积显然不能等于 n，矛盾.

综上所述，所求 n 的最大值为 192.

14. **解** 如图 4-19 所示，延长 CB 至 K，使得 $BK=DF$，连接 AK，延长 AH 交 EF 于 L. 由于 $AB=AD$，$\angle ABK=\angle D=90°$ 得 $\triangle ADF\cong\triangle ABK$，故 $DF=BK$、$AF=AK$，$\angle BAK=\angle DAF$. 由此得 $\angle FAK=\angle FAB+\angle BAK=\angle FAB+\angle DAF=\angle DAB=90°$.

由于 $\triangle CEF$ 的周长是正方形 $ABCD$ 周长的一半，故

$$EF=2AB-(CE+CF)=BE+DF=BE+BK=EK,$$

又 $AE=AE$、$AF=AK$，故 $\triangle AFE\cong\triangle AKE$，因此

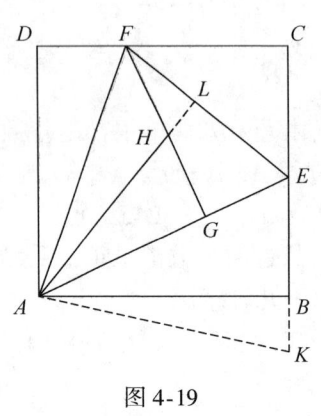

图 4-19

$\angle FAE = \angle EAK = \dfrac{1}{2}\angle FAK = 45°$.

因为 $FG \perp AE$,所以 $\triangle AGF$ 为等腰直角三角形,故 $AG = FG$.

结合 $AH = EF$、$\angle FAK = \angle AGH = \angle FGE = 90°$ 得 $\triangle AGH \cong \triangle FGE$,由此得
$$\angle FLH = 180° - \angle FHL - \angle HFL = 180° - \angle AHG - \angle GAH = 90°,$$
即 $AH \perp EF$,证毕.

评注 证得 $EF = EK$,5 分;证得 $\angle FAE = 45°$,5 分;证得 $AG = FG$,5 分;证得 $AH \perp EF$,5 分.

15. **解** (1)将图 4-20 所示的小正三角形涂黑,则无法在此大正三角形内放置任何一片四正三角形块而不盖住任何涂色的小正三角形. 若将旋转翻转视为相同,则只有此唯一的方法.

(2)假设结论不成立,即存在一种将 6 个小正三角形涂色的方式,使得无法在此大正三角形内放置任何一片四正三角形块而不盖住任何涂色的小正三角形. 在下左图中,下面两个用红线标示的正六边形内(图 4-21),必然至少各要将 2 个小正三角形涂色,否则显然可找出四正三角形块;上方用红线标示的三角形里必然也要至少要将 1 个小正三角形涂色,中间靠左用红线标示的凹六边形里必然也要至少要将 1 个小正三角形涂色,这说明 6 个被涂色的小正三角形都要在已用红线标示的四块封闭区域中,也就是说,中间靠右的两个小正三角形不能再被涂色,否则涂色的数量超过 6 个.

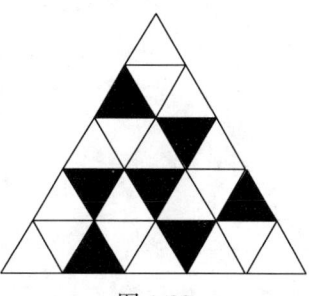

图 4-20

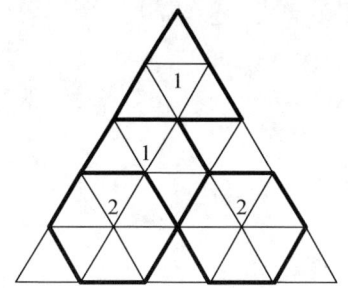

图 4-21

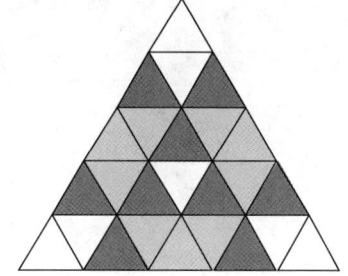

将纸版旋转翻转,由对称性可知图 4-21 右图中黄色的小正三角形都不能被涂色,故绿色的小正三角形必须都被涂色,否则可以找到四正三角形块,但绿色小正三角形有 9 个,矛盾!

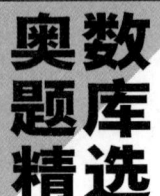

综上所述，无论如何挑选 6 个小正三角形涂色，都一定可以在此大正三角形内放置一片四正三角形块而不盖住任何涂色的小正三角形，证毕.

评注 (1)小题:给出正确涂色方法,4 分. (2)小题:说明图 4-21 左图内的两个红色凸六边形各至少要挖除 2 个小正三角形,4 分;说明左图内的红色凹六边形至少要挖除 1 个小正三角形,4 分;说明左图内的红色三角形至少要挖除 1 个小正三角形,4 分;说明右图的小正三角形必须都被挖除,4 分.

第5章　第5届国际中小学生数学能力检测(IMAS)(初中组)

5.1 第一轮英文试题

考试时间:75分钟

Questions 1–10, 3 marks each

1. What is the value of $\sqrt{(-2)^8}+(1+2+2^2+\cdots+2^{2015})^0+|-16|$?

(A) 0　　　　　　　　(B) 32　　　　　　　　(C) 33

(D) $2^{2016}-1$　　　　(E) $2^{2016}+31$

2. Someone set the alarm clock for 1:30 pm and fell asleep at 12:35 pm. When he was awaken by the alarm clock, for how long had this person been sleeping?

(A) 1 hour and 5 minutes

(B) 55 minutes

(C) 95 minutes

(D) 105 minutes

(E) 11 hours and 5 minutes

3. In a quadrilateral $ABCD$, $AB//DC$, $BC//ED$, $AD=AE$ and $\angle C=110°$. What is the measure of $\angle A$?

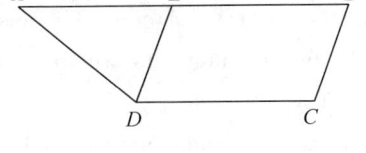

(A) 20°　　(B) 35°　　(C) 40°

(D) 55°　　(E) 70°

4. In a sale, each dress is reduced to 49% of its price and if two dresses are purchased at the same time, both are reduced to 45% of their prices. Lily buys two dresses together and pays 90 dollars for both. By doing this instead of buying them separately, how many dollars has she saved?

(A) 10　　(B) 8　　(C) 6　　(D) 4　　(E) 3.6

—115—

5. Sixteen points are arranged in a 3 cm by 3 cm formation. Four of them are removed, leaving behind twelve points as shown in the diagram. If we choose three of these twelve points as vertices of a triangle, what is the largest possible area of this triangle, in cm²?

(A) 9   (B) $\dfrac{9}{2}$ (C) 3

(D) 2   (E) $\dfrac{3}{2}$

6. Class A has 17 students more than Class B, which has 15 students less than Class C. Of the following five numbers, which can be the total number of students in these three classes?

(A) 150   (B) 151   (C) 152   (D) 153   (E) 154

7. From 0, 1, 2, 3, 4 and 5, we choose two different numbers x and y. What is the largest possible value of $2(x+y)^2+(x-y)^2$?

(A) 75   (B) 163   (C) 175   (D) 187   (E) 200

8. Divide the rectangle $ABCD$ into four isosceles right triangles and one square, as in the diagram below. If the area of square $EFGH$ is 100 cm², what is the area of rectangle $ABCD$, in cm²?

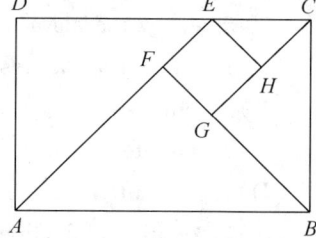

(A) 750   (B) 1000   (C) 1100

(D) 1200   (E) 1600

9. A group of students are staying in a hotel. If five of them share a room, then there is no room for six of them. If six of them share a room, there are just enough rooms, one of which has less than six students. Of the following five numbers, which cannot be the number of students?

(A) 46   (B) 51   (C) 56   (D) 61   (E) 66

10. In a pentagon, one angle is 48°. The second angle is three times as large as the first. The third angle is 30° less than the second. The fourth angle is 10° less than the fifth. What is the measure of the fourth angle, in degrees?

(A) 112   (B) 122   (C) 132   (D) 142   (E) 152

Questions 11–20, 4 marks each

11. There are three shirts, three pairs of trousers and three pairs of shoes. Of

each type, one is red, one is black and one is white. In how many different ways can we choose one of each type so that something white is chosen?

(A)8　　　(B)9　　　(C)18　　　(D)19　　　(E)27

12. In triangle ABC, AB is perpendicular to BC. D and E are points on BC such that $\angle BAD = \angle DAE = \angle EAC$ and $\angle ADC - \angle C = 56°$. What is the measure of $\angle BAC$?

(A)42°　　　(B)45°　　　(C)51°

(D)60°　　　(E)84°

13. If $\dfrac{a}{b} = a+1$ and $\dfrac{b}{a} = a-1$, what is the value of $\dfrac{b^2}{(a-1)^2}$?

(A)1　　　(B)2　　　(C)3　　　(D)4　　　(E)5

14. C and D are points on AB such that $AC:CD:DB = 1:2:3$. Semicircles are drawn on the same side of AB with respective diameters AB, AC, CD and DB. What fraction of the area of the largest semicircle is the total area of the other three semicircles?

(A)$\dfrac{1}{4}$　　(B)$\dfrac{1}{3}$　　(C)$\dfrac{13}{36}$　　(D)$\dfrac{7}{12}$　　(E)$\dfrac{7}{18}$

15. Each coin is worth either 1 dollar, 5 dollars or 10 dollars. Their total worth is 60 dollars. They may be divided into three, four or five piles of equal worth. What is the minimum number of coins?

(A)6　　　(B)11　　　(C)15　　　(D)16　　　(E)20

16. From a cube of side length 10 cm, a cylinder with diameter 6 cm and depth 8 cm is hollowed out. What is the volume, in cm³, of the remaining part of the cube? Take $\pi = 3.14$.

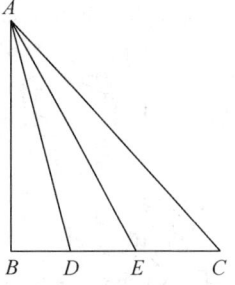

(A)426.08　　(B)517.46　　(C)573.94

(D)717.46　　(E)773.92

17. If a, b and c are all positive integers, which of the following numbers can be the value of $(a+b+c)(a+b-c)(a-b+c)(-a+b+c)$?

(A)44　　(B)46　　(C)48　　(D)50　　(E)52

18. A three-layer structure consists of 14 unit cubes. The bottom layer consists of 9 cubes in a 3 by 3 configuration. The middle layer consists of 4 cubes in a 2 by 2 configuration. The top layer consists of a single cube. The exposed surface area of this structure is painted, including the bottom. What is the total area of the unpainted surface of the individual cubes?

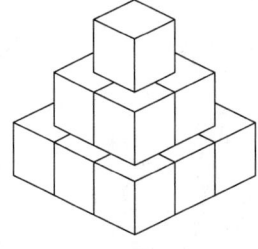

(A)20　　(B)31　　(C)42　　(D)53　　(E)64

19. In an election between four candidates, they are supported respectively by 11,12,13 and 14 of the first 50 voters. Six more votes are to be cast, each for one of the four candidates. In how many ways can the candidate currently with 13 supporters become the uncontested winner?

(A)16　　(B)17　　(C)18　　(D)19　　(E)20

20. Let x, y and z be distinct positive prime numbers such that $x+y+z$ and $x^2+y^2+z^2$ are also prime numbers. What is the minimum value of $x+y+z$?

(A)17　　(B)19　　(C)23　　(D)29　　(E)31

Questions 21–25, 6 marks each

21. $ABCDEF$ is a regular hexagon. G is the midpoint of AB and H is the point on AF such that $FH=2AH$. If the area of triangle AHG is 1cm^2. What is the area, in cm^2, of $ABCDEF$?

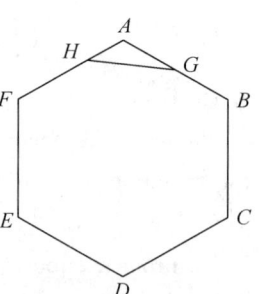

22. What is the value of abc where a, b and c are positive real numbers such that $a(b+c)=48, b(c+a)=70$ and $c(a+b)=88$?

23. What is the value of b^a where a and b are real numbers such that $b=\sqrt{a^2-6a+b}+|b-9|+9$?

24. What is the maximum value of a if $a^2 \mid (10\times11\times12\times\cdots\times19)$?

25. For any permutation of 1,2,3,4,5,6,7 and 8, add the second number to the first, multiply the sum by the third number, add the fourth number to the product, multiply the sum by the fifth number, and so on. What is the minimum value of the final sum?

5.2 第一轮中文试题

1–10题,每题3分

1. 请问代数式 $\sqrt{(-2)^8}+(1+2+2^2+\cdots+2^{2015})^0+|-16|$ 的值是什么?
 (A)0 (B)32 (C)33
 (D)$2^{2016}-1$ (E)$2^{2016}+31$

2. 某人午睡时将闹钟定在下午1时30分,并在12时35分睡着,请问当闹钟响时,他总共睡着了多长时间?
 (A)1小时5分 (B)55分 (C)95分
 (D)105分 (E)11小时5分

3. 在四边形 ABCD 中.已知 AB//DC、BC//ED、AD=AE、∠C=110°,如图5-1所示,请问∠A 等于多少度? 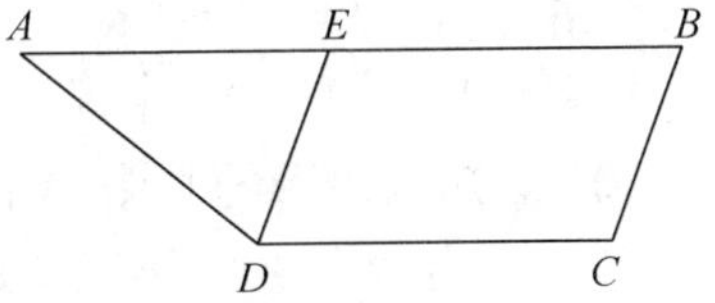
 (A)20° (B)35° (C)40°
 (D)55° (E)70°

图5-1

4. 某服装店举行优惠活动,购买衣服一件减价51%,一次购买衣服两件则减价55%.小莉花费90元一次购买两件衣服,如果她分为两次购买,请问会多花费多少元?
 (A)10 (B)8 (C)6 (D)4 (E)3.6

5. 从3cm×3cm 的16个格点中移除4个,剩下的12个格点之排列方式如图5-2所示.连接其中3个点构成一个三角形,请问这个三角形的面积的最大可能值为多少 cm²?
 (A)9 (B)$\frac{9}{2}$ (C)3
 (D)2 (E)$\frac{3}{2}$

图5-2

6. A 班的学生比 B 班多17人、B 班的学生比 C 班少15人.请问下列哪一个选项可能是这三个班级的学生总人数?
 (A)150 (B)151 (C)152 (D)153 (E)154

7. 从 0、1、2、3、4、5 中选出两个相异的数 x、y，请问 $2(x+y)^2+(x-y)^2$ 的最大可能值是什么？

(A)75 (B)163 (C)175 (D)187 (E)200

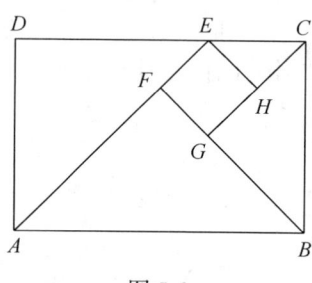

图 5-3

8. 将矩形 $ABCD$ 分割为四个等腰直角三角形与一个正方形，如图 5-3 所示. 已知正方形 $EFGH$ 的面积为 $100cm^2$，请问矩形 $ABCD$ 的面积为多少 cm^2？

(A)750 (B)1000 (C)1100 (D)1200 (E)1600

9. 有一群学生到旅馆住宿，若每 5 个人同住一间房间，则有 6 个人没房间住；若每 6 个人同住一间房间，则房间刚好足够但只有其中一间房间没住满 6 个人. 请问下列哪一个选项不可能是这群学生的总人数？

(A)46 (B)51 (C)56 (D)61 (E)66

10. 已知五边形的其中一个内角为 $48°$，第二个内角是它的 3 倍，第三个内角比第二个内角小 $30°$，第四个内角比第五个内角小 $10°$. 请问第四个内角是多少度？

(A)112 (B)122 (C)132 (D)142 (E)152

11-20 题，每题 4 分

11. 有衣服三件、裤子三件、鞋子三双，每样都有红、白、黑色各一. 现在要从中选出一件衣服、一条裤子与一双鞋子，请问有多少种不同的选择方式使得至少有一样是白色的？

(A)8 (B)9 (C)18
(D)19 (E)27

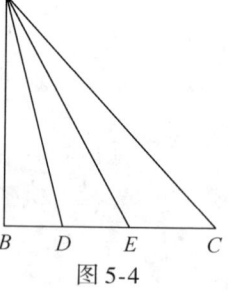

图 5-4

12. 在 $\triangle ABC$ 中，已知 $AB \perp BC$、$\angle BAD = \angle DAE = \angle EAC$、$\angle ADC - \angle C = 56°$，如图 5-4 所示，请问 $\angle BAC$ 为多少度？

(A)$42°$ (B)$45°$ (C)$51°$ (D)$60°$ (E)$84°$

13. 已知 $\dfrac{a}{b}=a+1$、$\dfrac{b}{a}=a-1$，请问 $\dfrac{b^2}{(a-1)^2}$ 的值为多少？

(A)1 (B)2 (C)3 (D)4 (E)5

第5章 第5届国际中小学生数学能力检测(IMAS)(初中组)

14. 以线段 AB 为直径画一个大半圆,并且在线段 AB 上取两点 C、D,使得 $AC:CD:DB=1:2:3$,分别以 AC、CD、DB 为直径在大半圆内部画三个小半圆,如图 5-5 所示. 请问三个小半圆的面积总和占大半圆面积的几分之几?

(A) $\dfrac{1}{4}$ (B) $\dfrac{1}{3}$ (C) $\dfrac{13}{36}$ (D) $\dfrac{7}{12}$ (E) $\dfrac{7}{18}$

15. 有 1 元、5 元与 10 元的硬币总值 60 元,这些硬币恰好可分别分为等值的三堆、四堆、五堆,请问这些硬币总共最少有多少枚?

(A) 6 (B) 11 (C) 15 (D) 16 (E) 20

16. 有一个立体模型是将一个边长为 10 cm 的正立方体金属,在正中央挖除一个直径为 6cm、高为 8cm 的圆柱体,如图 5-6 所示,请问这个立体模型的体积为多少 cm³?(π 取 3.14)

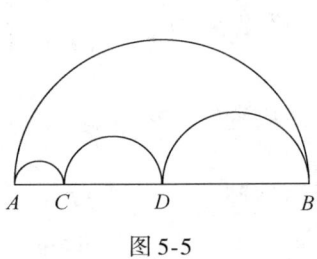

图 5-5 图 5-6

(A) 426.08 (B) 517.46 (C) 573.94 (D) 717.46 (E) 773.92

17. 已知 a、b、c 都是正整数,请问 $(a+b+c)(a+b-c)(a-b+c)(-a+b+c)$ 可能取下面哪一个选项的值?

(A) 44 (B) 46 (C) 48 (D) 50 (E) 52

18. 一个三层的立体模型是由 14 个单位正立方体构造成的,底层由 9 个正立方体排成 3×3 的形状,中间层由 4 个正立方体排成 2×2 的形状,顶层则只有 1 个正立方体,如图 5-7 所示. 现将这块积木的表面部分(包括底部)全部涂上红色,请问这 14 个正立方体中未被涂色部分的表面积总和为多少单位?

(A) 20 (B) 31 (C) 42
(D) 53 (E) 64

19. 某次选举共有四位候选人,当开完前 50 张票时,他们的得票数分别为 11、12、13、14 张票,且尚有六张投给这四位候选人的有效票. 请问这四位候选人总共有多少种不同的得票情况可使得目前得到 13 张票的候选人之得票数赢过其他三人?

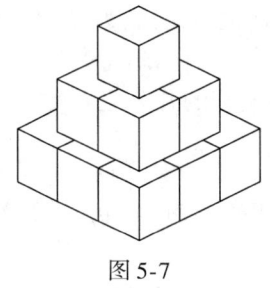

图5-7

(A) 16   (B) 17   (C) 18
(D) 19   (E) 20

20. 已知 x、y、z 是三个相异的正质数,且 $x+y+z$ 与 $x^2+y^2+z^2$ 也都是质数,请问 $x+y+z$ 的最小可能值是多少?

(A) 17   (B) 19   (C) 23
(D) 29   (E) 31

21—25 题,每题 6 分

21. 在正六边形 $ABCDEF$ 中,点 G 为边 AB 的中点,点 H 为边 AH 上的一点,使得 $FH=2HA$,已知 $\triangle AHG$ 的面积为 $1\,cm^2$,如图 5-8 所示. 请问正六边形 $ABCDEF$ 的面积为多少 cm^2?

22. 设三个正实数 a、b、c 满足 $a(b+c)=48$、$b(c+a)=70$、$c(a+b)=88$,请问 abc 的值是多少?

23. 已知 a、b 为实数且 $b=\sqrt{a^2-6a+b}+|b-9|+9$,请问 b^a 的值为多少?

24. 正整数 a 满足 $a^2 \mid (10\times11\times12\times\cdots\times19)$,请问 a 的最大值是多少?

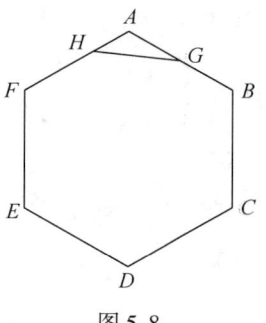

图5-8

25. 对于 1、2、3、4、5、6、7、8 的任意排列作以下的运算:将第一个数加上第二个数,所得的结果再乘以第三个数,所得的结果再加上第四个数,所得的结果再乘以第五个数,依此类推. 请问可能得到的最小结果是多少?

5.3   第一轮试题解答与评注

1. 答案:(C).

解 原式 $=16+1+16=33$,故选 (C).

2. 答案:(B).

解 可知 12 时 35 分到下午 1 时共 25 分钟、下午 1 时到下午 1 时 30 分共 30 分钟,所以他总共睡着了 $25+30=55$ 分,故选 (B).

3. 答案:(C).

解 由于 $BCDE$ 为平行四边形,可知 $\angle DEB = \angle C = 110°$,因此 $\angle DEA = 70°$,故 $\angle A = 180°-2\angle DEA = 180°-2\times70° = 40°$,故选 (C).

第5章 第5届国际中小学生数学能力检测(IMAS)(初中组)

4. 答案:(B).

解 两件衣服的原价为 $90 \div 45\% = 200$ 元,如果分为两次购买需要 $200 \times 49\% = 98$ 元,所以多费花了 8 元,故选(B).

5. 答案:(B).

解 因为三角形的面积为 $S = \frac{1}{2} \times$ 底 $\times$ 高,要使面积最大,则底乘高的值必须最大.从图 5-2 中可知,两个格点在水平方向之最大距离为 3cm,在垂直方向之最大距离为 3cm,所以,三角形面积的最大可能值为 $\frac{1}{2} \times 3 \times 3 = \frac{9}{2}$ cm². 任意选取在最外层正方形的四个顶点中的三个格点,所构成的三角形的面积即是最大的. 故选(B).

6. 答案:(C).

解 可先假设 B 班没有学生,则此时学生总数为 $17+15 = 32$ 人. 接着可以每次都同时将每一班都增加 1 人而不会影响到各班之间的人数差异,因此将学生总数除以 3 之后所得的余数必为 2,选项中只有 152 符合,故选(C).

7. 答案:(B).

解 由于 $2(x+y)^2 + (x-y)^2 = 3x^2 + 3y^2 + 2xy$,所以要取 x、y 尽可能地大,所以原式之最大值为 $3 \times 5^2 + 3 \times 4^2 + 2 \times 4 \times 5 = 163$,故选(B).

8. 答案:(D).

解 由于正方形 EFGH 的面积为 100cm²,它的边长为 $EH = GH = 10$cm,可知四个等腰直角三角形的腰长分别为 10cm、20cm、30cm、$20\sqrt{2}$ cm,即矩形 ABCD 的面积为 $100 + \frac{1}{2} \times (100 + 400 + 900 + 800) = 1200$ cm²,故选(D).

9. 答案:(E).

解 设旅馆总共有 x 间房间,则学生总人数为 $5x+6$,依题意得 $5x+6 = 6(x-1)+y$,其中 $y = 1、2、3、4、5$,化简得 $12-x = y$,故对应的 x 可取值 11、10、9、8、7,学生总人数 $5x+6$ 可能为 61、56、51、46、41,因此不可能为 66,故选(E).

10. 答案:(A).

解 可知第二个内角为 144°,第三个内角为 114°,设第四个内角为 x°,则第五个内角为 $x+10$°,因此 $48+144+114+x+(x+10) = 540$,解得 $x = 112$,故选(A).

11. 答案:(D).

解 所有的选择方式共 $3 \times 3 \times 3 = 27$ 种,其中没有任何一样是白色的有 $2 \times 2 \times 2 = 8$ 种选择方式,故至少有一样是白色的有 $27-8 = 19$ 种不同的选择方式,故选(D).

12. 答案:(A).

解 设 $\angle BAD$、$\angle DAE$、$\angle EAC$ 的度数为 $x°$,则 $\angle C=90°-3x°$,$\angle ADC=\angle C+56°=146°-3x°$.

在 $\triangle ADC$ 中,$(146-3x)+(90-3x)+2x=180$,解得 $x=14$,因此 $\angle BAC$ 为 $42°$,故选(A).

13. 答案:(B).

解 两式相乘可得 $1=\dfrac{a}{b}\times\dfrac{b}{a}=(a+1)(a-1)=a^2-1$,因此 $a^2=2$,又由 $\dfrac{b}{a}=a-1$ 可得 $\dfrac{b}{a-1}=a$,因此 $\dfrac{b^2}{(a-1)^2}=a^2=2$,故选(B).

14. 答案:(E).

解 令 AB 的长度为 12 单位,则 AC、CD、DB 的长度分别为 2、4、6 单位,可知三个小半圆面积总和与大半圆面积之比为 $\dfrac{\frac{1}{2}\pi\times(1^2+2^2+3^2)}{\frac{1}{2}\pi\times6^2}=\dfrac{7}{18}$,故选(E).

15. 答案:(D).

解 因可将这些硬币分为五堆,每堆 12 元,故知至少有 10 枚 1 元硬币,即这些硬币总共最少有 15 枚.若恰为 15 枚,则必有 5 枚 10 元硬币,此时可知无法将这 15 枚硬币分为四堆,每堆 15 元,因此这些硬币总共最少有 16 枚,而 10 枚 1 元、2 枚 5 元、4 枚 10 元即恰为 16 枚的情况且可满足题意,故选(D).

16. 答案:(E).

解 这个立体模型的体积为 $10^3-\pi\times3^2\times8=1000-72\pi=773.92 \text{ cm}^3$,故选(E).

17. 答案:(C).

解 由于 $a+b+c$、$a+b-c$、$a-b+c$、$-a+b+c$ 的奇偶性相同,故取值为偶数时必定为 $2^4=16$ 的倍数,而当 $a=b=c=2$ 时,可取值为 48.故选(C).

18. 答案:(C).

解 从这个立体模型的上方与下方可各看到 9 个单位正立方体,而从这个立体模型的每个侧面可各看到 6 个单位正立方体,因此有 $9\times2+6\times4=42$ 单位的表面积暴露在外而被涂上红色,从这 14 个正立方体的总表面积扣除这些即为所求,即未被涂色部分的面积总和为 $14\times6-42=42$ 单位,故选(C).

19. 答案:(D).

解 为了使目前得到 13 张票的候选人保证赢过其他三人,他至少要从剩下的 6 票中获得 2 票. 令这四位候选人最终的得票数分别为 $15+x$、$14+y$、$12+z$、$11+t$ 票,其中 x、y、z、$t \geq 0$,则有 $x+y+z+t=4$. 故有以下情况:

当 $x=4$ 时,$y=z=t=0$,只有 1 种可能.

当 $x=3$ 时,$(y,z,t)=(1,0,0)$ 及其轮换,有 3 种可能.

当 $x=2$ 时,$(y,z,t)=(1,1,0)$、$(2,0,0)$ 及其轮换,有 6 种可能.

当 $x=1$ 时,若 $y=0$ 时,则 $(z,t)=(3,0)$、$(2,1)$、$(1,2)$、$(0,3)$;若 $y=1$ 时,则 $(z,t)=(1,1)$、$(2,0)$、$(0,2)$. 此情况共有 7 种可能.

当 $x=0$、$y=0$ 时,$(z,t)=(1,3)$、$(2,2)$,有 2 种可能.

因此,总共有 $1+3+6+7+2=19$ 种可能的得票情况,故选(D).

20. 答案:(C).

解 不妨假设 $x<y<z$. 可知 x 不可能为 2,否则 $x+y+z$ 为偶数,不符合题意;

若 $x>3$,则 $x^2 \equiv y^2 \equiv z^2 \equiv 1 \pmod{3}$,因此 $x^2+y^2+z^2$ 为 3 的倍数,不符合题意;

故可推知 $x=3$. 此时可得知 $x+y+z$ 不可能为 17,否则 $x=y=3$ 或 $y=z=7$,不符合题意;若 $x+y+z=19$,则 $(x,y,z)=(3,5,11)$,但 $x^2+y^2+z^2$ 的个位数码为 5,不符合题意;因此知 $x+y+z$ 的最小值为 23,此时 $(x,y,z)=(3,7,13)$. 故选(C).

21. 答案:36.

解 设 O 为正六边形 $ABCDEF$ 的中心,由 $AG=GB$ 可知 $\triangle ABH$ 的面积等于 2 倍 $\triangle AHG$ 的面积,故 $\triangle ABH$ 的面积为 2cm^2,由 $FH=2HA$,可知 $\triangle ABF$ 的面积等于 3 倍 $\triangle ABH$ 的面积,即等于 $2 \times 3 = 6\text{cm}^2$. 显然 $ABOF$ 为平行四边形,故 $\triangle ABO$ 的面积等于 $\triangle ABF$ 的面积,因此六边形 $ABCDEF$ 的面积是 $6 \times 6 = 36\text{cm}^2$.

22. 答案:165.

解 将三式相加可得 $ab+bc+ac = \dfrac{48+70+88}{2} = 103$,因此 $ab=15$、$bc=55$、$ac=33$,故 $(abc)^2 = 15 \times 55 \times 33 = 165^2$,由 a、b、c 为正实数可得 $abc=165$.

23. 答案:729.

解 由 $b-9 = \sqrt{a^2-6a+b} + |b-9| \geq |b-9|$ 可得 $b \geq 9$,因此 $\sqrt{a^2-6a+b} = 0$ 且 $b \geq 9$,当 $b>9$ 时,$a^2-6a+b = (a-3)^2+(b-9) > 0$,矛盾,所以 $b=9$、$a^2-6a+9=0$,解得 $b=9$、$a=3$,故 $b^a = 9^3 = 729$.

24. 答案:720.

解 分解质因子可得 $10 \times 11 \times 12 \times \cdots \times 19 = 2^8 \times 3^4 \times 5^2 \times 11 \times 13 \times 17 \times 19$,因此 a 的最大值是 $2^4 \times 3^2 \times 5^1 = 720$.

25. 答案:81.

解 因为只有进行加法与乘法运算,所得结果是递增的,为使得到的结果最小必须将数 1、2、3 安排在乘法运算的位置,且要依照 3、2、1 的顺序. 而其他五个数则安排在加法运算的位置,且要依照渐大的顺序. 所以可能得到的最小结果为 $(((4+5)\times 3+6)\times 2+7)\times 1+8=81$.

5.4 第二轮英文试题

考试时间:120 分钟

Questions 1–5, 4 marks each

1. Michael bought 6 pens and 3 notebooks while Wallace bought 3 pens and 6 notebooks. The pens are identical and so are the notebooks. Michael's bill is 6 dollars higher than Wallace's. How many dollars is the price of a pen higher than the price of a notebook?

(A) 1　　(B) 2　　(C) 3　　(D) 4　　(E) 5

Answer:＿＿＿＿

2. If all the divisors of 2016 are arranged in decreasing order, by how much is the third divisor larger than the fourth divisor?

(A) 12　　(B) 48　　(C) 168　　(D) 672　　(E) 2016

Answer:＿＿＿＿

3. Which of the following is equal to $xr+ys$ if $r=3x+2y$ and $s=xy-x-y$?

(A) $x^2y-x^2+2xy+2y^2$

(B) $xy^2+3x^2+xy-y^2$

(C) x^2y+2x^2+xy

(D) xy^2+2x^2+2xy

(E) x^2y^2+x+y

Answer:＿＿＿＿

4. E is a variable point on the side BC of a square $ABCD$. $DEFG$ is a rectangle with FG passing through A. As the point E moves from B towards C, how does the area of $DEFG$ change?

(A) Steadily increasing

(B) Steadily decreasing

(C) Decreasing and then increasing

(D) Increasing and then decreasing

(E) Remaining constant

Answer: _____

5. The diagram shows a 6 by 6 board with three barriers. An ant is at the top left corner and wishes to reach the bottom right corner. It may only crawl between squares which share a common side, and only towards the bottom or the right. It cannot pass through any barrier. How many different paths can it follow?

(A) 88　　　(B) 90　　　(C) 92　　　(D) 96　　　(E) 112

Answer: _____

Questions 6–13, 5 marks each

6. One square in a 3 by 3 board is to be painted black, a second square blue and a third square red. If no two of these three squares are in the same row or in the same column, how many different ways of painting them are there?

Answer: _____ ways

7. The diagram shows a tile divided into regular hexagons of side length 1 cm. What is the total area, in cm^2, of the parts of the tile which are shaded?

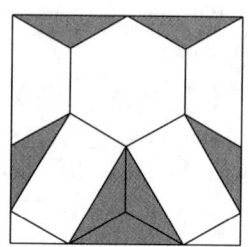

Answer: _____ cm²

8. Let a, b, c and d be real numbers such that $|a+b|, |a-b|, |c+d|$ and $|c-d|$ are 6, 7, 8 and 9 in some order. What is the value of $a^2+b^2+c^2+d^2$?

Answer: _____

9. A rectangle $ABCD$ with $BC = 3$ cm and $AB = \sqrt{3}$ cm is folded along AC so that the point B lands on the point K symmetric to it about AC. What is the area, in cm², of triangle KDE, where E is the point on the extension of BC such that $\angle CDE = 30°$?

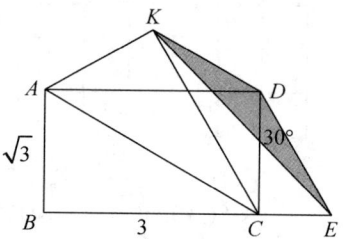

Answer: _____ cm²

10. In the expression $(((10\square2)\square2)\square2)\square2$, each $\square$ is to be replaced by a different one of $+, -, \times$ and $\div$. How many different values can this expression take?

Answer: _____

11. Let a, b and c be real numbers such that $abc = 1$, $(a+1)(b+1)(c+1) = 16$ and $(a+2)(b+2)(c+2) = 53$. What is the value of $(a-1)(b-1)(c-1)$?

Answer: _____

12. The area of triangle ABC is 120 cm² and $BC = 16$ cm. What is the minimum length, in cm, of the perimeter of ABC?

Answer: _____ cm

13. Let a, b, c and d be four different non-zero digits. The greatest common

divisor of the four-digit numbers $\overline{abcd}$ and $\overline{acbd}$ is n. What is the largest possible value of n?

Answer:＿＿＿＿＿

Questions 14–15, 20 marks each
Detailed solutions are needed for these two problems

14. The first diagram shows a 6 by 6 board, and the second diagram shows an L-shaped piece consisting of four 1 by 1 squares. Paint as few of the squares of the 6 by 6 board black so that wherever the L-pieced piece is placed on the board covering four squares, at least one of the squares will be black. The L-shaped piece may be turned about or flipped over

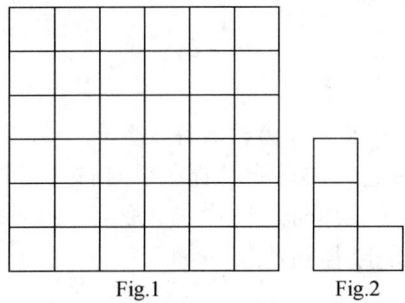

Fig.1　　　Fig.2

15. P and Q are points on the bisector of the exterior angle at A of triangle ABC, with A between P and Q, such that BP is parallel to CQ. D is the point on BC such that $DP=DQ$. Prove that AB is parallel to DQ.

5.5　第二轮中文试题

1–5题,每题4分

1. 小明买了6支笔与3本笔记本,小华买了3支笔与6本笔记本,他们买的笔与笔记本款式都相同,付款时小明发现自己比小华多花了6元. 请问笔的售价比笔记本的售价贵多少元?

(A)1　　(B)2　　(C)3　　(D)4　　(E)5

答:＿＿＿＿＿

2. 将2016的所有因子从大到小排成一列,请问第三个因子比第四个因子大多少?

(A) 12　　　(B) 48　　　(C) 168　　　(D) 672　　　(E) 2016

答：_____

3. 若 $r=3x+2y$、$s=xy-x-y$，请问 $xr+ys$ 等于下面哪一项？
(A) $x^2y-x^2+2xy+2y^2$　　　　　　(B) $xy^2+3x^2+xy-y^2$
(C) x^2y+2x^2+xy　　　　　　　　(D) xy^2+2x^2+2xy
(E) x^2y^2+x+y

答：_____

4. 如图 5-9 所示，在正方形 ABCD 的 BC 边上有一动点 E，以 DE 为边作矩形 DEFG，且 FG 边通过点 A，请问当点 E 从点 B 移动到点 C 的过程中矩形 DEFG 的面积是如何变化的？
(A) 一直变大　　　　　　　　　　　(B) 一直变小
(C) 先变小后变大　　　　　　　　　(D) 先变大后变小
(E) 保持不变

答：_____

5. 如图 5-10 所示，一张 6×6 方格表左上角的小方格中有一只蚂蚁，它想爬到右下角的小方格 A 中. 它每次只能沿着水平向右或竖直向下的方向爬到相邻的小方格，并且表格中有三块隔板（图中加粗的线条）不能从中穿过. 请问这只蚂蚁总共有多少条不同的路径到达 A？

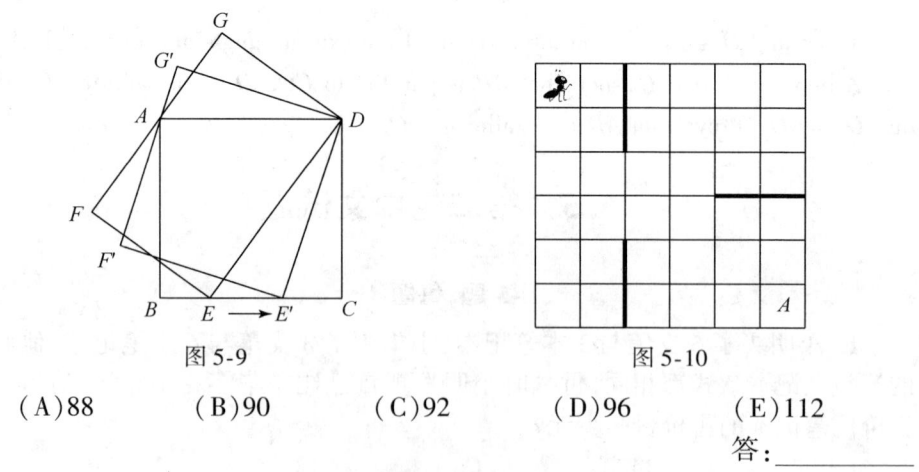

图 5-9　　　　　　　　　　　图 5-10

(A) 88　　　(B) 90　　　(C) 92　　　(D) 96　　　(E) 112

答：_____

6-13 题，每题 5 分

6. 如图 5-11 所示，在 3×3 的方格中选取 3 个方格分别涂黑、蓝、红三种颜色，每种颜色各涂一格，要求这三个方格中任意两个方格不在同行也不在同列.

请问总共有多少种不同的涂色方法?

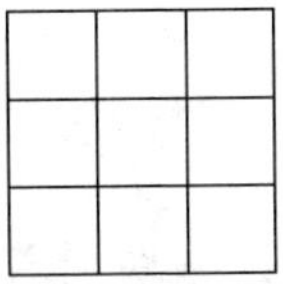

答:_____种

7. 一块长方形瓷砖的图案如图所示,已知每个正六边形的边长为 1cm,请问图 5-12 中涂上阴影部分的面积为多少 cm^2?

答:_____cm^2

图 5-11

8. 设 a、b、c、d 是四个实数,已知 $|a+b|$、$|a-b|$、$|c+d|$、$|c-d|$ 分别等于 6、7、8、9,请问 $a^2+b^2+c^2+d^2$ 的值等于多少?

答:_____

9. 在一个长为 3cm,宽为 $\sqrt{3}$ cm 的矩形 $ABCD$ 的 BC 边延长线上取一点 E,使得 $\angle CDE=30°$,将点 B 沿着对角线 AC 翻折后与 K 点重合,如图 5-13 所示,请问 $\triangle KDE$ 的面积为多少 cm^2?

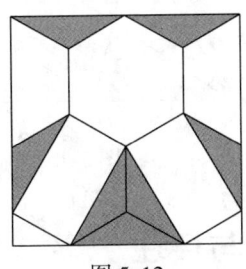

图 5-12

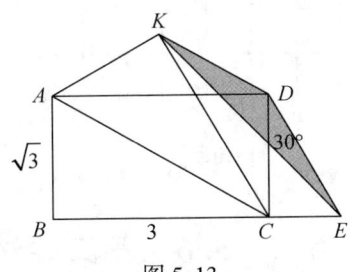

图 5-13

答:_____cm^2

10. 在算式 $(((10\square 2)\square 2)\square 2)\square 2$ 的四个 $\square$ 中填入加、减、乘、除四个运算符号(每个符号都恰只使用一次),请问可以得到多少个不同的值?

答:_____个

11. 已知实数 a、b、c 满足 $abc=1$、$(a+1)(b+1)(c+1)=16$、$(a+2)(b+2)(c+2)=53$,请问 $(a-1)(b-1)(c-1)$ 的值是多少?

答:_____

12. $\triangle ABC$ 的面积为 $120cm^2$,BC 边的长为 16 cm,请问 $\triangle ABC$ 周长的最小值是多少 cm?

答:_____cm

13. 已知 a、b、c、d 是两两相异的非零数码,四位数 $\overline{abcd}$ 和 $\overline{acbd}$ 的最大公因子为 n,请问 n 的最大可能值是多少?

答:_____

14、15题，必须填写详细计算过程或证明，每题20分

14. 图 5-14(a) 为一个 6×6 的方格表，图 5-14(b) 为一个 L-形四方块，它是由四个边长为 1 的小正方形组成的．将方格表的某些小方格涂上黑色，使得 L-形四方块沿着网格线无问论如何放入方格表内都至少会盖住一个黑色的小方格，L-形四方块可以旋转或翻转．请问至少要将几个小方格涂黑？

15. 在 $\triangle ABC$ 中，点 P、Q 在 $\angle BAC$ 的外角平分线上且在直线 AB 的异侧，使得 $BP//CQ$，点 D 在 BC 上使得 $DP=DQ$，如图 5-15 所示．证明：$AB//DQ$．

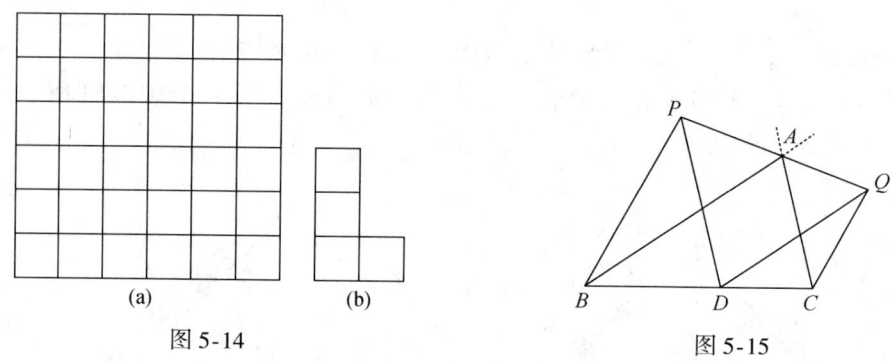

图 5-14　　　　　　　　　　图 5-15

5.6　第二轮试题解答与评注

1. 答案：(B)．

解　可知小明比小华多买了 3 支笔、少买了 3 本笔记本，且多花了 6 元，故可判断出笔的售价比笔记本的售价贵 $6\div3=2$ 元．

2. 答案：(C)．

解　因 $2016=2^5\times3^2\times7$，故知 2016 最小的四个因子依序为 1、2、3、$2^2=4$，故 2016 第三大的因子为 $2016\div3=672$、第四大的因子为 $2016\div4=504$，所以第三个因子比第四个因子大 $672-504=168$．

3. 答案：(B)．

解　$xr+ys=x(3x+2y)+y(xy-x-y)=3x^2+2xy+xy^2-xy-y^2=xy^2+3x^2+xy-y^2$．

4. 答案：(E)．

解　如图 5-16 所示，连接 AE，可知在正方形 $ABCD$ 中，$S_{\triangle AED}=\dfrac{1}{2}\times AB\times AD=\dfrac{1}{2}S_{\square ABCD}$，在长方形 $DEFG$ 中，$S_{\triangle AED}=\dfrac{1}{2}\times DE\times EF=\dfrac{1}{2}S_{\square DEFG}$，而点 E 从 B 移动到

点 C 的过程中，$\triangle AED$ 的面积保持不变，故知矩形 $DEFG$ 的面积一直保持不变.

5. 答案：(A).

解法1 如图 5-17 所示，设蚂蚁开始所在的小方格为 B，现在把蚂蚁的路径分为两类，第一类是由 B 途经 C 到达 A，第二类是由 B 途经 D 到达 A.

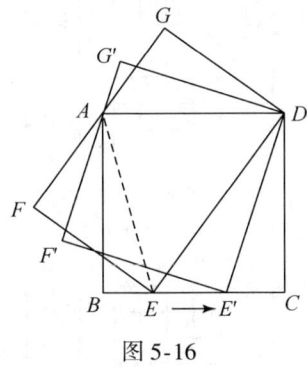

图 5-16

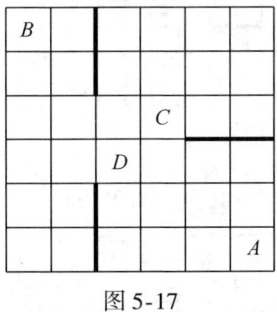

图 5-17

第一类路径：由 B 到 C，共有 3 条路径（图 5-18）.

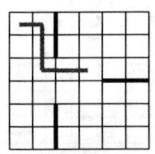 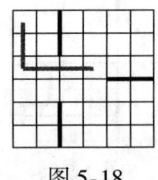 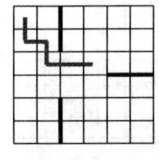

图 5-18

由 C 到 A，共有 6 条路径（图 5-19）.

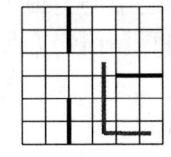 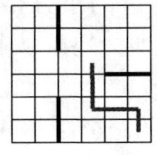 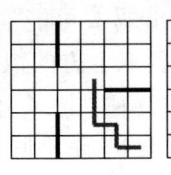 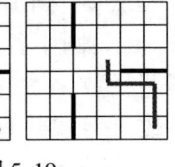 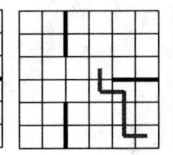 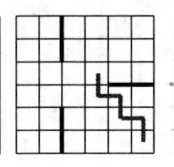

图 5-19

所以这一类路径共有 $3 \times 6 = 18$ 条.

第二类路径：由 B 到 D，共有 7 条路径（图 5-20）.

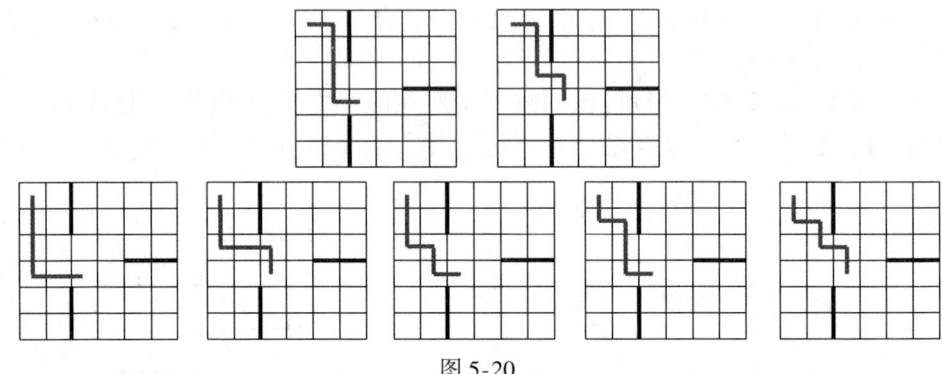

图 5-20

由 D 到 A，共有 10 条路径(图 5-21)．

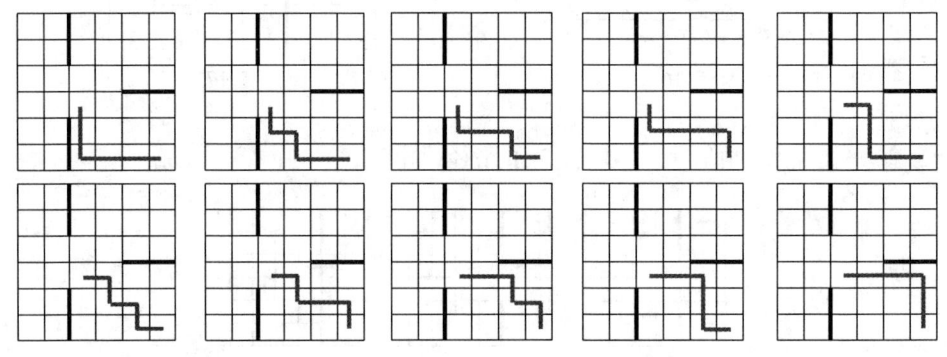

图 5-21

所以这一类路径共有 $7 \times 10 = 70$ 条．

综上所述，这只蚂蚁总共有 $18 + 70 = 88$ 条不同的路径到达 A．

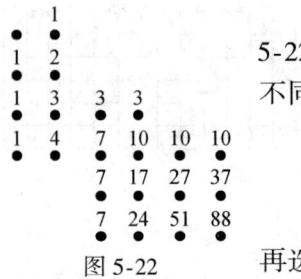

图 5-22

解法 2 画出蚂蚁可能通过的小方格之中心，如图 5-22 所示，图中各点上方的数即为蚂蚁从起点到该点的不同路径数．

故可得知共有 88 条不同的路径到达 A．

6. 答案：36 种．

解法 1 先选择涂黑色的方格，有 9 种选择的方式；再选择蓝色的方格，这时与黑格同行同列的格子都不能选取，故有 4 种选择的方式；最后选择红色的方格，这时与黑格、蓝格同行同列的格子都不能选取，故仅有 1 种选择的方式．由乘法原理知共有 $9 \times 4 \times 1 = 36$ 种选择的方式．

解法 2 可知选取三个方格中任意两个方格不在同行也不在同列的选取方法共有 $3×2×1=6$ 种方法,而对于每一种方法的三个方格都分别不重复地涂上黑、蓝、红其中一种颜色都有 $3×2×1=6$ 种涂法,故知总共有 $6×6=36$ 种涂色的方法.

7. 答案: $\dfrac{7\sqrt{3}}{4}cm^2$.

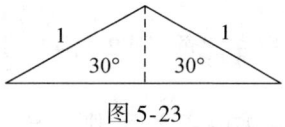

图 5-23

解 可知图 5-23 中阴影部分是由七个腰长为 1 cm、两底角皆为 30°的等腰三角形所构成. 而腰长为 1cm、两底角皆为 30°的等腰三角形底边上的高为 $\dfrac{1}{2}$ cm、底边长度为 $2×\dfrac{\sqrt{3}}{2}=\sqrt{3}$ cm,故这样的三角形之面积为 $\dfrac{1}{2}×\dfrac{1}{2}×\sqrt{3}=\dfrac{\sqrt{3}}{4}cm^2$,因此图 5-23 中涂上阴影部分的面积为 $\dfrac{\sqrt{3}}{4}×7=\dfrac{7\sqrt{3}}{4}cm^2$.

8. 答案:115.

解 可知 $(a+b)^2=(|a+b|)^2=6^2=36$、$(a-b)^2=(|a-b|)^2=7^2=49$,

故 $a^2+b^2=\dfrac{1}{2}((a+b)^2+(a-b)^2)=\dfrac{1}{2}×(36+49)$;

可知 $(c+d)^2=(|c+d|)^2=8^2=64$、$(c-d)^2=(|c-d|)^2=9^2=81$,

故 $c^2+d^2=\dfrac{1}{2}((c+d)^2+(c-d)^2)=\dfrac{1}{2}×(64+81)$;

因此, $a^2+b^2+c^2+d^2=\dfrac{1}{2}×(36+49)+\dfrac{1}{2}×(64+81)=\dfrac{1}{2}×230=115$.

9. 答案: $\dfrac{\sqrt{3}}{2}cm^2$.

解 因 $CD=AB=\sqrt{3}$ cm 且 $\angle CDE=30°$,故 $DE=2$cm. 因 $AB:BC=\sqrt{3}:3=1:\sqrt{3}$ 且 $\angle ABC=90°$,故可判断出 $\angle ACB=30°$,所以 $\angle ACK=30°$,即可推得 $\angle DCK=90°-30°-30°=30°$,因此知 $KC//DE$,所以 $\triangle KDE$ 在 DE 边上的高即为点 C 至线段 DE 的距离,再由 $CD=\sqrt{3}$ cm 可得知点 C 至线段 DE 的距离为 $\dfrac{\sqrt{3}}{2}$ cm,故 $\triangle KDE$ 的面积为 $\dfrac{1}{2}×2×\dfrac{\sqrt{3}}{2}=\dfrac{\sqrt{3}}{2}cm^2$.

10. 答案：5个.

解法1 将除以2改写为乘以$\frac{1}{2}$,然后将整个式子用乘法分配律打开,即变为10、2与-2各乘一个系数再相加,其中10的系数只能是$2\times\frac{1}{2}=1$,若乘以2在乘以$\frac{1}{2}$之前,则2与-2的系数只能是1或$\frac{1}{2}$,结果只能为9、10、11之一;若乘以2在乘以$\frac{1}{2}$之后,则2与-2的系数只能是1或2,结果只能为8、10、12之一.综上所述,共有5种不同的运算结果.

解法2 $(((10+2)-2)\times 2)\div 2=10$、$(((10+2)-2)\div 2)\times 2=10$、$(((10+2)\times 2)-2)\div 2=11$、
$(((10+2)\times 2)\div 2)-2=10$、$(((10+2)\div 2)\times 2)-2=10$、$(((10+2)\div 2)-2)\times 2=8$、
$(((10-2)+2)\times 2)\div 2=10$、$(((10-2)+2)\div 2)\times 2=10$、$(((10-2)\times 2)+2)\div 2=9$、
$(((10-2)\times 2)\div 2)+2=10$、$(((10-2)\div 2)\times 2)+2=10$、$(((10-2)\div 2)+2)\times 2=12$、
$(((10\times 2)-2)+2)\div 2=10$、$(((10\times 2)-2)\div 2)+2=11$、$(((10\times 2)+2)-2)\div 2=10$、
$(((10\times 2)+2)\div 2)-2=9$、$(((10\times 2)\div 2)+2)-2=10$、$(((10\times 2)\div 2)-2)+2=10$、
$(((10\div 2)-2)\times 2)+2=8$、$(((10\div 2)-2)+2)\times 2=10$、$(((10\div 2)\times 2)-2)+2=10$、
$(((10\div 2)\times 2)+2)-2=10$、$(((10\div 2)+2)\times 2)-2=12$、$(((10\div 2)+2)-2)\times 2=10$.

故知共可算出8、9、10、11、12共五个不同的值.

解法3 由交换律可知当加号与减号同时填入相邻的□时,若将此两个相邻的□填法互换,则值不会改变,而乘号与除号也有相同的性质.因$(((10+2)-2)\times 2)\div 2=10$,故只需观察加号与减号不同时填入相邻的□,以及乘号与除号不同时填入相邻的□的取值:$(((10+2)\times 2)-2)\div 2=11$、$(((10+2)\div 2)-2)\times 2=8$、$(((10-2)\times 2)+2)\div 2=9$、$(((10-2)\div 2)\times 2)+2=12$、$(((10\times 2)-2)\div 2)+2=11$、$(((10\times 2)+2)\div 2)-2=9$、$(((10\div 2)-2)\times 2)+2=8$、$(((10\div 2)+2)\times 2)-2$

= 12，故知共可算出 8、9、10、11、12 共五个不同的值.

11. 答案：2.

解 由 $(a+1)(b+1)(c+1) = abc+ab+ac+bc+a+b+c+1$ 可知 $ab+ac+bc+a+b+c$ $= 16-abc-1=14$；由 $(a+2)(b+2)(c+2) = abc+2ab+2ac+2bc+4a+4b+4c+8$ 可知 $ab+ac+bc+2a+2b+2c = \dfrac{53-abc-8}{2} = 22$；两式相减即可得知 $a+b+c = 22-14=8$，故 $ab+ac+bc = 14-8 = 6$.

所以知 $(a-1)(b-1)(c-1) = abc-ab-ac-bc+a+b+c-1 = 1-6+8-1 = 2$.

12. 答案：50cm.

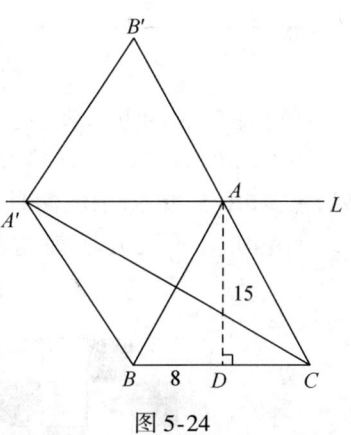

图 5-24

解 可知 BC 边上的高为 $\dfrac{120 \times 2}{16} = 15$cm，因此点 A 必在一条与 BC 的距离为 15 cm 的直线 L 上. 现验证当 $AB = AC$ 时，$\triangle ABC$ 的周长最小. 如图 5-24 所示，令点 A 在直线 L 上使得 $AB=AC$，且点 A' 是在直线 L 上异于点 A 的点. 以直线 L 为对称轴作点 B 的对称点 B' 并连接 $A'B'$、AB'，可知 $A'B' = A'B$、$AB' = AB$ 以及 $\angle BAA' = \angle B'AA'$.

由 $\angle BAA' = \angle B'AA'$ 可知 C、A、B' 三点共线，因此 $B'C = AB' + AC = AB + AC$. 而在 $\triangle CA'B'$ 中，恒有 $A'B' + A'C > B'C$，故得 $A'B + A'C = A'B' + A'C > B'C = AB+AC$. 所以可判断出 $\triangle A'BC$ 的周长大于 $\triangle ABC$ 的周长. 而当 $AB = AC$ 时，可令 BC 边的中点为点 D，则由 BC 边上的高 $AD = 15$cm、$BD = 8$cm 知 $AB = \sqrt{15^2+8^2} = 17$cm，此时 $\triangle ABC$ 的周长为 $16+17+17 = 50$cm.

13. 答案：225.

解 可知两个数的公因子必是此两个数之差的因子，所以 n 为 $\overline{abcd} - \overline{acbd}$ 的因子，且由 $d \neq 0$ 可判断出 n 的个位数码不为 0，即 n 没有质因子 2，或是没有质因子 5.

不失一般性，可令 $b > c$，则 $\overline{abcd} - \overline{acbd} = 90(b-c)$.

若 n 没有质因子 2，则 n 为 $\dfrac{90(b-c)}{2} = 45(b-c)$ 的因子，再由 $b-c \leq 9-1=8$ 知 n 至多为 $45 \times 7 = 315$. 若 $n = 315$，则由 n 的个位数码为 5 知 $d=5$、由 $b-c=7$ 知 $b=$

8、$c=1$,或者 $b=9$、$c=2$,再由 315 为 9 的倍数知 $\overline{abcd}$ 必为 4815 或 2925 之一,但两者均不能被 315 整除,故不合. n 的下一个可能值为 $45×5=225$,而当 $\overline{abcd}=4725=225×21$、$\overline{acbd}=4275=225×19$ 时,$n=225$.

若 n 没有质因子 5,则 n 为 $\dfrac{90(b-c)}{5}=18(b-c)$ 的因子,其值至多为 $18×8=144$.

综上所述,n 的最大可能值是 225.

14. 答案:12.

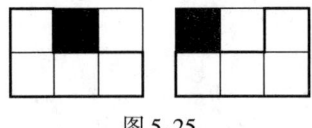

图 5-25

解 在 $2×3$ 的方格表中,若只涂黑一个小方格,则一定可放入一个 L-形四方块而不盖住此涂黑的方格(图 5-25):

故知在 $2×3$ 的方格表中,至少要涂黑两个小方格.(10 分)

因 $6×6$ 的方格表可分成六个 $2×3$ 的方格表,故知至少要将 $2×6=12$ 个小方格涂黑.如图 5-26 所示的两种涂色法,都是将 12 个小方格涂黑而使得 L-形四方块无论如何放入方格表内都至少会盖住一个黑色的小方格的涂色方式.(10 分)

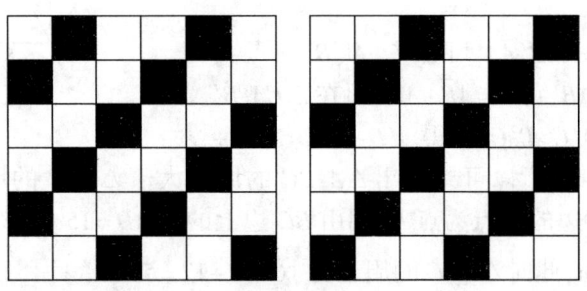

图 5-26

综上所述,至少要将 12 个小方格涂黑.

15. **解** 假设 $AB>AC$,延长 PQ、BC 交于点 X.令点 E 是 BC 上的点使得 QE 平行 AB,如图 5-27 所示.则可得 $\dfrac{XQ}{XA}=\dfrac{XE}{XB}$ 与 $\dfrac{XQ}{XP}=\dfrac{XC}{XB}$,即 $XA×XE=XB×XQ=XP×XC$,所以 $\dfrac{XA}{XP}=\dfrac{XC}{XE}$,可得知 $AC//PE$.(10 分)

第 5 章　第 5 届国际中小学生数学能力检测(IMAS)(初中组)

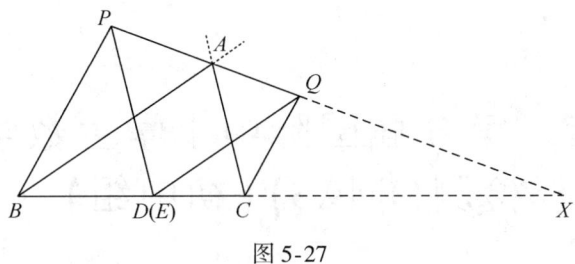

图 5-27

又知 $\angle EPQ = \angle CAQ = \angle PAB = \angle EQP$,可得 $EP = EQ$,因此点 Q、点 E 均为直线 PQ 的中垂线与直线 BC 的交点,此即点 E 与点 D 重合,故证得 $AB // DQ$.(5 分)

当 $AB = AC$ 且 $\angle BAC \neq 90°$ 时,同理可证.

当 $AB = AC$ 且 $\angle BAC = 90°$ 时,可知 $PQ // BC$,即上述作法的点 X 不存在.此时可知四边形 $PQCB$ 为平行四边形(图 5-28),因此 $\triangle ABC$ 与 $\triangle DCP$ 为底边长相同、面积相同的两个等腰三角形,故可判断出 $\triangle ABC$ 与 $\triangle DCP$ 为全等三角形,即有 $\angle PDQ = \angle BAC = 90°$,故 $AB // DQ$.(5 分)

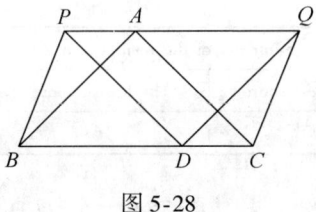

图 5-28

第6章 第6届国际中小学生数学能力检测(IMAS)(初中组)

6.1 第一轮英文试题

考试时间:75 分钟

Questions 1–10, 3 marks each

1. What is the value of $\sqrt{(-20)^2 + 16^2 - 15^2}$?
   (A)−19   (B)11   (C)21   (D)51   (E)61

2. The table below summarizes the results of a test in a certain class. What is the total score of this class?

Summary of the results of a test			
No. of students	The highest score	The lowest score	The average score
42	100	16	84.5

   (A)672   (B)3528   (C)3549   (D)4200   (E)4872

3. A three-digit number is not divisible by 24. When divided by 24, the quotient is a and the remainder is b. What is the minimum value of $a+b$?
   (A)5   (B)6   (C)7   (D)8   (E)9

4. In the trapezium $ABCD$, AB is parallel to CD. E and F are points on AD and BC respectively such that EF is also parallel to AB. The area, in cm², of triangles BAF, CDF and BCE are 8, 7 and 18 respectively. What is the area, in cm², of $ABCD$?
   (A)30   (B)32   (C)33
   (D)35   (E)36

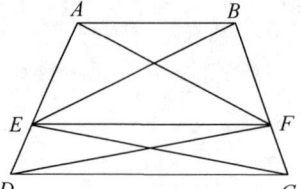

5. What is the value of the negative number x which satisfies $|x-3| = |3x|+1$?

第6章 第6届国际中小学生数学能力检测(IMAS)(初中组)

(A)−2 (B)−1 (C)−$\frac{2}{3}$ (D)−$\frac{1}{2}$ (E)−$\frac{1}{4}$

6. The radius of each wheel of Rick's bicycle is 25 cm. He rides to school at a constant speed and arrives after 10 minutes. During this time, each wheel makes 160 revolutions. Of the following five distances, which is closest to that between Rick's home and school?

(A)1km (B)1.5km (C)1.8km (D)2km (E)2.5km

7. How many two-digit numbers are there such that at least one digit is divisible by 3?

(A)48 (B)54 (C)60 (D)66 (E)80

8. The chart below shows the sale figures of a certain merchandise in 2014 and 2015 by the season. How many more items were sold in 2015 than in 2014?

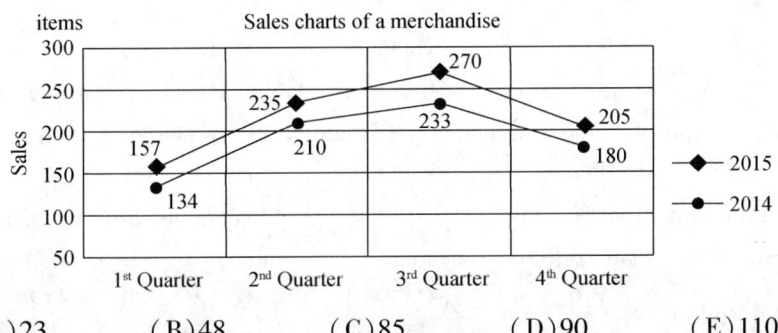

(A)23 (B)48 (C)85 (D)90 (E)110

9. ABC is an equilateral triangle. D is a point inside (ABC) such that BCD is a right isosceles triangle. The altitude BE of ABC intersects CD at F. What is the measure, in degrees, of ∠CFE?

(A)75° (B)70° (C)65°
(D)60° (E)55°

10. In how many ways can 36 be expressed as the sum of two prime numbers, the first larger than the second?

(A)1 (B)2 (C)3 (D)4 (E)5

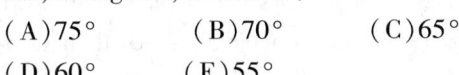

Questions 11–20, 4 marks each

11. Every student in a class is either in the mathematics club or the language club, and one third of them are in both. If there are 22 students in the language

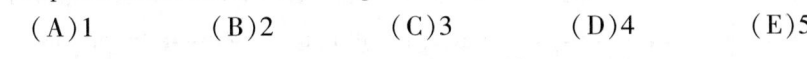

club, 4 less than the number of students in the mathematics club, how many students are there in this class?

(A) 12　　　(B) 18　　　(C) 24　　　(D) 30　　　(E) 36

12. The average of a group of numbers is 5. A second group contains twice as many numbers and its average is 11. What is the average when the two groups are combined?

(A) 6　　　(B) 7　　　(C) 8　　　(D) 9　　　(E) 10

13. What is the value of x^y if $\sqrt{x-1}+\sqrt{1-x}+y=2016$?

(A) 2015　　　(B) 2016　　　(C) $\dfrac{1}{2016}$　　　(D) 1　　　(E) 0

14. Each of A and B goes to the gymnasium 3 or 4 times a week. After n weeks, A has been there 57 times while B has been there only 47 times. What is the value of n?

(A) 15　　　(B) 16　　　(C) 17　　　(D) 18　　　(E) 19

15. D is a point on segarouf AB such that $AD=1$ and $BD=2$. How many points C are there in the plane such that both ACD and BCD are isosceles triangles?

(A) 2　　　(B) 4　　　(C) 5　　　(D) 6　　　(E) 8

16. From a 5×5 square piece of paper, two 2×4 rectangles are cut off along the grid lines. In how many different ways can this be done?

(A) 6　　　(B) 9　　　(C) 12　　　(D) 18　　　(E) 24

17. The number a is 5 more than its reciprocal. What is the value of $(a^2-1)^2 -125a$?

(A) 5　　　(B) 25　　　(C) 125　　　(D) $\dfrac{1+\sqrt{21}}{2}$　　　(E) $5\sqrt{21}$

18. With each vertex of a parallelogram $ABCD$ as centre, a circle is drawn. Exterior common tangents are then drawn, as shown in the diagram below. If the perimeter of $ABCD$ is 36 cm and the radius of each circle is 2 cm, what is the maximum area, in cm², of the figure enclosed by the circular arcs and tangents?

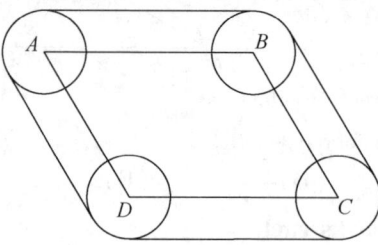

(A)$117+4\pi$ (B)$144+4\pi$ (C)$153+4\pi$ (D)$144+12\pi$ (E)$153+12\pi$

19. What is the smallest positive integer with 12 positive divisors such that it is relatively prime to (2016^3-2016)?

(A)7007   (B)9163   (C)26741   (D)39083   (E)52877

20. At most how many right triangles can be formed by five lines on the plane?

(A)4   (B)5   (C)6   (D)7   (E)8

Questions 21–25, 6 marks each

21. The International Article Number has 13 digits *ABCDEFGHIJKLM*. Here *M* is a check digit. Let $S=A+3B+C+3D+E+3F+G+3H+I+3J+K+3L$. If S is a multiple of 10, then *M* is chosen to be 0. Otherwise it is chosen to be $M=10-t$ where t is the remainder obtained when S is divided by 10. The Code for a certain Article Number is 6901020□09017. What is the missing digit?

22. What is the largest three-digit number which can be expressed as the sum of the cubes of three different positive integers?

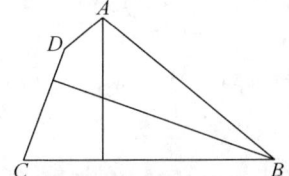

23. The diagram shows a quadrilateral *ABCD* with $\angle CDA=150°$. The bisector of $\angle DAB$ is perpendicular to *BC* and the bisector of $\angle ABC$ is perpendicular to *CD*. What is the measure, in degrees, of $\angle BCD$?

24. Let *a* and *b* be positive real numbers such that $a^2=b(b+1)$ and $b^2=a+1$. What is the value of $\dfrac{1}{a}+\dfrac{1}{b}$?

25. Each blouse cost 40 dollars, each skirt 70 dollars and each pair of shoes 80 dollars. Fanny bought at least one item of each kind, and spent at most 800 dollars. A outfit consisted of one item of each kind, and two outfits were different if they differed in at least one item. At most how many different outfits could there be?

6.2　第一轮中文试题

1-10题,每题3分

1. 请问代数式 $\sqrt{(-20)^2+16^2-15^2}$ 的值是多少?

(A)-19 (B)11   (C)21   (D)51   (E)61

2. 以下表格是某班级的数学期中考试得分统计表,请问该班学生数学期中考试的得分总和为多少分?

数学期中考试得分统计表

人数	最高分	最低分	平均分
42	100	16	84.5

(A)672　　(B)3528　　(C)3549　　(D)4200　　(E)4872

3. 将一个不是24的倍数之三位数除以24,所得的商是 a、余数是 b. 请问 $a+b$ 的最小值是多少?

(A)5　　(B)6　　(C)7　　(D)8　　(E)9

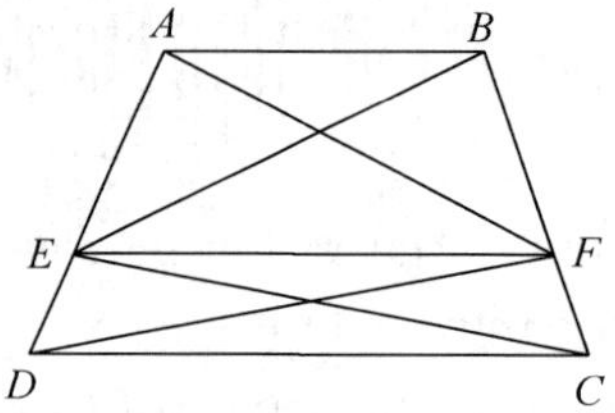

4. 在梯形 $ABCD$ 中,已知 $AB//CD$,点 E、F 分别在边 AD、BC 上,且 $EF//AB$,如图6-1所示. 若 $\triangle BAF$、$\triangle CDF$、$\triangle BCE$ 的面积分别为 $8cm^2$、$7cm^2$、$18cm^2$,请问梯形 $ABCD$ 的面积是多少 cm^2?

(A)30　　(B)32　　(C)33　　(D)35　　(E)36

图6-1

5. 已知负数 x 满足方程 $|x-3|=|3x|+1$,请问 x 的值是多少?

(A)-2　　(B)-1　　(C)$-\dfrac{2}{3}$　　(D)$-\dfrac{1}{2}$　　(E)$-\dfrac{1}{4}$

6. 小李从家中骑自行车去学校,已知自行车的车轮半径为25 cm,车轮每分钟转160圈. 假如从家中以此匀速骑到学校共费时10分钟,请问学校到小李家的距离最接近下面哪一项?

(A)1km　　(B)1.5km　　(C)1.8km　　(D)2km　　(E)2.5km

7. 请问数码中至少有一个是3的倍数的两位数总共有多少个?

(A)48　　(B)54　　(C)60　　(D)66　　(E)80

8. 图6-2为某商品在2014年与2015年各季度的销量折线图,请问2015年的总销量比2014年的总销量多几件?

(A)23　　(B)48　　(C)85　　(D)90　　(E)110

9. 等边三角形 ABC 中,已知 $BD=CD$、$BD\perp CD$、$BE\perp AC$,而 BE 与 CD 交于点 F,如图6-3所示. 请问 $\angle CFE$ 的大小为多少度?

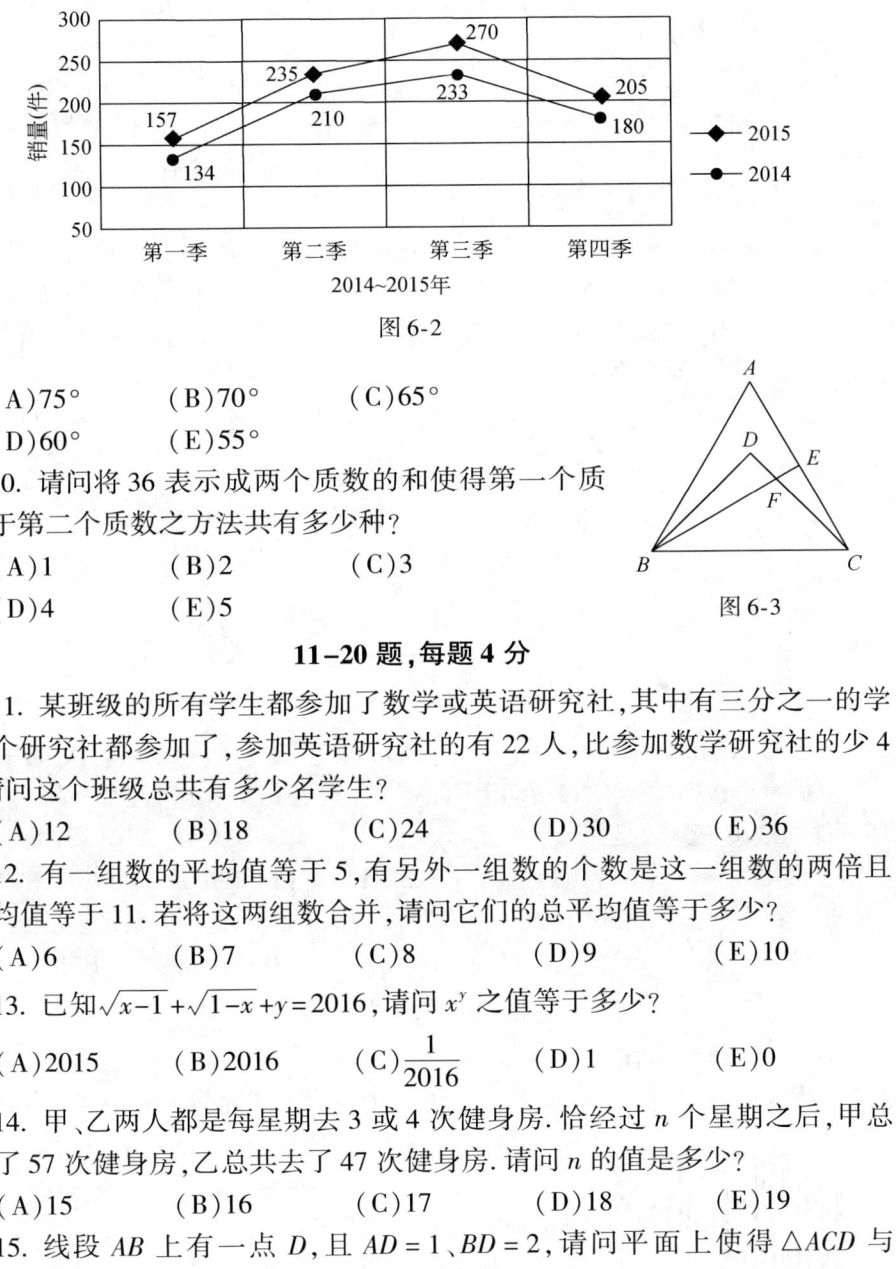

图 6-2

图 6-3

(A) 75°　　(B) 70°　　(C) 65°
(D) 60°　　(E) 55°

10. 请问将 36 表示成两个质数的和使得第一个质数大于第二个质数之方法共有多少种？

(A) 1　　(B) 2　　(C) 3
(D) 4　　(E) 5

11—20 题，每题 4 分

11. 某班级的所有学生都参加了数学或英语研究社，其中有三分之一的学生两个研究社都参加了，参加英语研究社的有 22 人，比参加数学研究社的少 4 人，请问这个班级总共有多少名学生？

(A) 12　　(B) 18　　(C) 24　　(D) 30　　(E) 36

12. 有一组数的平均值等于 5，有另外一组数的个数是这一组数的两倍且其平均值等于 11。若将这两组数合并，请问它们的总平均值等于多少？

(A) 6　　(B) 7　　(C) 8　　(D) 9　　(E) 10

13. 已知 $\sqrt{x-1}+\sqrt{1-x}+y=2016$，请问 x^y 之值等于多少？

(A) 2015　　(B) 2016　　(C) $\dfrac{1}{2016}$　　(D) 1　　(E) 0

14. 甲、乙两人都是每星期去 3 或 4 次健身房。恰经过 n 个星期之后，甲总共去了 57 次健身房，乙总共去了 47 次健身房。请问 n 的值是多少？

(A) 15　　(B) 16　　(C) 17　　(D) 18　　(E) 19

15. 线段 AB 上有一点 D，且 $AD=1$、$BD=2$，请问平面上使得 △ACD 与 △BCD 都是等腰三角形的点 C 总共有多少个？

(A) 2　　(B) 4　　(C) 5　　(D) 6　　(E) 8

16. 在一个 5×5 的方格纸上沿着网格线剪下两个 2×4 的矩形,请问总共有多少种不同的剪法?

(A)6 (B)9 (C)12 (D)18 (E)24

17. 已知有一个正数 a 比它的倒数大 5,请问 $(a^2-1)^2-125a$ 的值是什么?

(A)5 (B)25 (C)125 (D)$\dfrac{1+\sqrt{21}}{2}$ (E)$5\sqrt{21}$

18. 平行四边形 $ABCD$ 的周长为 36cm,分别以 A、B、C、D 为圆心,作半径为 2cm 的圆,然后再分别作每两个相邻的圆在平行四边形外部的外公切线,四条公切线与外侧的圆弧围成一个封闭图形,如图 6-4 所示.请问这个封闭图形的面积之最大可能值为多少 cm²?

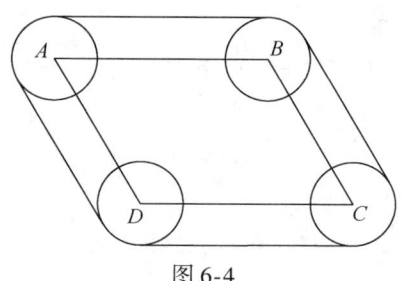

图 6-4

(A)117+4π (B)144+4π (C)153+4π (D)144+12π (E)153+12π

19. 一个正整数恰有 12 个正因子,且它与 (2016^3-2016) 互质.请问满足上述条件的最小正整数是什么?

(A)7007 (B)9163 (C)26741 (D)39083 (E)52877

20. 在平面上画五条直线,请问最多能构成多少个直角三角形?

(A)4 (B)5 (C)6 (D)7 (E)8

21-25 题,每题 6 分

21. 每件商品都有一个 13 位数码的国际商品条码:$ABCDEFGHIJKLM$,其中最后一位数码 M 是检查码,它的生成方式如下:令 $S=A+3B+C+3D+E+3F+G+3H+I+3J+K+3L$,若 S 除以 10 所得的余数为 0,则 $M=0$;若 S 除以 10 所得的余数为 $t\neq 0$,则 $M=10-t$. 现有一个国际商品条码为 6901020□09017,请问「□」内的数码是什么(图 6-5)?

图 6-5

22. 请问能表示成三个不同正整数的立方和的三位数之最大值是什么?

23. 在四边形 $ABCD$ 中,已知 $\angle CDA = 150°$、$\angle DAB$ 的平分线与 BC 垂直、$\angle ABC$ 的平分线与 CD 垂直,如图6-6所示.请问 $\angle BCD$ 的大小是多少度?

24. 已知 a、b 是满足 $a^2 = b(b+1)$ 与 $b^2 = a+1$ 的正实数,请问 $\dfrac{1}{a} + \dfrac{1}{b}$ 的值是什么?

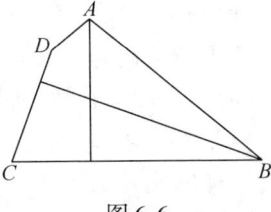

图 6-6

25. 上衣之售价为40元一件、裙子之售价为70元一条、鞋子之售价为80元一双.小芳有800元,每种服饰她都至少买一件.若将一件上衣,一条裙子与一双鞋子称作一种搭配,两种搭配里只要有一项服饰不是同一件,就称作不同的搭配.请问小芳购买的服饰最多能做出多少种不同的搭配?

6.3 第一轮试题解答与评注

1. 答案:(D).

解 $\sqrt{(-20)^2} + 16^2 - 15^2 = 20 + 256 - 225 = 51$.故选(D).

2. 答案:(C).

解 该班学生数学期中考试的得分总和为 $84.5 \times 42 = 3549$ 分.故选(C).

3. 答案:(B).

解 由于 $100 = 4 \times 24 + 4$,所以当被除数变大时,商 $a \geq 4$.若 $a = 4$,则可判断出余数 $b \geq 4$,因此 $a + b \geq 8$;而若 $a \geq 5$,则由此数不是24的倍数知 $b \geq 1$,故可得知 $a + b \geq 6$.若取此三位数为121时,有 $a = 5$、$b = 1$ 且 $a + b = 6$.故选(B).

4. 答案:(C).

解 由 $EF // AB$ 知 $\triangle BAE$ 的面积与 $\triangle BAF$ 的面积相同;由 $EF // CD$ 知 $\triangle CDE$ 的面积与 $\triangle CDF$ 的面积相同,所以梯形 $ABCD$ 的面积 $= \triangle BAE$ 的面积 $+ \triangle CDE$ 的面积 $+ \triangle BCE$ 的面积 $= 8 + 7 + 18 = 33 \text{cm}^2$.故选(C).

5. 答案:(B).

解 由于 x 是负数,所以 $x - 3 < 0$、$3x < 0$,原方程可化为 $3 - x = -3x + 1$,解得 $x = -1$.故选(B).

6. 答案:(E).

解 由于题目求的是大约的距离,可取 $\pi = 3.14$.自行车的车轮转一圈,自行车约前进 $2 \times 3.14 \times 25 = 157 \text{cm}$,故学校到家的距离大约为 $157 \times 160 \times 10 = 251200 \text{cm}$,即为 2512m,约 2.5 km.故选(E).

7. 答案:(B).

解法 1 若十位数码是 3、6、9 之一,这样的两位数显然满足条件,共有 30 个;若十位数码是 1、2、4、5、7、8 之一,则个位数码为 0、3、6、9 之一,这样的两位数共有 $6 \times 4 = 24$ 个. 故满足题目条件的两位数总共有 $30 + 24 = 54$ 个. 故选(B).

解法 2 可判断出不满足条件的两位数之两个数码都是 1、2、4、5、7、8 之一,这样的两位数共有 $6 \times 6 = 36$ 个,而所有的两位数共有 90 个,因此满足题目条件的两位数总共有 $90 - 36 = 54$ 个. 故选(B).

8. 答案:(E).

解法 1 2015 年总销量为 $157 + 235 + 270 + 205 = 867$ 件、2014 年总销量为 $134 + 210 + 233 + 180 = 757$ 件,即 2015 年总销量比 2014 年总销量多 $867 - 757 = 110$ 件. 故选(E).

解法 2 2015 年第一季度销量比 2014 年第一季度销量多 $157 - 134 = 23$ 件、第二季度多 $235 - 210 = 25$ 件、第三季度多 $270 - 233 = 37$ 件、第四季度多 $205 - 180 = 25$ 件.

所以 2015 年总销量比 2014 年总销量总共多 $23 + 25 + 37 + 25 = 110$ 件. 故选(E).

9. 答案:(A).

解 由 $BD = CD$、$BD \perp CD$ 可以得知 $\angle BCD = \dfrac{180° - 90°}{2} = 45°$. 又由 $\triangle ABC$ 是等边三角形可以得知 $\angle BCA = 60°$,故 $\angle DCA = 60° - 45° = 15°$,最后由 $BE \perp AC$,因此知 $\angle CFE = 90° - 15° = 75°$. 故选(A).

10. 答案:(D).

解 考虑较大的质数,它只能在 18 到 35 之间,而 18 到 35 之间的质数只有 19、23、29、31,而用 36 减这些数分别可得 17、13、7、5,它们正好都是质数,故知共有 4 种表示方法. 故选(D).

11. 答案:(E).

解法 1 由题意可得,参加数学研究社的学生有 $22 + 4 = 26$ 名. 有三分之一的学生两个研究社都参加,所以参加数学研究社与英语研究社的总人数等于全班人数的三分之四,故这个班级总共有 $(22 + 26) \div 4 \times 3 = 36$ 名学生. 故选(E).

解法 2 由题意可得,参加数学研究社的学生有 $22 + 4 = 26$ 名.

设两个研究社都参加的学生有 x 名,则这个班级共有 $3x$ 名,因此有 $22 + 26 - x = 3x$,解得 $x = 12$. 所以这个班级总共有 $12 \times 3 = 36$ 名学生. 故选(E).

第6章　第6届国际中小学生数学能力检测(IMAS)(初中组)

12. 答案:(D).

解法1 第二组数的个数是第一组数的两倍,不妨设第二组有 2 个数、第一组有 1 个数,可知它们的总平均值等于 $\frac{5+11\times 2}{1+2}=9$. 故选(D).

解法2 设第一组有 k 个数,则第二组有 $2k$ 个数. 可知第一组所有数之和为 $5k$,而第二组所有数之和为 $11\times 2k=22k$,因此知所有数的平均值为 $\frac{5k+22k}{k+2k}=9$. 故选(D).

13. 答案:(D).

解 由于 $\sqrt{x-1}$ 与 $\sqrt{1-x}$ 都有意义,所以 $x-1$、$1-x$ 都是非负数,而它们互为相反数,故 $x-1=1-x=0$,即 $x=1$,代入原式解得 $y=2016$,即 $x^y=1^{2016}=1$. 故选(D).

14. 答案:(A).

解 由条件知 $3n\leq 47$ 且 $4n\geq 57$,解得 $14\frac{1}{4}\leq n\leq 15\frac{2}{3}$. 由于 n 是正整数,所以 $n=15$. 故选(A).

15. 答案:(B).

解 注意到 $\angle ADC$ 与 $\angle BDC$ 互补,它们之间必然有一个不是锐角,即必然有一个是等腰三角形的顶角. 若 $\angle BDC$ 是顶角,则 $DC=2$,由三角形的两边和大于第三边、两边差小于第三边知 $1<AC<3$,故只能 $AC=DC=2$,这样可能的点有两个(图 6-7 中的 C_1、C_2 点);若 $\angle ADC$ 是顶角,则 $DC=1$,由三角形的两边和大于第三边、两边差小于第三边知 $1<BC<3$,故只能 $BC=DB=2$,这样可能的点也有两个(图中的 C_3、C_4 点). 因此总共有 4 个满足条件的点. 故选(B).

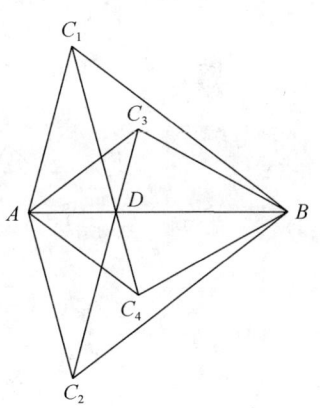

图 6-7

16. 答案:(E).

解 显然两个矩形必须同时为 2×4 的矩形或同时为 4×2 的矩形. 先考虑同时为 2×4 的矩形. 当第一个 2×4 的矩形位于由上往下数第 1、2 列时,另一个 2×4 的矩形可以位于第 3、4 列或第 4、5 列;当第一个 2×4 的矩形位于由上往下数第 2、3 列时,另一个 2×4 的矩形只能位于第 4、5 列,故有 3 种不同的占据列的方式. 当占据列的方式已确定时,每个矩形都有 2 个不同的位置,故有 3×2×2=

12种剪法.由对称性知 4×2 的矩形时也有 12 种剪法,所以总共有 12+12 = 24 种剪法.故选(E).

17. 答案:(B).

解 由题意知 $a - \dfrac{1}{a} = 5$,再由 a 不为 0 知 $a^2 - 1 = 5a$,即 $a^2 - 5a = 1$.因此
$$(a^2-1)^2 - 125a = (5a)^2 - 125a = 25(a^2 - 5a) = 25.$$
故选(B).

18. 答案:(C).

解 由四个圆心 A、B、C、D 分别与其所在之圆的两个切点连接,如图 6-8 所示.此时封闭图形可分成原来的平行四边形、四个矩形与四个扇形.因每一个圆的圆心所在之角都恰为两个矩形的直角、原平行四边形的一个内角与一个扇形的圆心角,所以可得知这四个扇形的圆心角分别等于平行四边形内角的补角,再由四边形内角和为 $360°$ 知四个扇形面积之总和恰等于一个圆的面积,即 $4\pi \text{cm}^2$;四个矩形的面积之和恰等于圆形半径乘以平行四边形周长,即 $2 \times 36 = 72 \text{cm}^2$;当平行四边形的周长固定时,它的面积之最大值会发生在此平行四边形恰为正方形,其值为 $\left(\dfrac{36}{4}\right)^2 = 81 \text{cm}^2$,故所求最大值为 $4\pi + 72 + 81 = 153 + 4\pi \text{cm}^2$.故选(C).

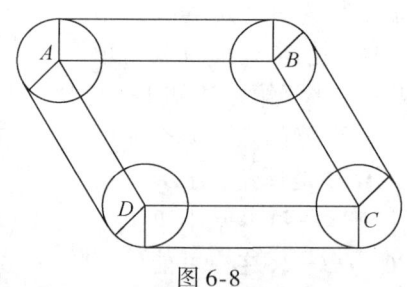

图 6-8

19. 答案:(D).

解 $2016^3 - 2016 = 2016 \times (2016^2 - 1) = 2015 \times 2016 \times 2017 = 2^5 \times 3^2 \times 5 \times 7 \times 13 \times 31 \times 2017$.所以满足条件的正整数之质因子只能是 11、17、19、…、29、37、…、2011、2027、….此正整数恰有 12 个正因子,故知此数之形式必为 p^{11}、$p^5 q$、$p^3 q^2$ 或 $p^2 qr$,其中 p、q、r 为相异的质数.可知前三种形式都会超过 10^5,而最后一种形式的最小值是 $11^2 \times 17 \times 19 = 39083 < 10^5$.故选(D).

第6章 第6届国际中小学生数学能力检测(IMAS)(初中组)

20. 答案:(D).

解 设这五条直线为 a、b、c、d、e. 若两条直线互相垂直,则固定这两条直线,第三条直线在剩余 3 条中任选一条,最多可以得到 3 个直角三角形. 因此,若图6-9中只有1组或2组直线互相垂直,则最多只能有6个直角三角形. 若图6-9中有至少3组直线互相垂直,则必然有两条直线 a、b 垂直于同一条直线,故 a、b 互相平行,这样 a 与 c、d、e 中任两条直线可能构成一个三角形,最多共 3 个三角形;b 与 c、d、e 中任两条直线可能构成一个三角形,最多共 3 个三角形;c、d、e 可能构成一个三角形. 故图6-9中最多有 $3+3+1=7$ 个三角形,因而最多有 7 个直角三角形. 图6-9即为构成 7 个直角三角形的例子. 故选(D).

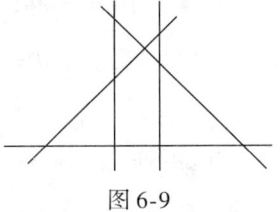

图6-9

21. 由题意可得,

解 $S=6+3\times9+0+3\times1+0+3\times2+0+3\times\square+0+3\times9+0+3\times1=72+3\times\square$,

已知 $M=7$,故 $72+3\times\square$ 除以 10 所得的余数为 $10-7=3$,即 $3\times\square$ 的个位数码为 1,所以 $\square=7$.

评注 国际商品条形码的设计使得
$A+3B+C+3D+E+3F+G+3H+I+3J+K+3L+M$ 可被 10 整除.

22. 答案:980.

解 因 $10^3=1000$,故可判断出题目的意思实际上是在 $1^3=1$、$2^3=8$、$3^3=27$、$4^3=64$、$5^3=125$、$6^3=216$、$7^3=343$、$8^3=512$、$9^3=729$ 中选取三个不同的数,使得它们的和小于 1000 且尽量接近 1000.

若不选 8^3 与 9^3,那么三个数之和最大是 $5^3+6^3+7^3=684$;

若选 9^3,则不能选 8^3 与 7^3,在选取 6^3 的情况下,此时所得的和为 $729+216=945$,故知接下来最大可选 3^3,总和为 972;在不选取 6^3 的情况下,此时所得的三个数之和最大为 $4^3+5^3+9^3=918$;

若选 8^3,因 $6^3+7^3+8^3=1071>1000$,故三个数的和最大为 $5^3+7^3+8^3=980$.

综上所述,所求三位数之最大值为 980.

23. 解法1 令 $\angle DAB$ 的平分线与 BC 之垂足为点 X、$\angle ABC$ 的平分线与 CD 之垂足为点 Y,且令 AX 与 BY 之交点为 O.

由 $\angle BCD+\angle XOY=180°$ 知 $\angle BCD=\angle XOB=\dfrac{1}{2}(\angle DAB+\angle ABC)$,即 $\angle DAB+\angle ABC=2\angle BCD$.

由四边形内角和知 $360°=\angle DAB+\angle ABC+\angle BCD+\angle CDA=3\angle BCD+150°$,

可解得 $\angle BCD = 70°$.

解法 2 设 $\angle ABC = 2x°$,由 $\angle ABC$ 的平分线与 CD 垂直知 $\angle BCD = 90°-x°$、由 $\angle DAB$ 的平分线与 BC 垂直知 $\angle DAB = 2(90°-2x°)$.再由四边形内角和为 $360°$ 知 $360° = 150°+2x°+90°-x°+2(90°-2x°)$,化简得 $3x° = 60°$,即可解得 $x = 20$,因此 $\angle BCD = 90°-20° = 70°$.

24. **解** 由 $b^2 = a+1$ 知 $a = b^2-1$,故再由 $a^2 = b(b+1)$ 知 $a(b^2-1) = b(b+1)$,即 $a(b-1) = b$,因此 $ab = a+b$,等式两边同除以 ab,得 $\dfrac{1}{a}+\dfrac{1}{b} = \dfrac{a+b}{ab} = 1$.

25. **解法 1** 设小芳买了 x 件上衣、y 条裙子、z 双鞋子,则 $40x+70y+80z \leq 800$,在此不等式下求 xyz 的最大值.

先将不等式两边除以 40,可得 $x+\dfrac{7}{4}y+2z \leq 20$,接下来将对 y 的取值作讨论.

注意到 x、y、z 都是正整数,故得 $\dfrac{7}{4}y \leq 17$,因此 $y \leq 9$.

当 $y=1$ 时,$x+2z \leq 18$.由算几不等式知 $\sqrt{2xz} \leq \dfrac{x+2z}{2} \leq 9$,因此 $xz \leq \dfrac{9^2}{2} = 40\dfrac{1}{2}$,即 xz 的最大值为 40,故此时 xyz 的最大值为 40,且会发生在 $x=8$、$z=5$;

当 $y=2$ 时,$x+2z \leq 16$.由算几不等式知 $\sqrt{2xz} \leq \dfrac{x+2z}{2} \leq 8$,因此 $xz \leq \dfrac{8^2}{2} = 32$,即 xz 的最大值为 32,故此时 xyz 的最大值为 64,且会发生在 $x=8$、$z=4$;

当 $y=3$ 时,$x+2z \leq 14$.由算几不等式知 $\sqrt{2xz} \leq \dfrac{x+2z}{2} \leq 7$,因此 $xz \leq \dfrac{7^2}{2} = 24\dfrac{1}{2}$,即 xz 的最大值为 24,故此时 xyz 的最大值为 72,且会发生在 $x=6$、$z=4$;

当 $y=4$ 时,$x+2z \leq 13$.由算几不等式知 $\sqrt{2xz} \leq \dfrac{x+2z}{2} \leq \dfrac{13}{2}$,因此 $xz \leq \dfrac{13^2}{8} = 21\dfrac{1}{8}$,即 xz 的最大值为 21,故此时 xyz 的最大值为 84,且会发生在 $x=7$、$z=3$;

当 $y=5$ 时,$x+2z \leq 11$.由算几不等式知 $\sqrt{2xz} \leq \dfrac{x+2z}{2} \leq \dfrac{11}{2}$,因此 $xz \leq \dfrac{11^2}{8} = 15\dfrac{1}{8}$,即 xz 的最大值为 15,故此时 xyz 的最大值为 75,且会发生在 $x=5$、$z=3$;

当 $y=6$ 时,$x+2z \leq 9$.由算几不等式知 $\sqrt{2xz} \leq \dfrac{x+2z}{2} \leq \dfrac{9}{2}$,因此 $xz \leq \dfrac{9^2}{8} = 10\dfrac{1}{8}$,即 xz 的最大值为 10,故此时 xyz 的最大值为 60,且会发生在 $x=5$、$z=2$;

当 $y=7$ 时,$x+2z \leq 7$.由算几不等式知 $\sqrt{2xz} \leq \dfrac{x+2z}{2} \leq \dfrac{7}{2}$,因此 $xz \leq \dfrac{7^2}{8} = 6\dfrac{1}{8}$,即 xz 的最大值为 6,故此时 xyz 的最大值为 42,且会发生在 $x=3$、$z=2$;

当 $y=8$ 时，$x+2z\leqslant 6$。由算几不等式知 $\sqrt{2xz}\leqslant\dfrac{x+2z}{2}\leqslant 3$，因此 $xz\leqslant\dfrac{3^2}{2}=4\dfrac{1}{2}$，即 xz 的最大值为 4，故此时 xyz 的最大值为 32，且会发生在 $x=2$、$z=2$；

当 $y=9$ 时，$x+2z\leqslant 4$。由算几不等式知 $\sqrt{2xz}\leqslant\dfrac{x+2z}{2}\leqslant 2$，因此 $xz\leqslant\dfrac{2^2}{2}=2$，即 xz 的最大值为 2，故此时 xyz 的最大值为 18，且会发生在 $x=2$、$z=1$。

综上所述，小芳购买的服饰最多能做出 84 种不同的搭配，此会发生在买 4 件裙子、7 件上衣、3 双鞋子时。答案：084

评注 本题的背景是加权的均值不等式。设小芳买了 x 件上衣、y 条裙子、z 双鞋子，则 $40x+70y+80z\leqslant 800$，在此不等式下求 xyz 的最大值。

由算几不等式知 $\sqrt[3]{40x\times 70y\times 80z}=\sqrt[3]{224000xyz}\leqslant\dfrac{40x+70y+80z}{3}=\dfrac{800}{3}$，等式两边都同时三次方可得 $224000xyz\leqslant\dfrac{512000000}{27}$，$xyz\leqslant\dfrac{512000000}{27\times 224000}=84\dfrac{127}{189}$，故 xyz 的最大值为 84，且会发生在 $x=7$、$y=4$、$z=3$。

6.4 第二轮英文试题

考试时间：120 分钟

Questions 1–5, 4 marks each

1. Which of the numbers below cannot be expressed as a sum of two prime numbers?

(A) 19   (B) 20   (C) 21   (D) 22   (E) 23

Answer:_____

2. In $\triangle ABC$, $AB=AC$ and $\angle ACB=80°$. Construct square $ACDE$ with the given side AC. Lines BE and AC intersect at point F, as shown in the figure. What is the measure of $\angle BFC$?

(A) 55°   (B) 60°   (C) 65°
(D) 70°   (E) 75°

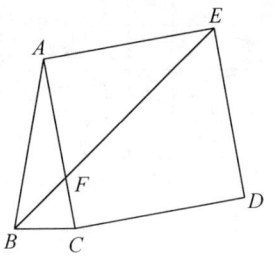

Answer:_____

3. Alex and Charles were both sending parcels. The postage rates are as follows: For the first 10 kg and below, the postage price is $6 per kg; for each successive kilogram after 10 kg, the postage price per kg is slightly lower than that of the first 10kg. It is known that the weight of Alex's parcel is 20% heavier than Charles' parcel, and that the postage prices for Alex and Charles are $92 and $80 respectively. How much more is the postage price per kg of the first 10 kg than that of each succeeding kg above 10 kg?

(A)1.5　　　(B)2　　　(C)2.5　　　(D)3　　　(E)3.5

Answer:＿＿＿＿＿

4. It is given that $A = 3x^2 + 3x$, $B = -x^2 + x + 5$ and $C = x^2 + x - 1$. $4A - (B - 2(2B - 3C) + 2A) - 2B = ?$

(A) $-x^2 + x + 11$　　　　(B) $-x^2 - x + 11$　　　　(C) $-x^2 + x + 1$

(D) $-x^2 + x - 1$　　　　(E) $x^2 + x + 11$

Answer:＿＿＿＿＿

5. On the bookshelf of Mar, there are Literature, Mathematics, History and Science books. If the number of Mathematics Books is 5 times that of the Literature books, and the number of Science books is 4 times that of the History books, which of the following is not a possible number for the total number of books on the bookshelf?

(A)21　　　(B)23　　　(C)26　　　(D)29　　　(E)30

Answer:＿＿＿＿＿

Questions 6–13, 5 marks each

A	4		
B		1	
1	2	3	4
3	4	2	1

6. Fill in the 4×4 box so that the numbers 1, 2, 3, and 4 appear exactly once in each row and column. Referring to the figure below, what is the sum of the values of A and B?

Answer:＿＿＿＿＿

7. The lengths of two sides of a triangle are 6 cm and 13 cm respectively. It is known that the length of the third side is also an integer (in cm). What is the minimum perimeter (in cm) of this triangle?

Answer:＿＿＿＿＿cm

8. It is given that Figure 1 shows a circle with diameter of 9 cm. Figure 2 shows an Olympic symbol which consists of five circles, each of diameter 9 cm. The distance between two of the tangents to the circles is 4 cm as shown. Find the length

of the Olympic symbol (Figure 3)?

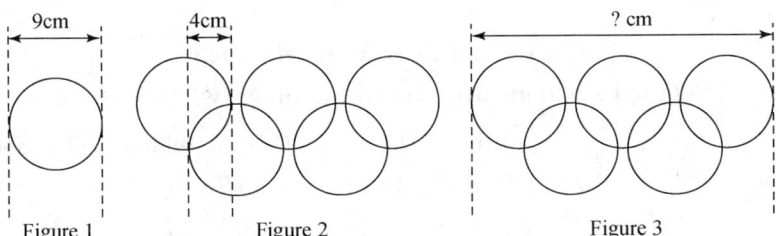

Figure 1   Figure 2   Figure 3

Answer:_____cm

9. The diagram below is composed of many right angled isosceles triangles. Suppose an ant wants to travel from point A to point C, in how many ways can this be done if the ant is only allowed to move up, right or diagonally?

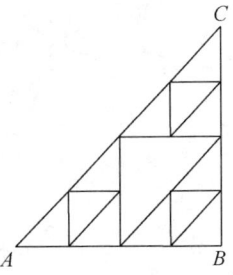

Answer:_____ways

10. Among the 1000 positive integers from 1 to 1000 inclusive, find the number of positive integers n such that $n^3 + n^2 + n$ is divisible by 8.

Answer:_____numbers

11. Given that $a^2 + b^2 + c^2 = (a+b+c)^2$, where a, b and c are non-zero real numbers. What is the value of $\frac{b+c}{a} + \frac{c+a}{b} + \frac{a+b}{c}$?

Answer:_____

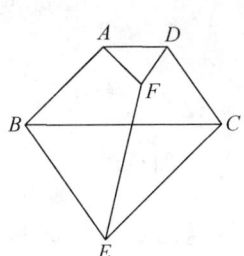

12. Refer to the diagram below, in trapezium $ABCD$, $AD//BC$. The line passing through B and parallel to CD intersects the line passing through C and parallel to AB at point E. Point F lies inside $ABCD$ such that $\angle FAD = \angle ABC$ and $\angle FDA = \angle DCB$. Given that the area of $ABEF$ is 20 cm^2 and the area of $DCEF$ is 16cm^2, what is the area of $ABCD$?

Answer:_____cm^2

13. A 4-digit number is said to be 'good' if it uses exactly 3 different digits from the set $\{2,0,1,7\}$ (at most one of the digits used can be repeated). For example, 8712 and 7200 are said to be 'good' numbers, while 2017 and 7175 are

not. How many 'good' numbers are there?

Answer: _____ numbers

Questions 14–15, 20 marks each
(Detailed solutions are needed for these two problems)

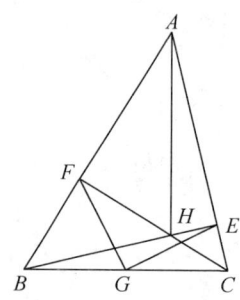

14. In $\triangle ABC$, point G is the midpoint of segment BC, $BE \perp AC$, $CF \perp AB$ and lines BE and CF intersects at point H. If $\angle EGF = 90°$, prove that $AH = BC$.

15. It is known that the equation $x^2 + (x+k)^2 = y^2$ has positive integers solutions (x, y), where x and y are relatively prime. If k is a positive integer greater than 1, what is the minimum value of k?

6.5　第二轮中文试题

1–5题,每题4分

1. 请问下列哪个数不能表示成两个质数之和?

(A) 19　　(B) 20　　(C) 21　　(D) 22　　(E) 23

答:_____

2. 在 $\triangle ABC$ 中, $AB = AC$、$\angle ACB = 80°$, 以 AC 为边向外侧作正方形 $ACDE$, 连接 BE 与 AC 相交于点 F, 如图 6-10 所示. 请问 $\angle BFC$ 等于多少度?

(A) 55°　　(B) 60°　　(C) 65°

(D) 70°　　(E) 75°

答:_____

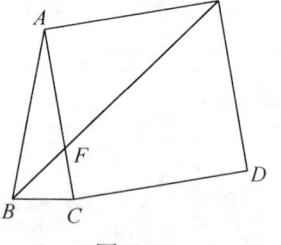

图 6-10

3. 小虎与小亮都要邮寄一件包裹, 邮局的收费标准为: 不超出 10kg 的包裹每千克的运费为 6 元, 超出 10kg 的部分每千克平均运费略低一些. 若小虎邮寄的包裹比小亮邮寄的包裹重 20%, 两人的运费分别为 92 元、80 元. 请问超出 10kg 部分比 10 kg 以内每千克的平均运费低了多少元?

(A) 1.5　　(B) 2　　(C) 2.5　　(D) 3　　(E) 3.5

答:_____

4. 已知 $A=3x^2+3x$、$B=-x^2+x+5$、$C=x^2+x-1$，请问
$$4A-(B-2(2B-3C)+2A)-2B=?$$
(A) $-x^2+x+11$ (B) $-x^2-x+11$ (C) $-x^2+x+1$
(D) $-x^2+x-1$ (E) x^2+x+11

答：_____

5. 小华的书架上放有文学书、数学书、历史书与科普书．其中数学书的册数是文学书的 5 倍、科普书的册数是历史书的 4 倍．请问书架上书的总册数不可能是下列哪个值？

(A) 21   (B) 23   (C) 26   (D) 29   (E) 30

答：_____

6–13 题，每题 5 分

6. 将数 1、2、3、4 分别填入 4×4 方格表的小方格内，使得每一行、每一列上的四个数都不相同．已在部分的小方格内填入数，如图 6-11 所示，请问图 6-11 中 A、B 位置上的数之和是多少？

	A	4	
B		1	
1	2	3	4
3	4	2	1

图 6-11

答：_____

7. 一个三角形的两条边之长度分别是 6cm 与 13cm，已知第三条边的长度也是整数 cm，请问这个三角形的周长最少是多少 cm？

答：_____

8. 图 6-12(a) 显示一个直径为 9cm 的圆，图 6-12(b) 由五个直径为 9cm 的圆组成一个奥运五环，其中显示两条与圆相切的虚线，其距离为 4 cm，请问图 6-12(c) 这个奥运五环的图案从左到右的总长度为多少 cm？

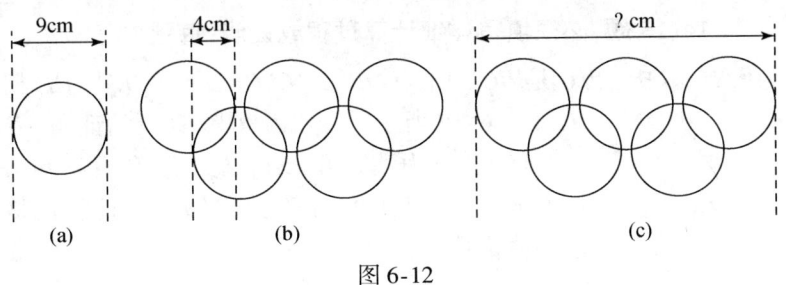

图 6-12

答：_____

9. 图 6-13 是由一些等腰直角三角形拼成的图形,若一只蚂蚁欲沿着三角形的边从 A 点爬到 C 点,规定在爬行的过程中只能向右方、上方或者斜右上方爬行. 请问这只蚂蚁总共有多少条不同的爬行路径?

答:_____条

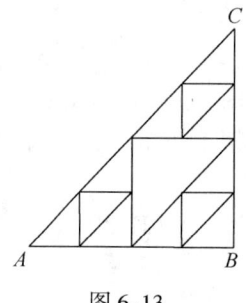

图 6-13

10. 在 1~1000 这 1000 个正整数中,请问总共有多少个正整数 n 使得 n^3+n^2+n 之值是 8 的倍数?

答:_____个

11. 已知 $a^2+b^2+c^2=(a+b+c)^2$,其中 a、b、c 为非零实数,请问 $\frac{b+c}{a}+\frac{c+a}{b}+\frac{a+b}{c}$ 的值是什么?

答:_____

12. 在梯形 $ABCD$ 中,$AD // BC$. 过 B 且平行于 CD 的直线与过 C 且平行于 AB 的直线交于点 E,点 F 为 $ABCD$ 内部的点使得 $\angle FAD = \angle ABC$、$\angle FDA = \angle DCB$,如图 6-14 所示. 已知四边形 $ABEF$ 的面积为 20cm²、并且四边形 $DCEF$ 的面积为 16cm²,请问梯形 $ABCD$ 的面积为多少 cm²?

答:_____cm²

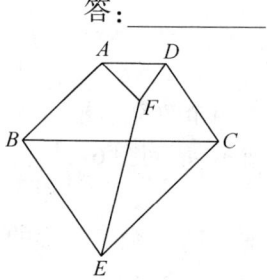

图 6-14

13. 在一个四位数中,若恰好出现 2、0、1、7 这四个数码中的三个(重复出现的数码只算一个),则称这个四位数是一个"好数". 例如,8712 与 7200 都是"好数",而 2017 与 7175 都不是"好数". 请问所有的四位数中总共有多少个"好数"?

答:_____个

14、15 题,必须填写详细计算过程或证明,每题 20 分

14. 在 $\triangle ABC$ 中,点 G 是 BC 的中点,$BE \perp AC$、$CF \perp AB$,BE 与 CF 相交于点 H,如图 6-15 所示. 已知 $\angle EGF=90°$,请证明 $AH=BC$.

15. 若 k 为整数且 $k>1$,已知不定方程 $x^2+(x+k)^2=y^2$ 有满足 x、y 互质的正整数解 (x,y),请问正整数 k 的最小值是什么?

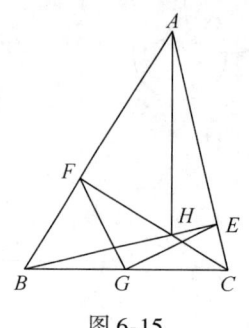

图 6-15

6.6 第二轮试题解答与评注

1. 答案:(E).

解 $19=2+17$、$20=3+17$、$21=2+19$、$22=3+19$,而若能将 23 表示成两个质数之和,这两个质数必为一奇一偶,故偶质数必为 2,因此奇质数为 $23-2=21$,与 21 不是质数矛盾.

2. 答案:(A).

解 由 $AB=AC$ 知 $\angle ABC=\angle ACB=80°$,故 $\angle BAC=180°-2\times80°=20°$. 由于 $ACDE$ 是正方形,故 $AE=AC=AB$;又 $\angle BAE=90°+20°=110°$,所以 $\angle AEB=\dfrac{180°-110°}{2}=35°$,因此 $\angle BFC=\angle AFE=180°-90°-35°=55°$.

3. 答案:(B).

解法 1 由题意知,10kg 包裹的运费为 60 元,故小虎与小亮两人的包裹都超过 10 kg. 超出 10 kg 部分的运费,小虎为 $92-60=32$ 元、小亮为 $80-60=20$ 元. 设小亮的包裹重为 x kg,则小虎的包裹重为 $(1+20\%)x=1.2x$ kg,可得 $\dfrac{x-10}{1.2x-10}=\dfrac{20}{32}$,解方程知 $x=15$. 即超出 10kg 部分每千克的平均运费为 $20\div(15-10)=20\div5=4$ 元,故超出 10kg 部分每千克平均运费比 10kg 以内的低了 $6-4=2$ 元.

解法 2 由题意知,10kg 包裹的运费为 60 元,故小虎与小亮两人的包裹都超过 10kg. 超出 10kg 部分的运费,小虎为 $92-60=32$ 元、小亮为 $80-60=20$ 元. 若设超出 10kg 部分每千克运费为 x 元,则小虎的包裹重为 $10+\dfrac{32}{x}$ kg、小亮的包裹重为 $10+\dfrac{20}{x}$ kg,并由题意得 $10+\dfrac{32}{x}=1.2\times\left(10+\dfrac{20}{x}\right)$,解方程知 $x=4$. 即超出 10kg 部分每千克的平均运费为 4 元,故超出 10kg 部分每千克平均运费比 10kg 以内的低了 $6-4=2$ 元.

4. 答案:(A).

解 $4A-(B-2(2B-3C)+2A)-2B=2A+B-6C=B+2(A-3C)=-x^2+x+11$.

5. 答案:(E).

解 设文学书有 x 册,历史书有 y 册,其中 x、y 为正整数,则书架上书的总册数为 $x+5x+y+4y=6x+5y$. 当 $x=1$、$y=3$ 时,$6x+5y=21$;当 $x=3$、$y=1$ 时,$6x+5$

$y=23$;当 $x=1$、$y=4$ 时,$6x+5y=26$;当 $x=4$、$y=1$ 时,$6x+5y=29$. 而若 $6x+5y=30$,则 $6x$ 必为 5 的倍数,故 x 也是 5 的倍数,这将导致 $6x\geq 30$,即 $5y\leq 0$,矛盾.

6. 答案:5.

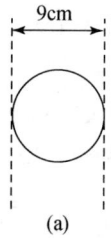

图 6-16

解 A 下方的空格不能填 1、2、4,故只能填 3,因此 A 格只能填 1;B 上方的空格不能填 1、3、4,故只能填 2,因此 B 格只能填 4. 故 A+B=1+4=5,完整的填法如图 6-16 所示.

7. 答案:27cm.

解 由三角形的两边之差必小于第三边之长度,知第三边的长度大于 $13-6=7$cm,故其长度至少为 8 cm,因此周长最少为 $13+6+8=27$cm.

8. 答案:29cm.

解 奥运五环图案的第一行有 3 个圆,根据图 6-17(a)与图 6-17(b)所示,相邻两个圆之间距为 $9-4-4=1$cm,故图 6-17(c)显示此奥运五环从左到右的总长度为 $3\times 9+2\times 1=29$cm.

9. 答案:42 条.

解 如图 6-18 所示,图中各点的数即为蚂蚁从起点到该点的不同路径数:故从 A 点爬到 C 点共有 42 条不同的爬行路径.

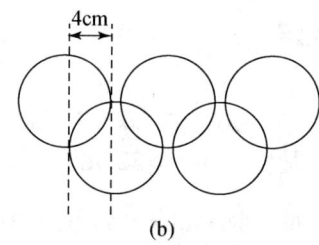

(a)   (b)   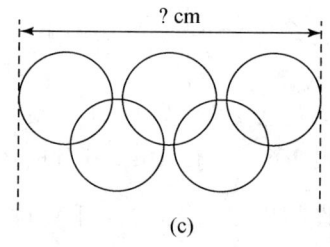 (c)

图 6-17

10. 答案:125 个.

解 由于 $n^3+n^2+n=n(n^2+n+1)$,而当 n 是正整数时,n^2 与 n 的奇偶性相同,所以 n^2+n+1 必为奇数,故 n^3+n^2+n 之值是 8 的倍数的充要条件为 n 是 8 的倍数,因此满足条件的正整数 n 总共有 $\dfrac{1000}{8}=125$ 个.

11. 答案:-3.

解 将已知等式展开整理得 $2(ab+bc+ca)=0$,即

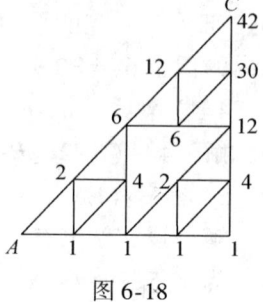

图 6-18

第6章　第6届国际中小学生数学能力检测(IMAS)(初中组)

$ab+bc+ca=0$.

由于 a、b、c 为非零实数,故 $\dfrac{ab+bc+ca}{abc}=0$,即 $\dfrac{1}{a}+\dfrac{1}{b}+\dfrac{1}{c}=0$,因此 $\dfrac{b+c}{a}+\dfrac{c+a}{b}+\dfrac{a+b}{c}=(a+b+c)\left(\dfrac{1}{a}+\dfrac{1}{b}+\dfrac{1}{c}\right)-3=-3$.

评注　本题也可以使用代入特殊值的方法.

12. **答案**:18m².

解　延长 BA、CD 交于点 G,如图6-19所示.

显然 $GBEC$ 是一个平行四边形,故 $S_{GBEC}=2S_{GBC}$. 由 $\angle FAD=\angle ABC=\angle GAD$、$\angle FDA=\angle DCB=\angle GDA$、$AD=AD$ 可以得知 $\triangle FDA\cong\triangle GDA$,故 $S_{FDA}=S_{GDA}$,因此 $S_{GAFD}=2S_{GDA}$. 所以

$$S_{ABEF}+S_{DCEF}=S_{GBEC}-S_{GAFD}$$
$$=2(S_{GBC}-S_{GDA})$$
$$=2S_{ABCD}$$

故得知 $S_{ABCD}=\dfrac{20+16}{2}=18\text{cm}^2$.

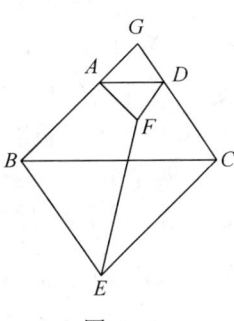

图 6-19

13. **答案**:576个.

解法1　我们分五种情况计算"好数"的个数.

情况1　四位数的四个数码都不相同且没有0.则其中三个数码必为2、1或7,另一个数码需选自3、4、5、6、8、9,共有六种选择方式.而当这四个数码被选定后,它们有 $4\times3\times2\times1=24$ 种排列方式,故此情况下共有 $6\times24=144$ 个"好数";

情况2　四位数的四个数码都不相同且有0.则另有两个数码选自2、1或7,最后一个数码需选自3、4、5、6、8、9,故有 $3\times6=18$ 种选择方式.而当这四个数码被选定后,因为首位数码不得为0,它们有 $3\times3\times2\times1=18$ 种排列方式,故此情况下共有 $18\times18=324$ 个"好数";

情况3　四位数有一个重复数码,且四个数码没有0.则所有数码必须为2、1或7. 从2、1、7中选择一个重复的数码有3种方式.而当这四个数码被选定后,它们有 $\dfrac{4\times3\times2\times1}{2}=12$ 种排列方式,故此情况下共有 $3\times12=36$ 个"好数";

情况4　四位数有一个重复数码,且四个数码中恰有一个0.则在2、1或7中选择一个数码出现2次,另一个数码出现1次,故有 $3\times2=6$ 种选择方式.而当这四个数码被选定后,因首位数码不得为0,它们有 $\dfrac{3\times3\times2\times1}{2}=9$ 种排列方

式,故此情况下共有 $6 \times 9 = 54$ 个"好数";

情况5 四位数有一个重复数码,且四个数码中恰有两个0,则需在2、1、7中选择两个数码,故有3种选择方式. 而当这四个数码被选定后,因首位数码不得为0,它们有 $\frac{2 \times 3 \times 2 \times 1}{2} = 6$ 种排列方式,故此情况下共有 $3 \times 6 = 18$ 个"好数".

综上所述,共有 $144 + 324 + 36 + 54 + 18 = 576$ 个"好数".

解法2 我们先求出所有可能的数码排列的个数,最后删除掉0为首位数码的情况数.

若四个数码两两不同,则其中三个数码选自2、0、1、7,另一个数码选自3、4、5、6、8、9,共有 $4 \times 6 \times 4 \times 3 \times 2 \times 1 = 576$ 个排列. 在这类情况下,0为首位数码时,后面必然是2、1、7中的两个数码与3、4、5、6、8、9中的一个数码,共有 $3 \times 6 \times 3 \times 2 \times 1 = 108$ 个排列是以0为首位数码.

若四个数码有两个数码相同,则它们必然全部选自2、0、1、7,先选一个数码出现二次(有4种选法),再选两个数码各出现一次(有3种选法). 而当这四个数码被选定后,它们有 $\frac{4 \times 3 \times 2 \times 1}{2} = 12$ 种排列方式,故此情况下共有 $4 \times 3 \times 12 = 144$ 种排列. 然而在这类情况下,四个数码均选自2、0、1、7,每个数码在每个位置上都有四分之一的情况,故0为首位数码的情况有 $\frac{144}{4} = 36$ 个.

综上所述,共有 $576 - 108 + 144 - 36 = 576$ 个"好数".

14. 解 由于 $BE \perp AC$、$CF \perp AB$,点 G 是 BC 的中点,故 $GB = GC = GE = GF$. (5分) 故 $\angle FCG = \frac{180° - \angle FGC}{2}$、$\angle ECG = \frac{180° - \angle EGC}{2}$,所以

$$\angle ECF = \frac{180° - \angle EGC}{2} - \frac{180° - \angle FGC}{2} = \frac{\angle FGC - \angle EGC}{2} = \frac{\angle EGF}{2} = 45°. (5分)$$

又 $CF \perp AB$,故 AFC 为等腰直角三角形,即 $AF = CF$. (5分)

由点 H 是 $\triangle ABC$ 之垂心,可得知 $AH \perp BC$,$\angle FAH = 90° - \angle ABC = \angle FCB$,又 $\angle AFH = 90° = \angle CFB$、$AF = CF$,故 $\triangle AFH \cong \triangle CFB$,因此 $AH = BC$. (5分)

15. 解 当 $k = 7$ 时,不定方程有解 $(5, 13)$,下面证明 $k = 7$ 就是最小值. (5分)

首先注意到 x 与 k 必须互质,否则若它们有公共质因子 p,则 $p | y^2$,故 $p | y$,与 x、y 互质相矛盾.

若 k 是偶数,则 x 必须是奇数,但此时 x^2 与 $(x+k)^2$ 均被 4 除余 1,故 y^2 被 4 除余 2,但不存在这样子的 y,故不合. (5分)

第6章 第6届国际中小学生数学能力检测(IMAS)(初中组)

若 $3 \mid k$,则 x 不是 3 的倍数,但此时 x^2 与 $(x+k)^2$ 均被 3 除余 1,故 y^2 被 3 除余 2,但不存在这样子的 y,故不合.(5 分)

若 $5 \mid k$,则 x 不是 5 的倍数,但此时 x^2 与 $(x+k)^2$ 被 5 除的余数相同且为 1 或 4,故 y^2 被 5 除余 2 或 3,但不存在这样子的 y,故不合.

综上所述,k 不能是 2、3、5 的倍数,又 $k>1$,故 $k=7$ 就是最小值.(5 分)

评注 给出 $k=7$ 时的一组解并宣称最小 k 为 7 可得 5 分,证明 k 不能是 2、3、5 中某一个数的倍数得 5 分.